A SURGE OF LANGUAGE

A SURGE OF LANGUAGE

TEACHING POETRY DAY BY DAY

Baron Wormser and David Cappella

Foreword by Jeffrey D. Wilhelm

HEINEMANN ■ Portsmouth, NH

Heinemann
A division of Reed Elsevier Inc.
361 Hanover Street
Portsmouth, NH 03801–3912
www.heinemann.com

Offices and agents throughout the world

Credit lines for borrowed material begin on page xiii.

Library of Congress Cataloging-in-Publication Data
Wormser, Baron.
  A surge of language : teaching poetry day by day / Baron Wormser and David Cappella.
    p. cm.
  Includes bibliographical references.
  ISBN 0-325-00606-7 (acid-free paper)
  1. Poetry—Study and teaching (Secondary)—Fiction. 2. Creative writing (Secondary education)—Fiction. 3. Teacher-student relationships—Fiction. 4. High school students—Fiction. 5. High school teachers—Fiction. I. Cappella, David. II. Title.

PS3573.O693S87 2004
813'.54—dc22   2003024646

Editor: Lisa Luedeke
Production service: Denise Botelho
Production coordinator: Vicki Kasabian
Cover designer: Joni Doherty
Cover photographer: Marybeth Simonelli
Typesetter: Tom Allen
Manufacturing: Steve Bernier

Printed in the United States of America on acid-free paper
08 07 06 05 04   DA   1 2 3 4 5

For Jim, "The Poem Guy"

Contents

December and January

February and March

April, May, and June

Poems Included in This Book

Student samples also appear throughout the book.

Credits

"Nonesuch River" by James Provencher. Reprinted by permission of the author.

"Surrounding Blues on the Way Down" by Bruce Weigl from *Archeology of the Circle*. Copyright © 1999 by Bruce Weigl. Reprinted by permission of Grove/Atlantic, Inc.

Foreword

Every time I hear Baron Wormser and David Cappella speak professionally, an overpowering thought comes to mind. I think it every time I read their work, be it poetry or about the teaching of poetry. I think it when I have the good fortune to sit down and talk with them. But they never cease to surprise me, and I thought it again last night as I finished reading this manuscript for the second time. I thought it so hard that I spoke out loud in bed: "Does *anybody* think *harder* about teaching poetry than these guys?" My wife looked up from her own book with a flicker of her eyes. "*I don't think so!*" I told her. And that is exactly what I want to tell you. I have read widely about teaching poetry. In my considered opinion, no one does it better, thinks harder about it, or writes as refreshingly on the topic as Wormser and Cappella. The book you hold in your hands is a marvel and an elixir. All language arts teachers at any level should memorize it. As my friend Jeff Golub would contend, reading it will make you so smart you'll be able to see through walls!

A short introduction to the authors: Baron Wormser is a very fine poet who served as poet laureate of Maine during my tenure at the University of Maine. (Run, don't walk, to the nearest bookstore and pick up a book of his poems if you don't own one yet.) Both Baron and David Cappella are gifted and passionate teachers and powerful writers. More than that, they are great-hearted people, and their unique energy shines through this great-hearted book.

I was impressed enough with their work that several years ago I invited them to keynote our Maine Writing Project Annual Conference, and to lead a full day workshop on teaching poetry. The reception was so enthusiastic that we invited them to lead a full week advanced institute on teaching the reading and writing of poetry the following summer. The results were electrifying and transformative. The evaluations showed that everyone had been stimulated and provoked in deep ways to rethink their teaching—not just of poetry—but of everything.

At Orono's signature Pat's Pizza, I had my first chance to really visit with Baron and David. I became even more impressed. Unlike most work on teaching poetry—and indeed most work around any kind of composition instruction in schools—their teaching is firmly rooted in current cognitive science and a clear-sighted sense of composition theory. They spoke about George Hillocks' work on teaching writing, about the task and text-specific processes of reading and writing that teachers usually do not share with their student readers. They explained how "poetry" is too wide to be considered a useful genre and that to teach poetry well we must consider the particular demands of ironic monologues, oratorical poetry, lyric poetry, and the like. "Show me a poem and I'll show you a prompt," David boasted. "Poems can teach what readers need to know to read them. Poems can teach everything writers and human beings in general need to know."

David recited part of Paul Corrigan's "Tying a Bowline" and talked about assisting students to take on expert knowledge from a Vygotskian sociocultural perspective. (I remember marveling that "these guys think in poems!") Baron talked jazz to explain transactional theories of reading and writing poetry. He quoted Theolonius Monk's famous injunction: "I put it down! You gotta pick it up!" and talked about how careful teaching is required so students will know how to notice a poet's conventions and codes so that they can be "picked up." They talked about the importance of teaching poetry as poetry, and how poetry can be used as part of a sequence—a bridge to other kinds of learning that we privilege: issues like expert language use, judging narrator reliability, and a wide variety of other reading, writing, thinking, speaking and listening skills.

I was very interested in the dictation method they had demonstrated in their workshops. It was a technique my German and French teachers had used to teach foreign language. "It's about slowing down and feeling the language in your bones," David explained. Baron chimed in that "it's a kind of reading aloud to think aloud so you can live out loud. Poetry is life in the slow lane. Poetry tells us to slow down and to pay attention. Poetry directs our attention." Likewise, many of the methods demonstrated in this book show how poetry is muscular and physical, how it uses drama and language to convey deep meanings unavailable to other art forms—*but only if we know how to pay attention.* Their book shows many ways of learning how to pay that kind of attention.

Though most English teachers must know of the primal power that resides in poetry, poetry is seen in the larger culture as insular; as an arcane practice that has little bearing on everyday living. Unfortunately, this attitude has taken hold in schools and in many English and language arts classrooms as well. Perhaps this is because of an emphasis on perceived practicality, or because of our current mindless emphasis on standardized test scores as a measure of human achievement. This narrow perspective makes us teach what can be easily tested. In other words, we find ourselves teaching information, which unlike knowledge cannot be deeply felt, understood, used, revised, or applied in transformative ways.

Wormser and Cappella offer a vigorous defense of poetry as they highlight its various powers and the work poetry can do in English classrooms, across a school, and in our lived experiences and in the world. More than that, they show us numerous ways of enacting and unleashing these powers.

They show that poetry is immediate and "right *now*": a form of oral exploration, a deep kind of reflection and commentary, a tool for everyday learning and living and sharing about what is most important, They show how poetry can be infused into a classroom in a way that makes it an integral part—as it has been throughout history—of what it means to learn from the hard run of human experience and our intimate connection to each other and the world.

In the landmark study, *What Americans Read*, the researchers found that fewer than one percent of adult Americans would pick up a book of poetry each year. Hardly any more would read any kind of poem. Why is this so? My answer would be "school happened." So perhaps I should ask a more pointed question: What *didn't* happen in school that created this situation? This is a particularly important question for those of us who know how poetry has been so important to culture, family, and friendship over time. Wormser and Cappella show how to make poetry a natural part of everyday classroom discourse, historical reflection, and the most human kind of talk around the current events that strike us more closely—in Marianne Moore's phrase: about news that stays news.

Baron and David have written a wonderful story, a story that demonstrates how to create a culture of critical language use through the use of poetry. Their story tells how not only to include poetry into the curriculum, but how to infuse a joy of living and learning into the daily equation. Their book reads like a novel and the writing is fittingly poetic. It is a teaching memoir from two great teachers that provides a wealth of ways of thinking about teaching, poetry and life.

I was moved reading this and I trust that you will be too. The authors have captured for us many essential and enriching insights about poetry and about teaching. I am reminded of Rilke's poem "In the Churchyard," where he writes that "We two, at the bottom of the chasm into which the others have fallen, look up and see the sky" (my own translation from the German). Baron and David help us look up and see what is fulfilling, stimulating, challenging, and beautiful about teaching poetry—but more than that—about teaching and relating to our students so they can become more than they currently are. See, I learned a lot from this book. I can think in poetry too!

Jeffrey D. Wilhelm
Boise State University

Introduction

There are many secondary school English teachers in the United States who present poetry in their classrooms on a daily basis. These teachers have gone far beyond the famous (or infamous) poetry unit that lasts for a week or two in the spring. This book is an attempt to show what that kind of teaching can look like. The journal of a teacher we call Mr. P. presents a range of classroom situations and practices for teaching poetry. Mr. P.'s journal is not exhaustive. It does not provide an entry for every day. Its purpose is to indicate the lay of the land and what the issues are. Dealing with poetry each day is a challenge, but it's an incredible opportunity when one considers the richness and range of the material. Mr. P. has been teaching for quite a while but he is still as keen as his first year. He has—in no small part—poetry to thank for that.

The United States seems to be in the midst of a poetry renaissance—at least in terms of the publicity that poetry is getting. The events of September 11th have turned many people in poetry's direction as they hanker for the emotional concision that poetry provides. Nonetheless, it would be safe to say that schools in the United States could do a good deal more with poetry.

In a way this is surprising because if one were making a pitch for poetry in schools, there is a lot to tout. What if we said to any educator that he or she had a resource within his or her grasp that would improve reading skills, verbal skills, and writing skills; that would require no additional outlays of money; that would make students better performers on standardized tests; that would provide daily inspiration in their lives; that would increase their self-esteem; that would help them enormously with the nuts and bolts of literacy, such as spelling, punctuation, and grammar; that would connect them with the multi-ethnic nature of democracy; that would improve vocabulary in meaningful and enjoyable ways; that would dramatically improve their listening skills; that would honor the integrity of their feelings; and that would be a solace and joy they could carry through their whole lives? Chances are any educator would say, Where do I sign?

The educator might ask, If poetry is so swell, why isn't it at the center of school curricula? It's a reasonable question to which there is a very long answer. Briefly, poetry in the twentieth century seemed difficult because it expressed the traumatic experiences of that century, beginning with World War I, a war that put an end to civilization as the human race once knew it. In keeping with modern art, poetry expanded its techniques, while many classrooms kept modernity at bay by enshrining the notion of poetry as a moralizing rhyme. As science and technology gained more and more prominence in people's daily lives, poetry, with its notorious subjectivity, seemed out of place and old-fashioned. As the American emphasis on practicality, pragmatism, and verifiable results grew and grew, poetry came to seem beside the point. As other media blossomed, the old oral ways of poetry appeared stagnant. As old people who passed on poetry to their grandchildren became more and more segregated, poetry was unheard at home.

Why societies discard their heritages and change their emphases are interesting and sobering points to ponder. Certainly the forces of the commercial republic (to use Benjamin Franklin's phrase) that emphasize novelty and the commodity value of everything haven't been kind to poetry. Poetry, a spirit gift, cannot be quantified. Similarly, objective testing results, a must-have these days, do not apply to poetry. A poem can never be reduced to a gist, much less a multiple-choice answer. On the contrary, poetry expands in a human mind and spirit more or less infinitely. It rejoices in the subtlety that our bodies enact with each second of life.

Along with any explanation of social forces at work in regards to poetry, one would have to note the forces that determine how poetry is taught. Poetry has faced some serious impediments here. For one, most teachers in their college careers never had an entire course that focused on the teaching of poetry, a course that recognized that poetry is not the same as prose and that it has different concerns from prose. For another, many teachers had bad experiences when they were students with poetry, experiences that shamed and humiliated them as they were quizzed about a poem and then told that their answers weren't the right ones. Little wonder that many very able teachers prefer to skirt poetry.

This is unfortunate, to put it mildly, because poetry—an oral and aural art—offers enormous possibilities for sustained literacy. Mr. P. loves to read poems aloud in his classroom and he loves to dictate lines of poems or whole short poems to students. What he finds in his students is that they like to hear poetry. They like experiencing a poem for the first time and not knowing what is going to happen next. It brings them to the primal level of experiencing literature—sheer curiosity. They like the incredible variety of poetry, how every day can be a fresh day as they experience a poem that is new to them. The oral approach and dictation slow the poem down so that they experience it fully and deeply. With time, Mr. P.'s students like being in touch with language in such a basic, word-by-word way. They start to internalize language, and that is a goal of all teachers.

Certainly students in this society need to foster their literacy throughout their school careers. Literacy isn't just something one picks up and then has forever. We may be able to read, but does our sense of language continue to grow? How does it continue to grow? What fosters it? How do we instill a love of language in students? How do we get students to actively build their vocabularies? What opportunities do we provide our students to actively respond to language as language rather than as the stuff of answers to conceptual and factual questions? Because of the modest size of a poem, it allows students to look very carefully at a given set of words—and stimulates them to begin writing their own poems. These are precious and important experiences, and surely worth doing on a regular basis. It would be fair to say that poetry, as it crystallizes the intuitions and rigors of the creative process, has something to say to all educators.

Mr. P. would like more people to be teaching poetry but his focus and pride are directed at his own classroom. If there is one word that sums up what poetry offers young people, we think it would be *inspiration*. Mr. P.'s classroom is the stuff of day-to-day school—late passes, loudspeaker interruptions, all manner of adolescent distress—but it's the stuff of inspiration, too. Poetry can be the center of that day-to-day classroom experience without anyone losing anything. On the contrary, students gain as they probe language each day. Poetry offers the best of both worlds: focused literacy and inspiration. What are we waiting for?!

August and September

Each summer in early August I go hiking by myself somewhere in northern New England. It's my get-away time; my on-my-own time. My wife understands it. School is coming and I need to be with trees, clouds, ferns, an occasional hawk—by myself. As a high school English teacher, I've taught the likes of Thoreau and it seems to me that it's not enough to know the text. You have to have some of your own feelings about the land in which the text is rooted. There's a lot to be said for getting in a canoe and paddling down the Merrimack River. You won't see exactly what Thoreau saw, but it's still a river and being on the river in a canoe is something like eternal.

In terms of my career I'm somewhere in the middle of it. I'm in my early forties, which means I have been teaching for a while, but I still want to teach more. I'm a lifer. I can't imagine doing something else. I love being in the classroom with the kids. But now I'm hiking in western Maine in the Bigelow Range. It's not hard hiking but it's challenging—trying to make so many miles a day. I've encountered some through hikers who started on the Appalachian Trail down south in the spring. Mostly they are young and you can feel energy in them that is more than physical. They are truly living on the earth. They are experiencing night as night and food as food and water as water without the mediations of social situations, advertising, technology, and a thousand other distractions. They tend to be quiet. You can feel how a degree of sheer awe has worked its way into their souls.

I ask them what they are reading on the trail and it turns out to be everything: a favorite childhood novel, the Bible, the *Tao Te Ching*, you name it. Occasionally someone has a book of poems. I can appreciate that because I take a book of poems with me when I hike. I'm not up for a lot of reading at night. It's dark for one and my little camp light is just that—little. The illumination of the page is precious and wants to shed its light on something that is precious. To my mind, that would be a poem. It's not big and it doesn't take long to read but it can echo in my soul for the rest of my days. I can carry it with me as I hike or pause to stare off into the distance or lie down exhausted. It's a companion and it has its own physical presence—rhymed or unrhymed, long lines or short lines, always filled with breath.

Over the years I've read any number of poets on the trail. There's a poem by Gary Snyder about reading Milton by firelight that speaks to this situation. I can recite the final lines by heart:

> Fire down
> Too dark to read, miles from a road
> The bell-mare clangs in the meadow
> That packed dirt for a fill-in
> Scrambling through loose rocks
> On an old trail
> All of a summer's day.

I have always been particularly fond of the last line, how it evokes the tradition of English literature in its old-fashioned syntax and its referring to the season. It's both simple and calm. It's how I feel when I bed down at night: I have experienced a summer's day. I can taste the poem and I can taste the day. When someone asks me why I read my students a poem or a part of a poem each day, I think of Snyder's poem. I want my students to feel how concentrated life can be when our senses are clear and when language is—to use Snyder's word—*packed*. I want my students to taste life on earth through the medium of language, hence poetry.

I'm not sorry school is coming, but I'd be a liar if I said I was in a hurry for it. When I'm up in these old mountains, I can feel a bit how slow time is and how ludicrous human time is. I can wait. I have a small book of poems in my pack. I have companionship all around me and inside me.

september 4

orality

I'm known as the "poem guy" around our school because the students know that I read a poem aloud every day. Some of my colleagues teach poetry; some do their best to avoid it. Our students take the same tests and my students do well year in, year out. I have all sorts of students, and to my mind their performances are not a mystery. I tell my students that the purpose of my classroom is to study and enjoy the uses of the English language. And what does that mean? It means we live with words. And what does that mean, Mr. P?

For starters it means we listen. Each day I begin with a poem. We may talk about the poem and we may not talk about the poem, but in every case we listen to the poem. I have always been impressed by a remark by the historian John Lukacs. He wrote that

> During the twentieth century the capacity and the practice of listening have deteriorated. In all walks of life, in all kinds of circumstances, the capacity of attention has become disrupted and curtailed because of the incredible—literally incredible—amount of noise and sounds and music and words and slogans whirling around people's heads and ears. This condition is, in itself, a matter worthy of the attention of a historian. It is the condition that the very consciousness of people changes through the ages: not only their ideas or the subjects of their thoughts but the functioning of their senses and their minds as well.

I don't see how anyone who teaches school can deny what he says. Our students are besieged by "noise and sounds and music and words and slogans." The advent of the Walkman has meant they can seal themselves off from the world in a socially approved manner. I have nothing against their listening to music. What I worry about is their ability to respond to language because they simply don't take the time to carefully listen to it. When I tell them that *of* is not *have* as in "You should of come here tonight," they agree with me but they also say, "You know what we mean. What does it matter?"

When we listen to a poem every word matters. The poem is a model of attention and care. We have to be quiet to hear the poem.

I read a poem (or part of a poem) first thing each period. The kids know the situation and they settle down immediately. They know a poem is coming. They don't know what the poem will be but they know that in order to hear that poem they have to be quiet because poems exist in relation to silence. Poems inform and shape silence but they don't shatter it. You can feel the silence around the edges of the poem. Ironically enough, reading poetry aloud is a great way of getting the class to settle down. Kids will shush other kids who are wound up about something or other. More than one teacher has asked me over the years how I get my kids to be on task right away. I tell them my students know that each period of their English education is consecrated to the word. They laugh at my language and I want them to laugh but it's true. We gather to attend to words and see what marvels words can perform. Poetry is urgent language.

The fact that the students never know what is coming is crucial. There is only one domain and that is poetry. All distinctions within that domain are intriguing but ultimately irrelevant. All that matters is the particular poem. What century it comes from and who wrote it are issues we often wind up exploring in some depth but the main issue is the poem that they are hearing for the first time. They are curious each day what will happen. Over the course of a year they have heard Allen Ginsberg and John Donne, Gerard Manley Hopkins and W.S. Merwin, John Keats and Gwendolyn Brooks. If I am reading it, they know I am taking that poem very seriously (even if the poem is goofy, such as a poem by Lewis Carroll or Gregory Corso)—we only have so many days together.

I read slowly. The only rule of thumb I know about reading poems aloud is don't read too fast. The poem wants to be heard and that means each syllable of each word wants its presence to be felt. This doesn't mean excruciatingly slow; it doesn't mean I don't speed up when speed seems wanted. It does mean that I am trying to let the poem be heard; it isn't the background to anything. It is the thing and it is in no hurry. I joke with the kids that poetry is life in the slow lane. It's true. Poetry doesn't care about nanoseconds. Poetry doesn't believe in progress. Poetry isn't hurrying anywhere or talking on a cell

> The only rule of thumb I know about reading poems aloud is don't read too fast.

phone. Poetry isn't busy. Poetry dwells and lingers and remains. It's conservative in the deep sense of the word: It seeks to conserve, via language, our sense of how amazing it is that we are alive. That's enough.

september 5

dictation

A few summers ago I read Barry Sanders' book *A Is for Ox*. One of Sanders' arguments is that literacy doesn't mean anything if students aren't actively hearing language in their classrooms. Literacy proceeds from orality and when the classroom abandons orality it undermines literacy. I think he is right. It's similar to what Robert Frost said when he noted that words don't live in books; they live in our mouths.

It seems obvious when one thinks about it but most classrooms I have been in don't acknowledge it. We wonder why students don't connect with language. For all the books that may be thrown at them, they remain language starved in the sense that they aren't hearing language, particularly language that is concentrated and concise, language that is jeweled. Language becomes to them a sort of macaroni and cheese that emanates from a cardboard box: It fills you up, but doesn't have much taste.

Part of the problem is that language spoken aloud is pleasurable and schools frown upon pleasure. According to Puritanism, learning is a task and a duty. Pleasure is far too wayward to enter into the equation. I can sympathize with generations of teachers who have sought the true and narrow path but I confess that a degree of pleasure has not produced pandemonium in my classroom. The pleasure of pleasing sounds is, in the scheme of things, a modest one but an undeniable one. Once students start to listen they start to hear how assonance and consonance and alliteration and all sorts of rhymes can captivate their ears. I don't come in with a list of those terms. On the contrary, I ask them what they noticed about the sounds in the poem. Many long *a*'s? Any consonants repeated? What was the dominant vowel sound? They start listening.

After a couple of days of reading short poems to my students and letting it go at that (just easing them into the situation), I dictated "In a Station of the Metro" by Ezra Pound to them today. It's a famous poem, but it's also a very short poem, two lines in its entirety:

> The apparition of these faces in the crowd;
> Petals on a wet, black bough.

When I dictate poems at the beginning of the school year, I indicate everything about the poem to my students: capital letters, punctuation, where lines stop and start. It takes time but I am not dictating lengthy poems. My interest isn't in causing anyone's hand to cramp but to get my students to write down poems word by word. They are not only listening but also getting the words on paper as they hear them. They are making the words their own because they are required to write them down.

It takes some time, but it's time that is well spent. They have to ponder each word and comma. I grade them on their dictations. At first, they think I am crazy (I am, after all, the poem guy). It seems the equivalent of handing out an "A." They write their dictations down in their poetry journals and I collect the journals. What I (and they) discover is that they tend to be careless. They aren't used to paying minute attention to another text. They are responsible for spellings, for instance. I tell them before they hand in their journals at the end of the week to check in the dictionary for spellings they aren't sure of. Sometimes they check, sometimes they don't. When their grade comes back a "C," they tend to start checking.

Pound's "In a Station of the Metro" inevitably sparks all sorts of questions from students, but before I allow the questions, I check the text with them. What, for instance, is that word *apparition*? It is a truism that students have to know all the words in order to discuss the poem. Some people call this vocabulary; I call it necessity. We look up words together or I have a student look the word up and read the definition for the class. We consider the word and where it comes from in terms of its etymology. The dictionary holds a central place in my classroom as it holds a central place in the lives of poets. The world got along before *Hot SAT Words* ever showed up. There's no substitute for looking up words so that we can talk about those words.

We considered today how thoroughly the three meanings of *apparition* seemed to function in the poem. Students felt that all three senses of the word were at work: that the image was ghostly; that the image was an unusual one for a crowd in a subway station; and that *apparition* had to do with appearance in the sense that the poem itself was the appearance of a vision. I'm putting these remarks in my own words after a day's work but the students came up with the different senses on their own. They were curious about how fully Pound was using what was for them a strange word. They were testing him. They were pleased when they could see he was using the word quite carefully. It wasn't a trick on his part; it was art.

By dictating the poem I can slow time down and get the words into my students' bodies. Poetry is physical and I want them to experience that physicality. By writing the words down—and I make allowances for students who are challenged in various ways, such as being hearing impaired—they have to grapple with the physical nature of each word. I told them today how *apparition* is spelled

> By dictating the poem I can slow time down and get the words into my students' bodies.

but sometimes I let them write down a word and then we check on it as a class to determine how to spell that word. It's not that I am on a crusade about spelling; it's that I want them to have to apprehend words in various situations—some more structured than others. I want them to be alive to words and spelling is part of that alive-ness.

I like to do the Pound poem at the beginning of the year because it's a way to get students thinking about what constitutes a poem. It challenges a lot of their notions: it isn't end-rhymed; there's no meter; it's ridiculously short; it's not about much in terms of subject. I ask them what they noticed as they were writing the poem down. (Dictation is not mechanical; it's focusing.) Today, after an initial pause, students started talking about how surprised they were that the poem ended so quickly. They thought he was just getting started and he stopped. I asked them why they thought he stopped. Immediately, Susan Sturtevant in my second period class raised her hand and said that the poet was making a point about what a poem could be, that a poem didn't have to go on and on. "A poem can just do its work and be done and that's that. See you later." Susan moved her hands together in a dismissive, school-is-out gesture. Everyone laughed but I could feel the thinking inside their laughter.

september 6

prompts/models

Once my students have written a poem down in their poetry journal (a notebook that holds their dictations, journal responses to poems, poems and lyrics they copy down, and drafts of their own poems) they can use that poem as a model for writing a poem of their own. Another reason I like to do Pound's "In a Station of the Metro" is that it serves as an excellent model for a student poem. Essentially it says to the kids, "See what you can do in two lines. See how much you can make every word count."

I am convinced that writing poetry makes for good prose writers. Among the lessons that poetry teaches is economy of language. Every word in a poem must be scrutinized because all the words have to be necessary. The phrases that students love to toss around on their papers—"on the other hand," "moreover," "we can see," and other pearls of established rhetoric—have no place in poems. Poems are the glowing bones of language. Frequently I will ask a student to justify a word in a poem I speak aloud or dictate: "Why is that word in the poem?" Because one word is connected intimately with all the other words in a poem, students come to see how a poem is an articulate tangle: Pull one thread and all the other threads are influenced.

To write their own poems students need good models. Because poetry is a multifarious art, there is no shortage of various models to spur student writing. "Show me a poem and I'll show you a prompt" has become my motto. What I find is that by defining the parameters carefully, for instance a two-line poem that uses image to compare one thing with another, the preconscious mind is opened up. Students don't have to fret about what to write about and how to

> "Show me a poem and I'll show you a prompt" has become my motto.

structure it. I have taken care of that already and that takes the worrying, conceptual, conscious mind out of the picture. They can just go to where their imaginations take them.

Some teachers feel prompts are artificial but I don't feel that way at all. For me the prompt that works from a model poem is more like a Zen koan. A *koan* is a Buddhist riddle that is designed to frustrate the rational mind and let intuition take over, as in the famous "What is the sound of one hand clapping?" When I offer a prompt, I am casting a line out into my students' preconscious minds. None of us know what we will get and that is as it should be. We write, after all, to find out what is inside us. Unless we do the writing, we won't know.

To be sure the classroom situation is artificial. Many students have said to me that they do their best imagining as they are floating off into sleep. Alas, we can't work in a dormitory right before lights out. Once students come to see that the prompts are designed to allow them maximum imaginative space within a defined structure, they start to loosen up and start to feel that their imaginations are always there. What the imagination wants is to be prodded.

The challenge for the teacher is to see how poems can become models. Obviously a poem with an enormously polished verbal texture can be too daunting. I may have students try to write a line that is as sensorily rich as a line from Keats' "To Autumn," but the whole poem would be way too much as a model. On the other hand (to quote my students), I may point to the ode form that Keats often used and have the students write a loose ode that praises any daily presence—coffee, clouds, shoe strings, or dogs. The twentieth century excelled in expanding the definition of what any form can be and I take advantage of that expansion. I may show them some other odes by the likes of Thomas McGrath, Donald Justice, or Pablo Neruda (especially the *Odes to Common Things*), and have them compare the forms.

What I am always looking for is what the blues singers called the key to the highway. I want my students to see how art sparks art, how poems are heuristic as they lead to further poems. I am not so much interested in imitation as I am in experiencing the art from the inside: its structures, its impulses, and its tasks. Students have to begin somewhere and other poems are excellent places to begin: they use long lines or short lines; they are written in third person or first person; they use metaphors freely or sparely, whatever. I want my students to think like artists in the sense that artists learn lessons from works of art. Painters are famous for this, but poets do it just as much. I want them to see poems from the inside.

You can't teach creativity but you certainly can encourage it. When I talk with adults about their days in English class in high school, I often encounter a certain ruefulness about the absence of creativity. We provide instruction about knowledge but how much instruction do we offer about creativity? There aren't, to be sure, "rules" about creativity but there are procedures in terms of giving oneself the time and space to try something. My own procedures are simple: Give the task a chance; feel free to discard; don't denigrate your effort; share with others (once you feel comfortable); don't worry about what should be because there is no should be. We are all in the same leaky boat of the first draft. Art is the random becoming focused and both sides of the equation need to be recognized.

Creativity Guidelines

1. Give the task a chance.
2. Feel free to discard.
3. Don't denigrate your effort.
4. Share with others (once you feel comfortable).
5. Don't worry about what should be because there is no should be.

To say that students want to write poems is an understatement. Quite a few of them are already doing it on their own. They are full of feelings and they need to get those feelings down on paper. By acknowledging the writing of poems as a public endeavor, it makes students see how poems are part of the world and not just something for their diaries. The diary has its place, I'd be the first to say, but so does the sense of the poem as something that can be shared in the light of day. When something one student writes moves another student, something truly precious has happened.

Every week of the school year, students read their own poems (or someone else's) in my classroom. Typically one student a week in each class gets to read something he or she wrote or a favorite poem (which could be well known or by another student or a parent or whatever) or song lyric. (Yes, I check the song lyrics ahead of time for school appropriateness. If swearing is being used for the sake of swearing—and it very often is—I say that there are plenty of lyrics out there that are appropriate.) Usually the student just reads the poem and that's that but if the student wants feedback (and my students know that means more than "Really nice poem, Kathy.") then the student says he or she would like to hear any responses. This can take more time in a class period but it's well worth it. The classroom becomes something more than Mr. P's stage; it's my students' stage also.

september 12

questions

I dictated a short poem by the contemporary American poet Jane Gentry today. The poem is entitled "Exercise in the Cemetery" and goes like this:

> At dusk I walk up and down
> among the rows of the dead.
> What do the thoughts I think
> have to do with another living being?
> In the eastern sky, blue-green as a bird's egg,
> a cloud with a neck like a goose
> swims achingly toward the zenith.

As usual we went over the words before I started asking questions. That meant in the case of this poem we talked about what *zenith* means and what part of speech *achingly* is. No one knew the word *zenith*. We wound up discussing other words that have to do with something being topmost.

When I ask questions, I ask questions about the poem's art. Because any given poem has so many facets, I find that I never really repeat a question. I also find that I don't have to ask questions that put the student on the spot by making presuppositions and creating anxiety. This means I never ask what a line or a poem means nor do I ask what the students think the poet had in mind. If you talk about art, meaning will take care of itself because art creates meaning. To talk about what the poet had in mind is to practice mind reading. I am interested in the text not in hypotheses about the poet's mind. When I hear (and I have heard) a teacher say "Now, what did Shakespeare mean to say here?" I cringe. It's what a friend of mine calls "the intentional fallacy."

Poems are not hierarchical—every word matters. That means the doors into a poem are as numerous as the words in the poem.

> Poems are not hierarchical— every word matters.

Accordingly my first question to the class usually will be a question about word choice. As my students say, "When we talk about poems, we talk about language." In the case of Gentry's poem this means I might ask what word is most surprising to my students or what word doesn't seem to belong or what word doesn't make sense to them or what word moves them the most. What I want is for my students to respond to the words in the poem as words. Poetry affords me the opportunity to focus on the lives of the words.

Ten Questions to Ask About Words
1. What word intrigues you most?
2. Is there a word that confuses you?
3. What word surprises you?
4. What word seems most metaphorical?
5. Is there a word that seems unnecessary?
6. What word is most important?
7. What is the most physical word in the poem?
8. What is the most specific word in the poem?
9. What is the strongest sound word in the poem?
10. What is the most dynamic verb in the poem?

Today, for instance, we wound up talking about *achingly*. We talked about why the word seemed important in the poem, how it lent an emotional note to the end of the poem. What was that note? We talked about the connotations of the word—that there seemed some pain in the word (*ache*) and also some longing (*ache* for someone or something). We talked about how both senses were important for the end of the poem. Teresa Caron in my first period class said that she felt heartache in the word. How true. So how much resolution can there be in a seven-line poem? And does this subject invite resolution? What happens in talking about a word is what always happens: from the single word we move on to other aesthetic and thematic issues.

Most of the time I make the opening question about the poem open-ended in the sense that I want to get various student responses. I don't want them to feel from me that one thing is more important than another. I want them to feel their own way through the poem. Hence my predilection for starting with a word choice question. Sometimes, however, I may choose a word I want to focus on. Often, it may be a word that doesn't seem at first glance a real important word in the poem. I think this approach is particularly important when we are confronting canonical poems that the kids already may have notions about. When I teach 'Out, Out—' by Robert Frost, I like to ask about the word *work* (Call it a day, I wish they might have said / To please the boy by giving him the half hour / That a boy counts so much when saved from work.) and how that word informs the poem. It's not a dramatic word, but it's a very important word in the world of the poem. Sometimes I ask my students to propose a word of their choosing that is modest but important to the poem. It gets them thinking about the different sorts of words that make up a given poem.

Whenever I teach a poem I prepare at least ten questions to ask my students. This allows me latitude as we proceed through the discussion. If it seems to be lagging, I have plenty of fresh questions. Here are the questions I had for Gentry's poem:

1. How many sentences is the poem made up of?
2. What happens in terms of structure in the three sentences? (What occurs in each sentence?)
3. What do the sentences have to do with one another? (What is the relationship, say between the second sentence and the third sentence?)

4. Why does the poem end with an extended image?
5. What feeling does the poem leave you with? What can you point to specifically in the language of the poem that causes that feeling?
6. What makes it a complete poem?
7. What effect does the personification in the last sentence have? (If my students don't remember the literary term, we define it then and there.)
8. What does the title have to do with the poem?
9. Given that this is a free verse poem, are the line breaks expected or unexpected?
10. If the word *achingly* is removed from the poem, what difference does it make?

I could make up ten more questions easily. Why is the poem written as one stanza? Why *eastern*? What connotations arise from *blue-green*? Are sentence structures repeated or varied? The point of the questions is to get the kids thinking about the near-infinite particularities of this one poem. If you make students aware that literature is art they respond to it as art. They come to see that art is a process, and that once upon a time the great poet was scratching out words and putting in new ones just as they do in their own writing. If you teach literature as knowledge then they start looking for the right answers. If you teach literature as art what they come to understand is that there aren't right answers; there are thoughtful and articulate and intuitive answers, but a poem can't be solved; it isn't a problem. It's a form of being and we would no more ask a poem what it means than ask a friend what he or she means by existing.

I'm passionate about poetry, and I want my kids to grow up and become readers and speakers and writers of poems. Poetry rides in the back of the bus in this society. I feel that kids who don't have poetry in their lives are missing a part of what it means to be human. It is possible to go through life without poetry, but it can be a positive influence, offering powerful solace and pleasure. As the poet writes, "What do the thoughts I think / have to do with another living being?" Poetry is our companion.

september 13

profile

What is the point of the questions? Where am I going in terms of goals and objectives? Once upon a time I worked in a school where every lesson plan had to be defined in terms of goals and objectives. We stopped doing it because no one ever checked on whether we were achieving our goals and objectives, but that's another story. I believe strongly as a teacher that I always want to have a sense of why I am doing what I am doing, where I am trying to go. I like to build—that seems one thing the school year is about.

What I am trying to create in my questions isn't an exhaustive meaning, but a profile of the poem. You can draw a profile with a couple of pencil marks, or you can fill in a profile with many small, meticulous strokes. It depends how thorough you want to be and what sense you want to communicate. The issue with teaching any poem is how much I want to fill in, how thoroughly I want to query the poem.

I could, for instance, ask one question about the Gentry poem from yesterday, say, the structure question. This would lead us to ponder how one structures a brief narrative poem, which would represent learning about writing and I could leave it there. (It carries over to their writing of both poetry and prose in terms of what one sentence has to do with another.) Or I could ask all of my ten questions about the poem and really investigate it thoroughly in order to convey a sense of what makes this poem tick. That seems very important at times—to take a class period and go as deeply as possible into a given poem. That sense of the poem's deep individuality is, after all, what makes students aware of what a work of art really constitutes. A work of art can support all of these questions effortlessly because it is a work of art. If we don't, on occasion, take the time to do a thorough profile, then the students won't have a sense of this.

Sometimes, I'll stop in the middle of my questioning and ask my students if they have had enough of the poem, if they want to go further. Once the kids understand that it's a serious question on my part, they respond seriously. More often than not they want to go ahead. They are curious how far we can go. When I ask just one question they know I am picking that question carefully. As they like to say, it signifies.

A few years ago I drew up a form for my students and me to use concerning a poem's profile. It looks like this:

Profile of a Poem

ELEMENTS	STRATEGIES	WHAT I NOTICED/ EXPERIENCED
Word Choice	Parts of speech Detail Sensory language Image Metaphor Repetition Etymology	
Organization	Line Stanza Form Structure Turns	
Ideas/Content	Subject matter Webbing/mapping Theme Narrative	
Voice	Tone/mood Point of view Drama Persona Audience	
Conventions	Spelling Punctuation Capitalization Grammar Rhythm Sound Margins	
Sentence Fluency	Syntax Lineation Variety	

The elements come from a standard approach to language arts that is used throughout our school district. We all try to focus on those elements in our students' writing. Of course, poetry enables me to focus closely on these elements in their reading, too—a fact that hasn't gone unnoticed by other teachers at other levels in the district.

The terms are pretty much self-explanatory. In the *Word Choice* area I want my students to note vivid, sensory language. I want them to pay attention to whether various parts of speech such as adjectives are being used and how they are being used. I want them to try to focus on how much image and metaphor a given poem uses. If a word is repeated I want to know why. I like students to check at least one etymology in a poem. Students need to delve into words in order to feel what words are. Everything feels as though it was made yesterday to them. That each word has a history comes as a surprise to them.

Organization speaks to how the poem is put together. Poems typically use lines and stanzas. Sometimes they involve a specific, predetermined form. Structure takes some time for students to get a handle on, but when they do they are excited. Basically I am asking them to examine what each specific sentence in the poem does: whether it sets a scene or asks a question, presents some images or shows a memory, or offers a metaphor. Similarly I like them to try to identify if there is a place in the poem where a decisive turn occurs that takes the poem to its outcome. All of this makes them think carefully about writing and how writers go about writing.

It's somewhat perplexing when we come to *Ideas/Content* because it doesn't function the way it does in prose. Indeed, this is where sins are committed against poems in the urge to reduce the poem to a concept or paraphrase or abstraction or that mythic "what the poet intended." One has to be wary because a poem is always a local endeavor whose every word has a vital presence. I try to keep this area quite simple and down to earth. Accordingly, I ask students to note quite simply what the poem is about—rabbits, baseball, war, first love. Often the title takes care of this. Then we do some mapping/webbing, which means I ask students to link a word that seems important to them with another word that seems important to them. They like the challenge of this activity and the openness of it, too.

When I ask about theme (and it's usually late in the discussion), I ask them to state it in a word or two or three—fear, loss, compassion, alienation. I am careful to note that theme isn't a reduction. Theme is an essence, an emanation, a sort of intellectual and emotional ghost the actual poem creates. Theme is a place the poem takes you to. First you have to travel with the poem to get there. As for narrative, I ask them how much of it is present in a poem. Does the poem tell a story? What sort of story? Who is in the story? These aspects are not airtight compartments: an aspect such as narrative may seem more relevant at times to organization, as, for instance, when we discuss how a poem turns. That's okay. I want my students to feel that a work of art is multidimensional. The profile form is an approximation, a means of approach.

> Theme is a place the poem takes you to. First you have to travel with the poem to get there.

Voice feels very personal to my students and they like that. It makes them scrutinize word choices carefully, as they note shades of feeling various words embody. Who is telling the poem is always an important issue, as is the audience the poem seems aimed at. The degree of drama in the poem asks students to gauge how much conflict is in the poem, how much pressure is felt, and what consequences are present in the poem. The notion of the persona makes students evaluate how close the narrator of the poem feels to the actual poet—sometimes as identical as language and flesh can be and sometimes utterly dissimilar.

The *Conventions* combine the standard mechanics with poetry's particular mechanics—*rhythm* (meter or free verse), *sound* (rhyme, assonance, consonance, alliteration, onomatopoeia), and what sorts of margins the poem on the page uses. One fascinating aspect of poetry (and why I ask students to note what they experience) is that conventions such as rhythm can be described in emotional, subjective terms: Rhythm can feel happy or sad, bittersweet, or slow or brisk, or hundreds of other descriptors. For that matter, I sometimes ask my students how they experienced the punctuation—intrusive, not noticeable, abrupt, or what? It puts a new spin on "comma-world" for them.

Sentence Fluency asks students to actively evaluate sentences: How they are constructed, how those sentences are stretched across lines, and what sorts of sentences, are represented in a given poem. Students aren't used to paying such close attention to sentences, but it benefits their own writing enormously. They start to become connoisseurs of sentences with very definite opinions. They note, for instance, whether a poet uses the same sentence structure over and over or whether (and how much) the poet varies the sentence structure.

At first the form looks somewhat overwhelming to the kids, but as they come to learn the terrain the form becomes second nature. They realize how many issues are floating around in any given poem and they are able in time to formulate which issues seem interesting to them in a given poem. They enjoy responding to the issues without getting stuck in the impasse of subjectivity. ("I think this is a good poem because I like it," as a student once put it.) In terms of getting them to scrutinize language carefully, I think the form is an aid to students at any level. Other teachers have agreed with me. With some modifications of language, a number of the elementary school teachers are using the form.

september 14

discussion (the ball field and mystery)

When we are talking about poems, I sometimes get remarks that come from I-don't-know-where. These remarks can be "That reminds me of . . ." or "I think this is about . . ." or "I get this feeling. . . ." Some of my students have the notion (and I'm not sure where they get it from) that a poem is a subjective bog and anything they want to say about that bog is okay. Subjectivity rules. Of course, subjectivity does rule in poetry in the sense that there are no definitive answers about a poem. It's a work of art and each of us brings something different to the poem. Our individuality does not cancel the actuality of the poem. It doesn't mean anything you want it to mean.

The analogy I like to use about the poem is from baseball. A poem is like a ball field in that it has fair ground and foul ground. Lines demarcate fair ground from foul ground. The text of the poem is fair ground and we, as readers and listeners, have to pay attention to the fair ground. Remarks that have, in essence, nothing to do with the actualities of the poem are off in foul ground. I simply say "foul ball" when students go off on a tangent. It's not disrespectful, just a statement of fact. I am trying to teach them to respond to the poem rather than immediately launching into what the poem reminds them of or what they think the poem is about. (Their interest in symbolizing is frightening sometimes. The mere poem doesn't satisfy their lust for deeper, hidden meaning.)

In essence, we talk about how the poem works. We commonly use the phrase *work of art* and in the classroom we honor the work that makes the poem what it is. That, after all, is how writers talk about writing when they get together. It's the premise of writing workshops and it's a reasonable one. How does Shakespeare write a sonnet compared to how Edna St. Vincent Millay writes a sonnet? Not merely in terms of the subject matter but the actual construction. How many rhetorical phrases are used? What sound devices, above and beyond the end rhymes, are present? How elaborate is the syntax? How do the final couplets function? These may seem fairly sophisticated questions but I have used them with sophomores in high school. Once the kids understand that they don't have to fear poetry as a dark cave containing answers they never can find, they become open to exploring how poems actually work. The elements that comprise poems—rhythm, sound, line, stanza, syntax—are finite. That's comforting.

Almost inevitably when we do this kind of talking someone will raise a hand and protest that by talking about the poem we are destroying the mystery of the poem. I like to throw the issue out to the class when it comes up rather than delivering a speech. I can remember very well a debate between two seniors a few years ago—Hale Anderson and Ruthanne Czernak. Hale's point of view was that poems are magic and you can't talk about magic. He said it would be like the magician David Copperfield telling you how he did his tricks. Ruthanne, however, told Hale it was just the opposite—poetry was "talkative magic" (her words—I wish I had thought them up). She said that the more we talked the more mysterious the poem became because the poem was "still the same words we started with."

What we typically decide as a class is that poetry is a mystery in the sense that the words can't be added up to a specific sum that is the same for each person. A poem can be utterly lucid and simple as in a brief William Carlos Williams lyric (think of the famous "The Red Wheelbarrow"), and be utterly mysterious in the sense that existence is mysterious—it just is. We don't know why. All we can know is how and how only takes us so far down the road. We are left with awe. To my mind (and I try to lay off my opinions so that the kids can work this out for themselves) discussing how a poem works furthers the sense of mystery. We can talk and talk about technique, but the whole of the poem and its corresponding emotional import is always greater than our miscellaneous perceptions. The mystery is the stronger for our talking about it.

What I often find is hiding behind the word *mystery* is a predilection for vagueness and incoherence. Some students like the idea of being able to read anything into a poem as if it were a Rorschach blob. Gently (though I have been known to become exasperated during last period on gray, cold Wednesday afternoons when I look hard at the runny noses and drooping eyelids) I point out that each word in a poem is chosen carefully and that focusing on those words in no way diminishes the mystery of their being those words rather than some other words. Poetry, as Robert Frost was fond of pointing out, is metaphorical thinking. Metaphors promote mystery in that they expand our sense of life rather than narrow it. When a number of metaphors consort (and that is one definition of what a poem is), the mystery deepens. This complication is one of the gifts art bestows. In a brief lyric, Emily Dickinson can move our heads around our necks effortlessly yet we remain in the same place. She doesn't create mystery; she elucidates mystery as in "#805":

> Poetry, as Robert Frost was fond of pointing out, is metaphorical thinking.

> This Bauble was preferred of Bees—
> By Butterflies admired
> At Heavenly—Hopeless Distances—
> Was justified of Bird—
>
> Did Noon—enamel—in Herself
> Was Summer to a Score
> Who only knew of Universe—
> It had created Her.

Each word is a world. That lucidity and mystery can be so intertwined is hard for us to accept. It seems a spiritual lesson that calls for humility. For my part, when my students raise the issue of mystery, I try to tread lightly. They are onto something important. They sense that poetry is ancient and emanates from the incantatory world of charms and spells and chants. A high school classroom of cream-colored cinder blocks that is lit by fluorescent lights is a pretty demystified place. I want them to feel that to approach the mystery is not to ruin it.

september 19

the affective domain

Typically, schools are being pulled in two directions. The demand for results keeps growing. *Accountability* has been a buzzword for decades—a long life for a buzzword. Students must produce verifiable results. Perhaps as a response to the experimental sixties, an often-acerbic wariness has characterized the attitudes of politicians toward public schools.

Yet, at the same time, a lot is said about paying attention to our students' feelings. We are advised to teach the whole child (something grade school teachers have been doing forever). We are told to respect our students' feelings and allow room for growth. When some horror such as Columbine occurs, there is a lot of hand wringing about the anonymity of large schools and the cultures of schools. How did this happen?

I don't pretend to have the answer to these social issues, but I do know that poetry could play a lot greater role in schools than it currently does. Students are told what to say "no" to, but I'm not so sure what they are being told to say "yes" to. They have plenty of entertainment and they have plenty of information. What they don't have plenty of is inspiration—the inrush of spirit. Poetry, of course, is based on inspiration. It is the lamp of the inner life. It is the spirit taking unaccountable leaps.

Many times when I read a poem a sort of stunned hush comes over the classroom. My students, like a lot of high school students, have the feeling—thanks to the media they have been imbibing since they were children—that they have seen it all. Yet when they hear a poem, they often say absolutely nothing. It moves them and it leaves them speechless. A day ago I read "Hard

Rock Returns to Prison from the Hospital for the Criminal Insane"
by Etheridge Knight. It's a very powerful poem about a black man
who is lobotomized and who, accordingly, is rendered a shell of
what he was. The last stanza goes like this:

> And even after we discovered that it took Hard Rock
> Exactly 3 minutes to tell you his first name,
> We told ourselves that he had just wised up,
> Was being cool; but we could not fool ourselves for long,
> And we turned away, our eyes on the ground. Crushed.
> He had been our Destroyer, the doer of things
> We dreamed of doing but could not bring ourselves to do,
> The fears of years, like a biting whip,
> Had cut deep bloody grooves
> Across our backs.

I could talk about racism for a long time before I would ever make
the impact this poem makes. No one said anything. No one was
looking at anyone else. Utter quiet. I stayed with the silence and
just let it be. A couple of minutes went by before I asked a small
question: "Why is the word *Crushed* all by itself?" The question
opened up a floodgate of feeling.

Poetry makes no apologies about its being the art of feelings.
It recognizes that we as human beings live and die as feeling creatures and that every moment of exis-
tence is colored by our neural subjectivity. It rejoices in our subjectivity as a
quality that makes us human. What
poetry gives my students is a safe area
in which they can try out their own
feelings. They are not being put on the
spot. They are not talking in generalities; they are talking about a
text. If they get personal, it is in relation to the text.

> What poetry gives my students is a safe area in which they can try out their own feelings.

What I have seen over the course of hundreds of discussions
(really thousands but I am afraid to do the math) is how students
will begin from the poem and then use the poem as a sort of rope
to go exploring their own feelings. When we talked about "Hard
Rock . . ." one student spoke about science. He asked whether
what was done to Hard Rock was considered science at the time.
He went on to say that he didn't believe in science. Another student immediately questioned him. How could he not believe in

science? What was our world without science? The student began talking about his own situation and how his father believed everything should be done for scientific reasons, how science had all the answers to life's difficulties. He said he respected his father but he didn't believe his father and that there was a difference between respect and belief. As a class, we were quiet and listened. I went back to the text, to how in that part of the poem Knight doesn't use metaphor to describe what happens to Hard Rock. He uses simple direct language. Why? I asked them.

I don't pretend to be a counselor. I always try to go back to the poem when personal feelings come out. That's not because I don't respect what students need to say. I respect them hugely. It's because I want them to stay with what elicited those feelings. I want them to see how the poem provokes them and that is one reason we read poems—to be provoked. If you want to go through life self-complacently you don't need poetry.

That may be one reason for nervousness about poetry. It elicits feelings and one can never predict where those feelings are going. Without a doubt, some poets are downright harrowing. Yet I always remember what a young woman said about reading Sylvia Plath. We were reading some of Plath's darkest poems, such as "Daddy" and "Lady Lazarus." What she said was that she felt much better from reading the poems because she realized she wasn't the only person who had hard, dark feelings. Scary as the poems were, they were a source of inspiration to her. She wasn't alone in her feelings. That Plath constructed the art she constructed was all the more inspiring. Students crave emotional honesty and poetry has never been interested in hypocrisy. Poetry cannot be put on a witness stand in a court of law. It isn't legal truth, or journalistic truth, or historical truth, but as emotional truth it is unassailable.

september 22

reading poems

For a long time, since I was a teenager, I have tried to read a poem every day. As is the case with many people who love poetry, I have a teacher to thank for my introduction to poetry. My junior year in high school I had Mr. Reiser. He was cool in a lot of ways—patches on the elbows of his sport coats, hair down over his shirt collar, records he would play in the morning before school started—jazz records. He was a devotee of poetry and played Dylan Thomas for us. He told us about Allen Ginsberg and the Beats. He loved all poetry and read Whitman with a fervor that I can still feel. He was the real thing and I knew I wanted to have what he had in my own life.

What surprised me was how easy it was to make it part of my life. I walked in a bookstore and bought Ferlinghetti's *Coney Island of the Mind*, *Leaves of Grass* by Walt Whitman, and a translation of the *Poet in New York* by Lorca. I was gone. Solid gone. I couldn't believe my good fortune, especially because a lot of my adolescent life was not the stuff of good fortune—parents divorcing, uncertainty on my part about both of them and their palpable anger, wanting desperately to connect with a girl and not connecting, drifting through most of school. I wasn't on the "A" track. Maybe that's why, in part, I took to poetry. I had more feelings than I knew what to do with and not much direction.

I'm still reading. After I have graded my last papers, taken the dog for a walk, made love (on the nights my wife and I remember we have bodies), turned the heat down, checked in with my fifteen-year-old son about his day, and twenty other things, I read some poems. Lately I have been reading an American poet who died very young. His name is Joe Bolton. He committed suicide at the age of twenty-eight.

Poets believe that the life vanishes but the poems may remain. In Bolton's case this seems true. His work is blue, dark blue—full of longing, desire, melancholy. It's romantic in the basic sense of the word, which is to say it considers feeling to be the touchstone of our being human. Feeling is a good in itself—even bad feeling is better than no feeling. It's an attitude that can make for powerful poetry, but it can be awfully hard in terms of living a coherent life.

What particularly charms me about Bolton is that he was rigorous about his versification, even as his feelings threatened to drown him. His work is quiet and decorous and carefully wrought. To my mind, it makes the sadness of his feelings all the stronger. Art can be a counterweight. Tonight I have been reading the same poem over and over. It's called "Elegy for Roland Barthes." It has an epigraph that is "'I don't think he needs an elegy.'—my ex-wife." Bolton had a sense of humor.

> They do not need us,
> Any more than last year's leaves
> Are signs of anything
> Unless we make them so for our sake,
> As I am doing now.
> Here on the back porch,
> In the twilight,
> It is merely spring,
> And the leaves that fell or the wind shook loose
> Make one darkness
> With the season's first green shoots.
> But the white gown you have hung from the line
> Shines. Phosphorescent.
> It catches what light the sky can manage yet
> And moves, and is alive.
> And if it is only wind,
> Say that the wind, for our sake,
> Needs a form,
> And that your white gown
> Lifting there in the dark
> Makes a possibility of wind and darkness,
> While the language of children
> Fades along the street.
> I cannot remember
> When spring seemed less than a miracle,
> When my body made any pretense it would last,
> When summer began like anything
> But a memory of summer.
> There is something beautiful
> About what returns inevitably,
> Though what is gone
> Is perhaps also beautiful
> By its own code,
> But which we translate:
> *Later*—the street silent, no wind;
> A white gown shining in starlight
> For no one.

It's quiet in the house when I read this and I just let the poem occur. The poem haunts me—I can feel the time of year and see the white gown and feel the poet's mind—and that must be one reason I like to read poetry. I like to remember how haunting it is to be alive, that it's nothing to take for granted. Sometimes students tell me they don't want to read poetry because they don't want to be depressed. I tell them that poetry isn't about being up or down. It's about being—period. Whatever forms being takes, poetry is going to be there. It's fearless. I go to bed with the italicized word in my head, how it shimmers all by itself.

> I tell them that poetry isn't about being up or down. It's about being—period.

september 24

rhythm

I like to stress the basics of poetry at the beginning of the year. When the kids are little kids as opposed to being kids who are taller than I am, they are emphatic about the rhythmic dimension of poetry. They chant, recite nursery rhymes, sing jumprope songs. One teacher in the elementary school in my neighborhood has her students march to lunch reciting nursery rhymes. I love her for that. I try to get down to her school once a year to see it in action: All these six-year-olds clomping down the hall reciting "Hey diddle diddle." They've got the beat.

As they get older the beat recedes. Self-consciousness, growing up, losing interest—you can take your choice as to why. It's my job to bring back the sense of the beat. I start by pointing out to them what they already know: English is an accentual-syllabic language. Meaning what? This means you can't go three syllables in English without wanting to put an accent on one of those syllables (assuming one is reading in a human voice rather than an android drone). I have my students say something like "It's got to be me." I ask them where the accents go and we talk about emphasis and inflection, how the voice calls the shots.

How does rhythm compel people? How is rhythm in our lives? We start talking about nature, about the tides and seasons and day and night. We talk about women's bodies. Often some of my female students acknowledge how menstruation is a profoundly rhythmic event in their lives. As one of them put it, "My body is the moon." We talk about rain on the roof and wind and snow falling. We talk about how people walk down the street, how no two people have exactly the same gait. I talk about the scene in the movie *Dead Poet's Society* when Robin Williams has his students walk around to illustrate my point about each person's rhythmic gait. (If I'm organized I show them the scene.)

We talk about how other languages work in terms of rhythm—how some languages are strictly syllabic, how pitch influences rhythm in other languages. If I have a foreign-language speaker in the classroom, we talk about the student's native language. When we get back to English, I ask them how English poetry compels people. I ask them by reading them some lines of Shakespeare. Today I chose the moment when Macbeth is mulling the murders he and his wife have planned:

> If it were done when 'tis done, then 'twere well
> It were done quickly. If the assassination
> Could trammel up the consequence, and catch,
> With his surcease, success, that but this blow
> Might be the be-all and the end-all here,
> But here, upon this bank and shoal of time,
> We'd jump the life to come.

After we have sorted out the language questions (*jump* means *risk*, etc.), we talk about what rhythmically is compelling here. Sometimes my students know what meter is, sometimes they don't; in any case, we wind up talking about where I began the lesson— English is an accentual-syllabic language. We talk about the pattern we hear, that alternation of unaccented and accented syllables. We talk about long words and how they are accented (*assassination*) and lines that consist wholly of monosyllables. Why is the opening, monosyllabic line particularly effective? What effect does it have on the listener? How slowly or quickly do the words want to be said? How plain is the pattern based on that line? How do the little, almost unnoticed words of the English language (*it*, *and*, and *of*, for instance) figure into the rhythmic equation here?

We identify *iambic pentameter* as the applicable literary term, but it's my students' ears I care most about. After we discuss the rhythmic element, I have some of them read the passage and we talk about the differences among the readings. It doesn't take long but it's fascinating for them because they really start listening to the language and thinking about what a powerful engine meter is; how, by and large, every other syllable is going to be emphasized. How is that going to affect the words that fall into the pattern? Do the words feel stiff for having to cohere to the pattern? How much do you notice the pattern when you read the passage? How do the elisions feel when you read them? *Elisions?* What does that mean?

september 25

rhythm continued

I pick up rhythm again today in *Macbeth*. We have a reasonably clear sense of meter from our discussion yesterday. I ask them if they remember any of the lines from yesterday's passage and I get bits and pieces of the speech. We talk some about how rhythm is *mnemonic* (new word for them) and how a rhythmic pattern can make words memorable. Then I ask them if meter is the sum of rhythm. Certainly it has been the main highway of English poetry for hundreds of years. But what about Shakespeare's plays? Don't they have prose in them? What is that?

I point out what those who have read the play often recall on their own, namely that just about everyone speaks in meter in the play except for the porter. When Macduff asks the porter, "What three things does drink especially provoke?" the porter replies in a prose paragraph:

> Marry, sir, nose-painting, sleep, and urine. Lechery, sir, it provokes and unprovokes. It provokes the desire, but it takes away the performance. Therefore much drink may be said to be an equivocator with lechery. It makes him and it mars him, it sets him on and it takes him off, it persuades him and disheartens him, makes him stand to and not stand to; in conclusion, equivocates him in a sleep and giving him the lie, leaves him.

Since they have heard the word *lechery*, I know my students are listening carefully—something involving sex is going on. They have encountered Mercutio so they know Shakespeare has some

double entendres up his sleeve. Once we sort the language out—
equivocate, for instance—we talk about rhythm. Is there rhythm
here? (I usually dictate the passage because it's not long. They can
consult what they have written down.)

We talk about sentence structure, repetition, and phrases. As
with yesterday, different students read the passage. What words
are being stressed? Can we say fairly definitively that certain
words are accented and other words not accented? Why is the
porter speaking in prose? Shakespeare could make his speech
metrical if he so chose. Why prose for the porter?

We come to the conclusion that rhythm very definitely is a
factor in the porter's speech but it isn't meter. It's a hybrid where
the accentual factor is noticeable but not predominant. It's looser
and feels, despite the balanced phrases, more wandering and
impulsive. This talk leads us to consider who the porter is. He's
not a noble like most of the leading characters. Nor is he a spirit.
Why do nobles and witches speak in meter but the porter (and we
have defined that word because some students don't know what a
porter is) doesn't. We talk about social ranks and who is important in a society and who isn't important.

From that point I take a big leap. I tell them (and I admit I love
to make such pronouncements—one reason I'm an English
teacher is because the classroom is a stage of sorts) that they are
all porters and that's why most poetry these days is free verse.
They stare at me and at each other and sometimes they laugh and
more often I get a "Say what?". I dictate to them the ending lines
from Frank O'Hara's "The Day Lady Died":

> and for Mike I just stroll into the PARK LANE
> Liquor Store and ask for a bottle of Strega and
> then I go back where I came from to 6th Avenue
> and the tobacconist in the Ziegfield Theatre and
> casually ask for a carton of Gauloises and a carton
> of Picayunes, and NEW YORK POST with her face on it
>
> and I am sweating a lot by now and thinking of
> leaning on the john door in the 5 SPOT
> while she whispered a song along the keyboard
> to Mal Waldron and everyone and I stopped breathing

After we have sorted out the language issues (an activity that
keeps my students honest day-in, day-out because part of walking

into the room is learning about words), we talk about rhythm. He has written these lines out so they look like Shakespeare's lines. What are the differences?

My students start looking for a pattern. There are accents but a pattern is another story. And what about the little words we talked about in Shakespeare? What's going on with the lines ending with *and*? What is that? What tone do we have here? Who is Mike? Is he a noble? Is Frank O'Hara a noble? Where is this poem occurring? What happened to punctuation? Why the run-on sentence?

"So if I tell you (I say) this is free verse, what does that mean?" We go back to the lines and talk about the rhythmic feeling that the lines communicate. There is a feeling—everyone is certain about that. Although things are casual (as O'Hara himself notes) someone important has died. The poet's learning about Billie Holiday's death "deserves a poem"—to quote Andrea, who sits in the third row and tends to play with her hair. Would the poem be better, if it were in meter? (I want to push it further.) What would meter offer? Most of the kids like the poem the way it is, but there usually are dissenters. Because, they say, we aren't nobles doesn't mean that meter can't speak to our lives. The pattern that meter offers matters. Death is profound and deserves all the dignity we can give it. We stop there for the day except for some questions as to who this guy Frank O'Hara is. I pass the book around.

september 26

rock 'n' roll

I'm not done with meter. I want to know how their ears are functioning in terms of what they listen to and what I listen to. They are, after all, drenched in lyrics. I could fill a blackboard with the names of bands they know and still have listed only a fraction of their music. Lyric, in the sense of matching words to notes, is at the heart of the Anglo-American poetry tradition, be it the ballad or the song, to say nothing of an African-American form such as the blues. I want them to connect lyric with lyrics, the song impulse with the words. I want them to feel the weight and drive of the syllables, as they comprise any given line.

I focus on Chuck Berry. My older sister, Marcie, was a fan and passed her enthusiasm on to me. For my money (admittedly a teacher's salary) Chuck Berry is as much a poet as anyone in the American tradition. Some of my students know him from their parents and some from listening to the oldies stations and some don't know him at all. I start off today by dictating this line from "Nadine": "And I was campaign shouting like a southern diplomat." My question is simple: What is the rhythm here?

The students hear the line. Lo and behold, Chuck Berry, American icon, is writing classic English meter. Weak/strong, weak/strong, the syllables chug across the line. What I ask my students to look at is whether the rhythmic units are equivalent to whole words. What my students tell me is that more often than not they don't match. The weak syllable of *was* is joined to the strong syllable of *cam*. The rhythmic units tend to split the words. What effect does that have? Students use different words to describe it, but they agree that the accents push you forward while you remain focused on the integrity of the words. One student says, "It's like walking on a log—steady but not so steady at the same time." Another student opines that "It's a left brain, right brain thing. Two mindsets at work simultaneously."

We look more closely at the words. What are those words that are longer than one syllable? Three of them are two-syllable words and the accent is on the first syllable. How does Berry join them? Well, the weak syllable of *-paign* is linked with the strong syllable of *shout*. The weak syllable *a* is linked with *south*. And then there is the three-syllable word *diplomat* that takes accents on both the first and third syllables.

What, some student is bound to ask me, does all this matter? My answer is that Chuck Berry is attending to the genius of the English language—lots of little, one-syllable words that don't have much presence, plus lots of two-syllable words that have an accent on the first syllable, plus some three-syllable words that can take accents on the first and third syllables. The movement of the various syllable combinations is energy and Chuck has tapped into that energy. Every syllable has its role. There are no mouthfuls of quickly spoken words à la Bob Dylan (nothing against Bob, of course). This is pure. In terms of the pattern of meter Chuck conforms absolutely. And you can dance to it. It sings.

We go back and look at the entire stanza the line comes from:

> I saw her from the corner when she turned and doubled back
> And started walkin' toward a coffee colored cadillac
> I was pushin' through the crowd to get to where she's at
> And I was campaign shouting like a southern diplomat.

How about the stanza as a whole? What do you notice about syllable combinations and rhythm? In some lines Berry works the monosyllables hard but sustains the pulse as in line three. In other places, such as line two, he begins with *a* and moves into two words that are two syllables and then a three-syllable word. (And the word we use for the repetition of beginning consonant sounds is? I keep the terminology coming.) When a two-syllable word crops up, it feels like an event if the line is dominated by one-syllable words as in *corner* and *doubled* in line one.

Every syllable is an event. That's another definition of poetry —an art that pays attention to syllables. How much attention the poet bestows on the combinations of syllables varies but the syllables are the primal facts of any line of poetry. How they are organized determines how the poem communicates the feeling it wants to communicate. Chuck is wry and crisp, good-natured and alert, imperative and fooling around at the same time. He is a wit, and careful attention to syllables repays wit because Chuck's words are pegged to notes. There is, of course, endless variation in matching a syllable to a note in terms of how brief or drawn out that syllable may be. Chuck tends to be dead on center. As a class, we count seven beats to a line.

> That's another definition of poetry—an art that pays attention to syllables.

"And what about what you are listening to?" I ask the class. Homework is to go home and write down some lyrics and bring them to class so we can discuss the syllables. I make no restrictions as to the genre—just so there are words. What I get back inevitably gratifies me—not because I am enamored of all the lyrics I receive but because they are starting to listen to the syllables and realize that rhythm is not just in the notes but in the syllables too. They start noticing the classic combinations of syllables and words—for instance, an article, a two-syllable adjective, and a one-syllable noun, as in *a vacant seat*. To say that English is an accentual-syllabic language starts to have some meaning for them. They realize that meter is right there on the radio, not just in Shakespeare and Frost.

Relevance is a badly damaged word, but if I don't connect poetry with my students' lived lives I have to wonder what I am doing. Mostly, poetry is able to carry the fight into their territory. Still, the language of past centuries becomes more dissimilar daily, as my students sometimes seem to disappear completely down the chute of computer-speak. When I can forge ties between the past and the present, I feel I am grounding them in their language. If Chuck Berry can help me do that, all the better.

september 30

threading the poems

Part of what the school year is about for me is what I call "threading the poems." That means how I try to join one poem to another poem in my students' minds. I'm reading them a lot of poems. When I teach them everyday (I, like many teachers, have taught under different schedules), that's 180 poems. There's no problem in finding poems (I have appended a list of favorite anthologies at the back of this journal). What concerns me is that they develop over the course of the year a feeling for the culture of poetry. What concerns me is that they come to feel that poems belong together, that they don't exist on their own as relics or statues we occasionally dust off for the purposes of school. The poems are always there and they are talking to each other. I want my students to feel that they are becoming part of this great conversation that takes place over centuries.

For instance, the day after the Chuck Berry session (so to speak), I read them a sonnet by Edna St. Vincent Millay. I asked them to listen extra carefully to rhythm. Were there any similarities between Edna St. Vincent Millay (I love to say her whole name) and Chuck Berry? My students were quick to hear the meter. We talked about how rhythm is one way to compare poems, how closely or loosely a poet seems to be adopting a pattern, or whether pattern is an issue at all.

Such a discussion is one way I can thread the poems—via technique. Technique or, more generally, art, is crucial to what makes a poem a poem. I always want my students to be thinking about how a poem does its work. But I don't want them to ignore what the poem says. Subject matter is crucial also. However much poems are focused on the struggle to get accents in certain places or maintain the same length stanzas throughout a poem, what is being said wants to be discussed too. Poems are not just assemblages of sound.

It's tricky, however, because I don't want my students to lose sight of technique when they talk about subject matter. Ideally, they come to see how the two fuse and how any separation of them is bound to be artificial. Do Millay and Berry have anything in common in terms of their attitudes about love? We consider Millay's lines from the end of one of her sonnets:

> This have I known always: Love is no more
> Than the wide blossom which the wind assails,
> Than the great tide that treads the shifting shore,
> Strewing fresh wreckage gathered in the gales:
> Pity me that the heart is slow to learn
> What the swift mind beholds at every turn.

Given that the rhythm is nominally the same, what's different? Students point to word choices, for starters. Some are struck by how down home Berry is compared to Millay, who is, in the words of one student, "quite literary." She points to a word such as strewing and says she can't imagine Berry using that word. Others note that Berry is telling a story but Millay is offering an overview.

Then one student says that the issue is where you are in a love affair when you write about the love affair. It makes a big difference if you are just starting or just ending the affair. There are some quiet sighs and amens in response to this and some head turning directed at the girl who said it. So, I ask, where is Berry and where is Millay? We keep talking and I'm pleased with how the students keep going back to the poems and noticing how they work even as they talk about the dynamics of love. The class decides that the fact that Berry writes longer lines seems integral to his vision of what love is. He likes the sense of love as something that's loose and wayward. Nadine has her mind and Chuck has his. Millay feels much tighter to them, much more high-strung. It's not, a female student is quick to say, "just a male/female thing. Guys can be tight about love, too, and girls can be"—she pauses, then laughs—"loose, too." There's more laughter and a few definite looks are exchanged among members of my second period class.

We stay with what *tight* means. The lines are shorter and it feels as though a lot is happening in every line. The lines feel weighty. You feel the pressure and force of love because love is a force and pressure. It's not just play. A number of students find Millay very convincing and moving. She knows what she's talking about. She's been there. Her metaphors express important feelings. Love wants to be talked about in terms of metaphor.

This discussion isn't a big, headline-grabbing deal, but I believe that the English classroom is one place where students can have humane discussions and that such discussions matter deeply. Where I am trying to go in the course of such a discussion is not just to profile the poem (though that is important to me), but also to keep my students thinking about what one poem has to do with another poem. *Higher order thinking* is the educational speak for it. I look at it as making sense of one poem in terms of another poem to the advantage of both poems. I want my students to get a sense of how vast the field of poetry is. Techniques echo and so do themes. Techniques vary and so do themes.

As the year proceeds I simply bring up dictated poems that they have written down in their notebooks and ask them what one such poem has to do with a poem I am presenting that day. I want them to forge ties on their own. They can be quite simple—issues of theme, for instance, or point of view ("This is a first person poem."), or form ("This is free verse.") What I strive for is continuity. I am not presenting poems so they can study them for a test and then forget about them. I am presenting poems to them because poems are part of life. Each person's life forms a thread that links poems. I want my students to sense how they can do that in their own lives.

October and November

The phone rings while I'm on my still sleepy way to the bathroom. It's a close colleague, a PE teacher I run with. One of our students died in a car crash last night. She was alone in the car. Details are sketchy as to how it happened, but first indications are that it seems like driver inexperience. We are having school but our schedule is modified for students to talk and grieve. There will be various counselors available. We will not be "business as usual."

I know who the student is but didn't have her in my classes. I picture her well: She was tall and stooped a bit. I can feel myself gagging on the past tense. She was in school yesterday. She was alive yesterday. What is this *was*?

Sometimes I get the question, "Why do poets write about death so much?" I don't have one answer to the question. Poetry is about unknowing. If you already know something, there's not much point in writing a poem about it. Because death is the great unknown (I'm prone to want to capitalize that phrase), it seems natural that poets would be writing about it. Poetry is about leaping and death is a leap from one realm of being to who knows where. And poetry is about the fate of the spirit. Since death is the termination of spirit in the person as we know that person, poetry has to go there. The animate spirit disappears but the poem remains to commemorate and mourn and celebrate.

When my first period class shuffles in, I can sense the edginess. Most of them I would guess have had experiences with death, but when it is someone who is your age it feels different from a grandparent dying. I get some small "hi's" but it's basically very quiet. They know there's going to be a poem and I tell them that today's poem is by a man named Leo Connellan. The poem is called "Scott Huff":

> Think tonight of sixteen
> year old Scott Huff of
> Maine driving home fell asleep at
> the wheel, his car sprang awake
> from the weight of his foot head on
> into a tree. God, if you need him
> take him asking me to believe in
> you because there are yellow buttercups,
> salmon for my heart in the rivers,
> fresh springs of ice cold water running away.
> You can have all these back for Scott Huff.

I read the poem twice and then Jody Thomas raises her hand and asks if I would mind dictating the poem because she wants to write it down. I look around the room and there are a lot of nods so I dictate the poem.

I ask my students to tell me a word from the poem that they think is an important word. I write the words down on the blackboard: *Scott Huff, Think, God, need,* and *home.* Someone says that it's the whole last line of the poem that is crucial and that we can't limit ourselves to a word. Fair enough. I ask her about the last line and she says it's precisely because the line is so plain and straightforward that it is so moving. In her words the line is "just a bunch of simple words and then there's his name. His name is so much stronger than all those little words. The name is a person, a living person. And that living person is dead." She takes a deep breath.

I agree with her. Sometimes it seems as though the most important thing I do is simple affirmation. Can we ever get enough of it? Then I say that I want to go back to the individual words. We go over them one by one. We talk more about the importance of naming the person and repeating the name in the poem. When I ask if the poet could have put in more details about Scott Huff, hands shoot up—adamant "no's." More detail would take away from the brutal fact of his death. The crucial detail is already there—his age. That's what matters—his age.

We move on to the other words. There is strong feeling that *Think* is a stroke of genius on the poet's part, that it engages the reader immediately. It's not only a reporting of the death; it's a command and a description. At once, it feels as though he's telling the reader to think of this person and that he himself is thinking about Scott Huff. We are caught, implicated, and made to feel the force of the death not only in its own right but also as it affects other people. We go on to talk about what God is doing in the poem and how heartbreaking the words *need* and *home* are. Jamey Marsullo, who sits in the last row and to whom I have spoken more than once about using that distant spot for the purposes of doing his geometry homework, says that what amazes him is "how simple the whole thing is. I mean I could have written this. I always thought poetry was supposed to be too hard to understand but I understand this."

The class wants to hear more poetry by Leo Connellan and I read them more poems. We listen and talk until the bell rings. I stand by the door to make eye contact with them as they leave. They variously shrug, smile sadly, nod, avoid eye contact, talk to one another, make various gestures with their hands. Jamey thanks me on the way out. He pauses and says, "I knew her. I knew her real well." He just looks at me and then says, "Yeah, I knew her." He nods a couple of times as though he is trying to convince himself of something and walks out the door. I have the usual minute and a half before the next class walks in. I go over to the window and stare down at the parking lot. Cars.

october 6

driving to work

Variously on the twenty-five minute drive to school I sing to myself, recite bits of poems, listen to the public radio station, play CDs, worry, plan lessons, daydream, or think. Sometimes, when I am in the thinking mode, I think about poems. I don't think about what they "mean." I don't know who does. Maybe people who write the standardized tests. I tend to think about words in poems.

Maybe it's not really thinking I am doing as much as just marveling at words. I was a kid who never minded using the dictionary. I never understood the attitude of other kids about dictionaries, as if using a dictionary were tantamount to being sent to Siberia. I can still hear Kenny Cox groaning in my fifth grade class: "The dictionary. Why do I want to go near the dictionary?" I thought it was fun to learn new words. I couldn't believe how many words there were. I thought it was exciting there were so many words.

I have encountered more than one Kenny Cox in my own classroom. I let them groan. I'm good-natured about it but I'm persistent about keeping their hands on the dictionary. It's the word-hoard and there's some magic in that word *hoard*. The word's origins have to do with hiding or covering things. It has overtones of treasure. I try in my own enthusiasm for language to make them feel that words are treasures. Out of the infinite realm of noises, we have this trove, this hoard of articulate sounds. We can do more than grunt and wheeze.

Of course we grow dull to language. Day-in, day-out we say the same words over and over. Maybe we encounter a new car name or a name of a person we have never heard before. Mostly it's the same words. That's where poems come in. Poems are wake-up calls for our sense of language. They tell us that even the words we already know are deeper and stronger than our daily usage acknowledges. Words can resonate way beyond their simple communicative tasks.

So today I am thinking about Gerard Manley Hopkins and his poem called "God's Grandeur." I'm an agnostic but that doesn't stop me from adoring the poem. It may make me appreciate it all the more—I'm not sure. I am thinking about the sestet (second stanza) of the sonnet. It goes like this:

> And for all this, nature is never spent;
> There lives the dearest freshness deep down things;
> And though the last lights off the black West went
> Oh, morning, at the brown brink eastward, springs—
> Because the Holy Ghost over the bent
> World broods with warm breast and with ah! bright wings.

Hopkins' obsession with sound is almost lascivious: The alliterations and the vowels incarnate physical presence as they turn sound into throbbing sense. I always feel a throb in this poem, almost as if I felt what it was like to create the world. It's a big feeling to be carrying around in my old Toyota and I try to be careful with it.

What I am thinking about this morning is how Hopkins inserts that exclamatory *ah*! in the last line. Sometimes I take a word out of a poem and ask my students what difference it makes to the

> Sometimes I take a word out of a poem and ask my students what difference it makes to the poem.

poem. If I take out *ah!* what difference does it make? Isn't the lovely final image that repeats the sounds in which the line has reveled quite enough? Well, no, it isn't. The interjection is the human presence making itself felt in the poem. We have the *Holy Ghost* in the previous line and whatever one's religious background, the mere words summon up a serious, supernatural presence. It's daunting. It's connected to Hopkins' beautiful words so it shouldn't be too daunting, but it still is. It's the *ah!* that makes the ending human. It's a blurt and an appreciation and a gasp all at the same time. The poet has to make his joy and amazement felt. And I feel it.

This is a bit of what's going through my mind as I drive. I love how poems are alive in our minds and hearts as we go through life. The old habit of quoting from poems could be tedious when it was used for moralizing purposes, but I love it when someone refers to a line of a poem in the course of daily life. When, later in the year, I ask my students to memorize, I ask them to choose a poem that not only do they like, but that they would like other people to learn about. I ask them to choose a poem that would give them pleasure to recite. They come up with every imaginable choice—from Shakespeare to Kerouac. Sometimes I will ask them if they can connect a line or two of a poem with an event or moment. How do poems speak to our lives?

For me, as I stare at the car in front of me at a traffic light, I find myself being reminded of my lungs and my ability to exclaim. That seems an important part of being alive. It's not dictionary learning, but then I would be the first to say that living is much more than dictionary learning. As Wendell Berry notes, "We live beyond words." Hopkins is making a sound. I find myself saying *ah!* to the air in the car. I say it again—fully and truly. The light changes. I say the sound again, but quietly this time. Then even more quietly so I can barely hear it.

october 9

sound and word play

There are days when I just ask the kids to say a word that they like to say—any word. I want them to sense the pleasure of words in

> There are days when I just ask the kids to say a word that they like to say—any word.

their mouths. It's self-conscious at first, but, as we go around the room, a sort of happy determination sets in. It's as if to say, "This is my word and I like to say it and here it is." The words, of course, turn out to be anything. Today in one class we heard among others: *lollapalooza, circumspect, idiot, bunk, chartreuse, teepee, yikes, sauerkraut,* and *rubbery*. Once in a while I use the words they churn up as a writing prompt, as in "Now write a poem that incorporates some of these words." I like them to generate a poem simply from language. Language inspires poets to write poems and I want my students to participate in that dynamic.

It takes time to get my students to understand that sound is as much of an inspiration to the writing of poetry as some lived experience that sparks a poem. They know about rhyme, but they don't know about how the overall sound texture of the poem (the *soundscape* to coin a word) is an incitement. I make a point when we look at a poem to focus on the soundscape: Are certain vowels repeated? Where? Is there a predominant vowel sound? Similarly, are consonants repeated? Where and in what combinations? Are there predominant consonants in the poem?

Sometimes I will start with a word on the blackboard, *brown*, for instance, and then have my students generate a list of words that play off any sonic aspect of the initial word. We go around the room so that the first student may say *down*. I only allow one direct rhyme per word so the next student has to come up with some variant on the sound—*darn*, for instance. The next student has to say a word that plays off *darn*. And on we go. I want them to sense where sound can take them. Sometimes when we are looking at drafts of student poems, I will do this, but I will make the student do it for his or her own work. I will choose a word from the poem (typically a trite word) and tell the student to come up with a list of words—ten, twenty, thirty, fifty sometimes—that play off the sound of the initial word. Invariably such play leads them to word choices the student otherwise would not have made. Sound is a very important avenue into the precon-

> Sometimes I will start with a word on the blackboard, *brown*, for instance, and then have my students generate a list of words that play off any sonic aspect of the initial word.

scious, which is where poems come from. Sound is primal and so, as they pride themselves on how they link sounds together, are poets.

Today I dictated a short poem by Thomas Hardy called "In Church":

> "And now to God the Father," he ends,
> And his voice thrills up to the topmost tiles:
> Each listener chokes as he bows and bends,
> And emotion pervades the crowded aisles.
> Then the preacher glides to the vestry-door,
> And shuts it, and thinks he is seen no more.
>
> The door swings softly ajar meanwhile,
> And a pupil of his in the Bible class,
> Who adores him as one without gloss or guile,
> Sees her idol stand with a satisfied smile
> And re-enact at the vestry-glass
> Each pulpit gesture in deft dumb-show
> That had moved the congregation so.

My question to the class is simple: "Beyond the end rhymes, what sound events can you identify in the poem?" There's some quiet time as the kids pore over the poem, then I start to see hands up. They note that Hardy uses alliteration at the ends of lines when he seems to want to reinforce his point—*bows and bends, gloss and guile, deft dumb-show.* They note that he puns with sound—*door* and *adores.* They note he will echo a vowel sound from one line to another as in *bows* in line three and *crowded* in line four, or *chokes* in line three and *emotion* in line four. That "knits the poem together more," in the words of a student.

You can go a long way with sound in any moderately artful poem. Hardy, of course, is immoderately artful. I find that students like him a great deal. They delight in how unflinching he is; how he calls them as he sees them and refuses to be taken in by appearances. We talk about how his work with sound allows him to carefully focus the scenes he presents. Over time, the kids see how unique poetry's tools are. They see how powerfully intuitive poetry is, and how it is a medium that must be respected in its own right.

Along these lines, I like to show them the chart of the Frequency Scale of English Vowel Sounds that is reprinted in John

Frederick Nims' classic introduction to poetry entitled *Western Wind*. Actually what I do first is write all the vowel sounds on the board randomly—there are fifteen of them—and ask my students to arrange them from the lowest frequency to the highest frequency: ōō(goof), ō (tone), ŏŏ(look), aw (sought), oi (toy), ow (shout), ah (car), ŭ (dud), u[r] (curd), ă (cat), ĕ (set), ĭ (sit), ī (sigh), ā (day), ēē(tree). I tell them to spend some time sounding the vowels out on their own and then writing down the order according to their own observations. Some students have internalized the sounds and feel they don't need to do that but many do. Then I ask for their orderings and write them on the board. We talk about vowels.

Vowel Sounds

1. Show the vowel sounds to students (not in the ascending order, but randomly)
2. Have students sound the vowels out
3. Have students list the vowels in ascending order from lowest to highest sound
4. Discuss students' lists
5. Ask questions about different vowels (refer to text)

Ordering the vowels is fun because the kids have a chance to use their voices in a way they don't usually get to. There is a lively discussion about different voices producing different senses of vowels: the differences between male and female voices, for instance. Once we have agreed on an order (and there are always holdouts that insist they are right no matter what Nims' chart says) we talk about the emotional overtones of vowels. What difference is there between that long double "o" in *moon* and the trill of the long "e" in *tree*? What happens to lines where low frequency vowels predominate? Or high frequency vowels? Does each vowel sound have a particular emotional ambience? Nims feels they do. We talk about the long "o" sound, for instance. What words do you associate with that sound? Can we draw any emotional conclusions from those words? What does this do to synonyms where the words mean the same thing, but the sounds are different? What is the difference in sound between *big* and *large*?

This sort of question brings us to the world of consonants, particularly consonant combinations. I ask them what the ugliest consonant combination is in the English language. What about the most pleasing? Are certain consonants associated with certain feelings: "He was dim, dumb, and dull"? These discussions are playful, but they show how art is a sort of serious playing around. I find that my students enjoy the sense that poets are actively thinking about the sounds that go into the poem, that the sounds are not wholly arbitrary. It also moves them away from their obsession with end-rhyme and into the whole of the poem.

There's a lot of talk in our world about different intelligences. I don't know if there is something called *poetic intelligence*, but the way poetry synthesizes various modes of perception seems unique to me. T.S. Eliot, who was admittedly less than objective about the matter, said that the poet had the hardest task as an artist because the poet was trying to fuse rhythm, sound, and meaning (in the sense of the connotations and denotations of words) together in every word of the poem. To my also less-than-objective mind, he was right. That is a tall task. My students come to feel that there is a lot more to a poem than writing some lines down and calling it a poem. The beauty of it is that though the art is daunting—they are awed by the likes of Hardy—they are also excited by what art can do. Even something as elementary as sound has infinite possibilities.

october 14

ben

I make a point of having coffee with my son once a week. It's not that we don't talk otherwise. We do. It's that I feel it matters if we go together somewhere to talk. Maybe it's because my own father would never have done it. It was the dinner table or nothing in the house in which I grew up. Maybe it's because I feel part of being father and son is doing all sorts of things together in the world. Having a cup of coffee at the Java Joint is definitely part of the world.

Ben is taller than I am already (not saying a whole lot as I am five nine), has wavy black hair, blue-green eyes, and pale skin. His girlfriend has informed my wife, Maura, and me that Ben is "real cute." Given his girlfriend's interest (and his reciprocating interest), and given that Ben is more interested in listening to music and drawing and fooling around with the guitar and playing soccer than sitting in classes, school is not at the top of his priority list. It never has been. Ben has been happy with school in the way I suspect many if not most kids are happy with school—it's a way to spend the day with other kids.

It's never easy being a teacher's kid. My mom was an English teacher and I made a point of going to another high school to stay away from her. I couldn't see myself walking down the hall and saying "Hi, Mom." I was way too self-conscious for that. She told me to do what I needed to do. But Ben doesn't feel that way. When he sees me during the school day, he looks surprised, as if to say, "You're here too, huh?" It may be something of an act but he seems quite calm about my being a teacher in his school and his being a student in my school. He takes the jokes from the other kids in good grace, which is to say he jokes back.

It may be harder for me. Other teachers figure a teacher's kid is going to be an academic whiz. Ben is not an academic whiz. If he is interested in the teacher and subject, he does B-to-C work. If not, then it can be rocky. Right now Social Studies is rocky. He got a mid-term warning that he is failing. I ask him today what's up with that. No judgments beforehand on my part, just what's up?

Ben leans forward rather than back in his seat so his head is over his cup of latte and he asks me how I feel about multiple-choice tests. I tell him the truth: I have never given one and never will. As a teacher I have no use for them. If you want to ask for a fact, ask for a fact. For my part, my students write. I hasten to add, however, that I don't feel multiple-choice tests are wrong in all situations.

Ben knows I'm begging the question and presses me further. "In Social Studies, for instance? Is it wrong in Social Studies where Mr. Howell lectures every day or shows a video and then gives the same multiple-choice test he has given for twenty years because, as he says, 'History doesn't change' like history was fixed in cement by George Washington or something. Is that okay, Dad?" Ben hasn't raised his voice, but there's a knife in it. What are my principles as a teacher worth?

I know Dick Howell well. Ben isn't exaggerating. Dick is on his own trip as a teacher and his trip is to let the kids know how much he knows about American history according to the textbook. If it's not in the textbook, then it didn't happen, as far as Dick is concerned. And the purpose of teaching is to get those textbook facts into kids' heads so they will grow up knowing some facts. In his teachers' room speech (most teachers have a teachers' room speech), Dick bemoans the softness of school nowadays. "Kids don't really learn any hard knowledge. Ask a kid for a specific date. They don't know one century from another. It's all a jumble in their heads." Some days I sympathize with this, most days I don't. Dick overdoes it, but he has been in the school forever and plans to keep teaching forever. He loves the sound of his own voice.

Our conversation about Social Studies doesn't go anywhere startling, which is to say Ben says he will try and I say I hope so because there is more than one Dick Howell in the school. On the way back home from the coffee shop, Ben puts a CD in the player. It's a band he is very involved with called Rage Against the Machine. *Intense* would be a very mild word to describe the music. The singing is hyperventilatingly vociferous and the guitar line squeals like a machine gun. It's music that welcomes anger. Ben sings along in a sort of squeaky bass, a boy–man's voice.

I've wondered more than once about what it's like for Ben to be sitting there in Dick Howell's class and having the lyrics of "Calm Like a Bomb" or "Born as Ghosts" floating through his head. I think how much school is something that kids endure because they have to endure it. I think about how school is a machine with its tracks and tasks and grades. We trust it's a benign machine, but the name of the band to which Ben is listening isn't lost on me.

I look over at Ben and he's lost in the music and his own thoughts. I tend to shrug about school situations and say, "This too will pass." I also tend to get upset: My collegial hypocrisy only goes so far. I've asked some of the poets I have brought to school to tell the class what poetry gives them and two words that come up over and over are *solace and inspiration*. Those are always valuable commodities in this world that numbs us. The song coming from the car speakers likens school to a tomb. I feel a shiver along my spine, but it's a good shiver. Young people want to seize the language and make it theirs. I can understand that impulse very well.

what is that?

Emerson remarks somewhere that each poem is a fossil word. Once upon a time someone made the leap from a feeling or a perception or notion (or all three simultaneously intertwined) to a sound. That sound—in its strangeness and hopeful aptness—was a poem. What I love about poetry is that it preserves the sense of each word as a poem. In an artful poem, each word is placed in a context that vivifies it. Each word is a jewel and the poem as a whole is the setting. But it goes further than that because the jewel metaphor is static and a poem is dynamic in the sense that each word is being explored. We thought we knew the word but we didn't. Each word represents a depth and the poem seeks to plumb that depth. It's as much a form of discovery as trekking to a place where you have never been. Indeed, when I teach the various great poets, I have my students draw maps of "Keats Land" or "Whitman Land." (Part of the exercise is to get students to figure out what geographic reality fits what poet—an island, a continent, a mountain, a city—what?) What distinguishes these places is up to my students to represent.

Poet Land Maps
  1. List different poems by a given poet
  2. List geographical traits associated with the poems (for example, Walt Whitman's "Mannahatta," "By Blue Ontario's Shore," and "A Broadway Pageant")
  3. List some details from the poems
  4. Draw a map that shows a land (for example, "Whitmania") where the poems exist. Details on the map should reflect details in the poems.

The mapping is also a form of questioning. The simple question any poem asks is "What is that?" Life, as it teaches us to believe that we know what a dog is or a marriage or a ninety-nine cent

The simple question any poem asks is "What is that?"

cheeseburger, could care less. For practical purposes, identification is insight. Poetry, however, shows us that isn't so. Everything is at once stranger and deeply simpler than we thought. Anything that human beings touch is going to have feelings attached to it and poetry seeks to realize those feelings. What is it like to stand at a window at dusk in a big city? What is it like to take a walk in a cemetery? What is a cat doing as it lies in the sun? What is happening? So much always is.

One reason to read and write and speak poems is to gain feeling for ourselves. This might seem an automatic aspect of being alive, but I don't think it really is. Talking about ourselves—something most of us do a fair amount of—isn't the same thing as having feeling for ourselves. When we talk about ourselves it's our ego venting. We need to do it but it's reflexive. It's sort of like psychic exhalation: This is what I think, this is what I want, etc. Poetry is more like an inhaling that we can feel and that makes us feel that our lives are incredibly particular and utterly regular—the mortal facts apply to all of us.

I feel some of my English-teacher-as-preacher predilection coming over me so I want to look at a poem I did today. It's by a contemporary American poet named Michael Waters. The kids like it and so do I. It's called "Horse":

> The first horse I ever saw
> was hauling a wagon stacked with furniture
> past storefronts along Knickerbocker Avenue.
> He was taller than a car, blue-black with flies,
>
> and bits of green ribbon tied to his mane
> bounced near his caked and rheumy eyes.
> I had seen horses in books before, but
> this horse shimmered in the Brooklyn noon.
>
> I could hear his hooves strike the tar,
> the colossal nostrils snort back the heat,
> and breathe his inexorable, dung-tinged fume.
> Under his enormous belly, his—

swung like the policeman's nightstick,
    a dowsing rod, longer than my arm –
        even the Catholic girls could see it
hung there like a rubber spigot.

When he let loose, the steaming street
    flowed with frothy, spattering urine.
        And when he stopped to let the junkman
toss a tabletop onto the wagon bed,

I worked behind his triangular head
    to touch his foreleg above the knee,
        the muscle jerking the mat of hair.
Horse, I remember thinking,

four years old and standing there,
    struck momentarily dumb,
        while the power gathered in his thigh
surged like language into my thumb.

Well, what is a horse? There are infinite poems that could be written because there are infinite human experiences with all the horses that have ever been in this world, to say nothing of mythical horses that haven't been in this world. Waters makes you feel "horse-ness" and surely that is what a poem seeks to do as it seeks to make you feel what something is, its "–ness"—its particular qualities of being.

Because the scene is set in the world of childhood Waters can capitalize on the freshness of perception that is a child's. The child is literally feeling, "What is that?" He knows a horse from a book, but a living horse is not a picture in a book. It is a creature of the senses, and Waters revels in the world of the senses. It is a poem that you can smell, see, hear, and feel. The horse is there and each word makes you feel that "there-ness." When I asked my students for a word that brought the horse to life for them, I was faced with virtually every word in the poem. "How did he find so many right words?" Angela Shortley asked me. As she said, even the holding back of a word—the line that substitutes for phallus—"was the right word. By not being there it is more there."

After talking about the words, including the words that weren't familiar such as *rheumy* and *inexorable*, we talked some about why the poem is in quatrains. Everyone was quiet for a while and then three people raised their hands all at once as if some energy were in the room that suddenly materialized. What each of them said in a somewhat different way was that the stanza managed the poem, that it made the reader aware he or she was reading a poem. The stanza felt "artificial" in one student's word, but she quickly went on to say that the artificiality was a good thing not a bad thing. It put the words in a frame, the way a picture is framed. It made the reader aware that the poem was made of words. As another student observed, the crucial, thematic word in the poem is *language*. She felt that the poem is a poem about language's ability to represent reality. I'm wary of statements about what poems are about, but I had to agree with her in this case. The aptness of the word is startling. We experience the child experiencing the horse through language and then, there is the word joined in a simile with the physical being of the child. What is a thumb? At that moment in the poem we feel what "thumb-ness" is just as we feel what language is. As one student said after our discussion, "I'm tired. I feel like I went somewhere and I experienced so much I got tired."

In terms of threading poems, I use physical poems throughout the course of the year. Probably there are anthologies of poems about animals, but on my own I have found a lot of poems about animals and I use them. D.H. Lawrence alone could keep me going for a long time. "What is a snake or a blue jay or a baby tortoise?" he asks and then, as a poet, answers.

october 25

student poems

Our school does portfolios of student writing. We assemble different examples of writing to show our students' competency in different areas. A number of years ago at a department meeting we were talking about portfolios and I asked why we weren't including student poems in our portfolios. In response, one of my colleagues asked me point blank, "Why would we do that? Poetry is poofy. We're here to prepare students for the real world of college and work. That's not poetry." Then, with a fair amount of glee, she repeated herself in saying that poetry is "poofy." It probably goes without saying that I differed from my colleague. We took, as a department, the path of least resistance (the path we usually take), which means that there are minimum requirements for the portfolio that all teachers have to meet. Teachers are free to dictate other requirements above that minimum. Democracy thrives on compromise. I'm not knocking it.

I ask for three finished poems per quarter. It's not a big requirement. It's tiny in fact. I realize some students are more comfortable than others are with writing poetry. I'm not out to turn everyone into a Dylan-Thomas-spewing bard. But I do want everyone to have a chance at it. I do want everyone to experience poetry from the inside in terms of writing one's own poems. At the least, it's a humbling experience and humility isn't a bad thing for a sixteen-year-old. At best, it frees students who instinctively are associative, metaphorical writers to write the way they want to write.

Over the years I have observed that the writing of poetry offers powerful lessons for writers. One is word choice. Typically when my students are writing an essay or a journal response or a report or a letter the words they find are "good enough." Their main concern is to get their thoughts down on paper. With poetry, the thoughts are the words and the exactitude of those words matters enormously. This focus on word choice creates a powerful paradigm for their writing. They become less inclined to say "good enough," because they come to realize that poetry has no use for that attitude.

Also the writing of poetry offers valuable lessons about patience and attentiveness. When I give students a prompt based on a model poem, I am showing them a way of paying attention. To pay attention means they must linger and dwell and not move on too quickly. Their conceptual minds typically are in a hurry to get from one place to another—next year college, next week a job interview, tomorrow two tests—but I want them to be still and notice whatever is occurring in a given situation. I like to point to James Joyce's *Ulysses* (an epic prose poem) as an example of staying with what is there: eight hundred or so pages about one day. There is more in any given moment of life than we will ever get down on paper. We can try, however, and see what may be there.

> When I give students a prompt based on a model poem, I am showing them a way of paying attention.

The poem I dictated earlier in the year (see page 11) by Jane Gentry entitled "Exercise in the Cemetery" is a fair example of how I get my students to write from a model. They have the poem in their poetry journals because they have written it down. Today I told them to go back to the poem and look it over. Then I asked them what the structure of the poem was. What happens in the three sentences? After some discussion we agreed that the first sentence sets the scene: The narrator is in a cemetery. The second sentence is a question about life that comes from where the narrator is. The third sentence is an imagistic look at the world around the narrator. Then I told them I wanted them to write a brief poem that mirrored Gentry's structure. As in the first sentence I want you to place yourself (the poem is in first person) somewhere, in the second sentence I want you to ask a question, and in the third sentence I want you to look around you and describe in images whatever you notice. I told them to use any of their senses in the third sentence to register what is there. It had to be in images however. I wasn't looking for summary statements; I wanted them to trust the physical world.

Then I said the words, "Now go there." Those, for me, are crucial words. Writing a poem is a journey and I want them to go somewhere and see what is there. I want them in whatever way, shape, or form to realize how much bigger life is than they are, and how that is an incitement to them as writers rather than a liability. I want them to think of all their senses when they write—another powerful reason to be writing poetry. I want them to experience what one thing has to do with another. Schools, with their different subjects, tend to compartmentalize; poetry unifies.

Using a Prompt to Write a Poem
1. Dictate the poem to students
2. Discuss the poem in terms of its art—how it works (word choice, line, etc.)
3. Examine the poem's structure on a sentence-by-sentence basis (Sentence one does what?)
4. Ask students to write a poem based on a simple structure the poem has exemplified as in the Gentry poem

The poems I received today from this model are far from "poofy." They register some powerful feelings. They are first drafts, but what I am looking for is engagement on their part, both as to perception and as to language. I want to feel that they have gone there—wherever that may be. Here is one by a young woman who has been very quiet so far this year. She didn't give the poem a title yet:

> I'm sitting beside my Dad
> As he drives our old clunker
> Toward the mall where he has promised
> To buy me the shoes he promised
> To buy me two months ago.
> How is it that you don't
> Get to choose who your father is?
> I look down at the floor
> Where the empty Old Milwaukee cans
> Make a sort of metal music
> If I tap lightly enough.

The funny thing about our world is that I don't think we want to recognize how good student poems can be. If we did, we would be asking for more of them. After all, a lot of lyric writers do very good work in their early twenties. My students' feelings are literally jumping out of their skins and poetry is rooted in strong feeling. When they encounter some degree of structure, they can, over the course of a year, go fairly far, fairly fast. Sometimes, I will bring in a poem from one of my students and ask my colleagues what they think of it. "Who wrote that?" they ask. Then I tell them a student's name. Some of them have stopped asking me and have started having their students write poems, and put them in their portfolios.

october 28
revision

The "R" word. More than one student has said to me, "What do you mean 'revise' a poem? You don't revise poems. Everyone knows that. You just write down what you feel and that's that. It's done. You said it." Sometimes students go even further and tell me that revision is a form of betrayal, that poems are about honoring one's initial impulse and to go back and change them is something like immoral. It goes against what a poem is.

I'm happy to grant them such feelings. I'm glad they feel strongly about what a poem is. What I ask of them is to talk some about what a poem can be. I ask them to talk about not just what a person might want a poem to be, but also what a person might want a poem to do. What I find (and it makes sense given the society they live in) is that their notions about poems are rooted in notions of self-expression. If you express yourself, you've done what you wanted to do. Only if you feel you haven't expressed yourself should you push further. And, I ask, how do you tell? There's some silence here and the language that does come out is a bit vague. Still, I'm willing to honor it because intuition is a large part of art.

What I ask of them is to consider the Army's slogan, "Be all that you can be." Does a poem fall under this heading? Can a poem be all it can be? Does a poem want to be all it can be? At this point someone usually looks at me with that somewhat puzzled and amused face that adolescents are so very good at and asks me what is going on: Do I think the poem is alive or something? Other kids shake their heads as if to say, "He is so squirrelly." I reply in the affirmative, that once the poem is down on paper (or on the computer screen) it does have its own life. It is a poem.

And that means what? I go on to ask them to consider what they want to do with a given poem. Do they want to give it to someone as a gift? Is it a Mother's Day gift, for instance? My students tell me that any poem they write about their moms is going to be a good poem as far as their moms are concerned. It's the thought that counts. Their moms are not going to critique their word choices. Good enough, I say. What if you just take the first draft and stick it in your desk. What is that? I get various responses ranging from privacy to oblivion to that's what writers do—they stick things in desks. I push them further on this. What if you take the poem out in six months? What do you do with it? "Read it and barf," is a fairly common response. And what if you don't want to "barf"? What if the poem wants to be honored as a poem, as a potential work of art that wants to be all that it can be?

By this point I'm starting to get some nods. They can see the method in the teacher's madness. Offhandedly I tell them that poets often put a poem through twenty or more drafts. Some reach much higher numbers. There's silence here. They're digesting this. Then I spring the big question on them: What is there to revise in a poem?

We go to the usual suspects: word choice, structure, syntax, form, point of view, metaphor, detail. Plus we talk about coherence: Can someone understand your poem? Is the poem all there on the page or is it, in part, still in your head? Are you making assumptions about what your reader should know based on what you know? Are you showing in your poem who your fourth grade teacher, Mrs. Lang, was or are you assuming your reader knows who she is and you can just put in your emotional responses to her? Already (late October) they are starting to get a feel for how involved the picture is as to what constitutes a poem. I want them to sense all this, but I don't want to inhibit them. Indeed, the point I make with them is that the question as far as revision is concerned is, "What if? What if I change this to that? What if I take line four out? What if I add some more adjectives? What happens?" In this sense revision is play.

> The question as far as revision is concerned is, "What if?"

What Is There to Revise?

1. Word choice
2. Structure
3. Syntax
4. Form
5. Point of view
6. Metaphor
7. Detail
8. Coherence (does it make sense?)
9. Length (not enough poem or too much poem)
10. Ending

The word *play* is not a school word and the kids are skeptical. I ask them what *play* is—not entertainment but play. (My classroom is rooted in Socratic questioning. I am always asking them what something *is*.) We talk some and we wind up talking about freedom. It is a structured kind of freedom, however. We talk about how little kids are always making up rules for their games. The rules matter a lot. And we say that we "play" the guitar. We don't bang it or hammer it; we play it.

Freedom feels like space. It is room to see how something might work differently. It's backing off from the poem and indulging in whatever energy is there—a word, a phrase, a point of view, the sense of what a stanza can be. It's latitude and permission to feel how something can emerge over time. It doesn't necessarily happen all at once. I show them drafts of poems by previous students of mine to give them a sense of how a poem can develop.

In this sense I feel the process of revision is a real gift to students. They are used to writing a paper, getting a grade, and filing the paper in the circular file. End of process. When I put them through multiple drafts of a poem, they have to take more time and consider what might be there. The process is, in part, about honoring themselves. A first draft is an impulse and impulses matter powerfully. I would never deny that. I always begin any look

> I always begin any look at a poem with praise.

at a poem with praise. There is always a word or two that deserves that praise and usually there's a lot more than a word or two. But there's more to writing than impulse. Consider that every time one starts a new sentence in a poem one has made a decision that affects where the rest of the poem is going. What if the poet reconsiders those decisions? What does sentence two have to do with sentence one? Does sentence two honor what is there in sentence one or just go off on its own? And what about sentence three?

Revising poems seems a powerful model for writing because the scale of a poem is so manageable. Revising a term paper or a report is a big task. A poem of twenty lines or so is not so daunting. This issue of scale is one of the compelling reasons to use a lot of poetry. It's not overwhelming in terms of size. The comfort factor should never be overlooked. A lot of kids bring a lot of trepidation to the English classroom. I want to lessen that fear.

october 29

peer revision and revision guidelines

The small size of poems makes them ideal for students to work with other students on revision. I have my students do a lot of peer work with poetry. I structure it carefully so the tasks are very defined. Peer revision only works, in my experience, if the tasks are very clear. I ask them, for instance, to suggest three words in one another's poems that could be bettered. They are responsible for identifying the words and explaining why they think those words could be better. I have a battery of different tasks I can assign for peer work along these lines. Does the point of view work? Is the narrative all there? Are there places where metaphor could be used? Does the poem need more details? Are all the parts of speech used in the poem? The questions sound mildly sophisticated, but the kids get them quickly. They see that a poem is something one can work on.

Peer Revision. **What If** *Questions*

1. What if the poem is longer/shorter?
2. What if more/less metaphor is used?
3. What if one moment in the poem is expanded?
4. What if more detail is used?
5. What if the poem begins at a different place?
6. What if the poem changes its point of view?
7. What if the verb tense changes?
8. What if more adjectives are used?
9. What if more strong verbs are used?
10. What if all abstract/subjective words are deleted?
11. What if all the senses are used?
12. What if the soundscape is intensified/lessened?
13. What if form is used?
14. What if the architecture (stanzas) changes?
15. What if more/less punctuation is used?
16. What if appositives are used?
17. What if line lengths change?
18. What if syntax is changed?

19. What if fragments are used rather than complete sentences?
20. What if questions are asked in the poem?
21. What if the ending changes?

My students take one another's suggestions to heart. The "what if" aspect takes away the defensiveness that comes with the ownership of the poem. No one's feelings are being criticized. What is being looked at is the work on paper, not anyone's fragile psyche or artistic pride. It may be that the changes do not improve the poem. It happens sometimes. The issue, however, is freedom to consider what could happen. I find my students very positive about using freedom in a constructive manner. They want freedom; our society lauds freedom. Revision gives them opportunities to exercise it practically.

I hand out a list to my students of suggestions for them to think about in the course of revision. It isn't prescriptive and it isn't all encompassing. It does give them some guidelines to think about when they are revising a poem or peer editing a poem. It takes time for them to learn about the different suggestions but that helps contribute to their thinking about what goes into the making of a poem. Sometimes I fantasize what it would be like if students were paying attention to these suggestions all the way through school. It's doable. It just would take some real live interest in poetry.

The list is as follows:

Suggestions for Revising Your Poems

1. Look at the beginning of your poem. Often the beginning of a first-draft poem turns out to be an introduction or preface to the poem. Does the poem begin immediately in a confident manner? Is there another line in the poem that might be effective as a first line? Remember that a poem doesn't have to begin with a flat, declarative sentence.

2. Don't be afraid to radically rearrange the poem. Part of the pleasure of revising lies in being both creative and ruthless. Once the poem is down on paper, it begins to take on a life of its own.

Often, there are avenues of exploration that one wasn't aware of when one began the poem. Writing a compelling poem does not mean being absolutely faithful to every original detail in your first draft.

3. Try to identify imagistic and thematic "hearts" of your poem, those lines that speak deeply and that you know you want to retain in some form. Often such lines can provide further direction, because they emotionally indicate what the poem is about.

4. Remember you have five senses. Try to use all of them when you write. Vivid poetry makes use of all our senses. Don't be afraid to combine senses in what is called synesthesia (e.g., *black roar, brittle fragrance*).

5. Is your ending too sudden? Does it emerge understandably from the rest of the poem? Or is it slapped on as if to say, "Well, here's the end." Or do you say too much and spell out in capital letters THE MEANING OF THE POEM? There is no set way to end a poem. Sometimes an image, sometimes a statement, sometimes a metaphor, or sometimes the narration of an action is appropriate.

6. Look at your word choices. Strong verbs and specific nouns are at the heart of most good poems. *She left* might be *she split, she ran away, she absconded,* or *she jumped into the blue Dodge with the bad ball joint and drove off into the imperturbable night. Said* might be *shouted, whispered, spat through a grimace,* etc. Only use generic nouns (*toy, tree, dog*) if you want a generic feeling. If you want to be specific, then let us know about roller skates, balsam firs, and cocker spaniels. We delight in the surprises of particularity.

7. Think about the sorts of words you are using: slangy, polysyllabic, plain, technical, fanciful. Do certain words not fit because they don't fit the poem's tone? Every word has a certain background of overtones to it. You should include only those words whose overtones are appropriate for the poem you are writing.

8. Keep a close watch on verbs of being. They slow the poem down. Too many such verbs will put a poem to sleep.

9. Speak your poem out loud as you work on it. Poems live in our mouths as much as they live on paper. Don't be afraid to let sounds

make suggestions: maybe some alliteration here or maybe too many unaccented syllables there. Maybe some near rhyme or assonance is wanted. Are certain combinations of sounds awkward and hard to say? Are certain sounds too easy or not right for the sense of the poem (an overdose of the letter s, for instance). Sounds make sense. A poem has to feel musically right in your mouth.

10. Is there any fat in your poem? Look out for padding: irrelevant details, discursive anecdotes and opinions, redundancies, words that are just words and not connected to emotions and experiences, metaphorical wanderings. Only what contributes to the poem's success should stay in the poem. Every word has to justify itself.

11. The title should come naturally from the poem and should serve as a sort of signpost. After the poem has been read the title should reverberate. Avoid cute titles, highfalutin titles, abstract titles, and hopelessly personal titles.

12. Look at the point of view of the poem. Is first person effective or might third person be an improvement? What qualities are you trying to communicate that go along with the voice you have chosen? Often a change in the point of view helps to clarify the poem and opens up new perspectives. The poem told in your voice might be better told in an impersonal third-person narrator's voice and vice versa. Occasionally, second person is what is called for.

13. Be willing to pose questions in the poem. Questions are a constant, for instance, in the poems of the Nobel Prize-winning poet Czeslaw Milosz. Questions invigorate the poem and make us aware the poem is not predetermined. We are full of questions about life and poems should have their share, too.

14. Try to keep an open mind as you proceed through revisions. Revising is, in some ways, a matter of playing around. What happens if I drop a stanza; what happens if I add more detail to a line? Part of the art lies in entertaining such "what if" questions.

15. Poems are not so much finished as abandoned. As long as the interest is there, keep revising. The poem will almost always benefit.

Can a poem be revised too much? Of course it can. Sometimes that's part of the process. You don't know what too much is until you do it. It's a valuable lesson and helps students learn about themselves and how their minds work. I do a fair amount of comparing student drafts throughout the year (sometimes current work and sometimes work I keep in my files). The kids are quick to voice their opinions about which drafts they prefer and whether they think a poem has been diminished more than it has been strengthened. I often will not identify which is the earlier draft and which is the later. Instead, I ask my students what they think. This makes them really scrutinize the poem's verbal texture.

Though a numbered list can seem mechanical, this one isn't. Revision is about learning to grow in constructive ways. I find that many of my students come to see revision as part of their growth as adolescents, of their growing up. They appreciate the impetuousness of the first draft, but they also come to see how their spirits can be deepened and filled in on the page. They come to see the poem as something that is crafted over a period of time. I think their reading of literature deepens because they start to feel how much work goes into the making of a poem. The finished poem did not just fall out of bed and call itself a finished poem. All those poems that are surrounded by boxes and notes and little histories in their textbooks start to seem a bit more human. Even Shakespeare must have crossed out some words on occasion.

november 1

assessment

As a teacher once said to me, "It's one thing to have the kids write poems; it's another to give them grades for their poems." I can understand her remark. A guy whom I met at a state teachers' conference and with whom I became friendly told me that he gave everyone an "A" for his or her poem. His reasoning was that anything less than an "A" would be crushing emotionally. "There's a bit of your soul in a poem," he said. "What am I going to do? Flunk a kid's soul?" This attitude reminds me of a woman who used to teach with me who praised everything that kids did in their poems—including clichés. Again, her feeling was that a poem was deeply personal and that a grade could be emotionally devastating.

I sympathize with these attitudes. Even when they are written in response to a model or a prompt, poems are personal. They are a bit of inner spark and our inner spark is precious stuff. I don't feel however that this means everyone gets an "A" or that nothing can be said to students about poems. Indeed, I feel such an attitude is demeaning to students and to poetry. To my mind, it says, in effect, "It's a poem, which is a subjective loosey-goosey kind of writing, so we won't hold you accountable. Just do your thing." A poem that goes through the revision process is looking to be made better. Published poets know that. There's nothing wrong with our students knowing that. I've listed below some criteria I look for when grading poems.

Criteria for Grading Student Poems

1. *Originality.* It seems obvious, but if I give an assignment outside of class, I occasionally run into someone submitting something out of a book or off the Internet or from who knows where. Usually the language is a giveaway. It's not the tenth grader who has been in my classroom; it's someone else's language. I tend to talk with the student first when this happens and let him or her know what I am thinking. I'm not interested in pressing charges as much as I am interested in finding out why the student did it. Mostly, they come clean and mostly it's from laziness or fear. More than one student has said to me, "I never wrote a poem and I don't know how. So I thought I would copy something. It's a poem. What's the difference?" We talk about the difference. Word gets out to the rest of the class fairly quickly.

2. *Fresh language.* I don't abide clichés. There's a big "C" in my room and there's a diagonal line drawn through the "C." It means to my students that they are in a "No Cliché Zone." We talk about what clichés are and I put them on notice that I am looking for them. No dead language allowed. If someone is feeling cold in one of his or her poems, it better not be compared to "ice." (As I noted earlier when talking about sound, having the students improvise new words based on sound often opens up doors that purge them of clichés.)

3. *Does the poem make sense?* Again, it's obvious but there's a gap between what goes on in someone's head and what gets down on paper. Some students get stubborn about their private visions. I tell them I have nothing against their visions; I just want to read a coherent poem. If the images are utterly unrelated; if the poem can't keep its focus; then the grade is going to show it.

4. *What use has been made of the tools of the art?* Rhythm, sound, stanza, form, line, image, metaphor, detail, and syntax are basic tools. Because I am only grading a few poems each quarter I feel I have the right to lean hard on my students in terms of seriously revising what they are writing. When I ask them to pay attention to a certain aspect, I expect them to do it in their next drafts.

5. *Mechanics.* I expect the poem to be properly punctuated and properly spelled. If I ask about capitalization, I expect a rationale for why the poem is capitalized the way it is. I expect grammar to be utilized properly. Poems aren't holidays from mechanics.

6. *Effort.* Has the student worked with the revision process? Can the student explain what he or she was trying to do in a draft? Or is it a case of "good enough"?

These modest criteria yield the usual run of grades. The kids come to understand that a poem is not an automatic "A." They also come to understand that art has standards, and that I want them to try to think like artists. I assign very definite parameters when I make an assignment so there is no confusion about what I am looking for. When, for instance, I made the assignment to write a poem based on the Jane Gentry poem, I explained what I was looking for. I wanted, for instance, images in the last sentence rather than explanations or statements. I wanted them to create a definite setting in the first sentence. I wanted them to use language economically. It's not a long poem I am asking them to write and every word in it counts. If there are redundancies, then the grade suffers.

This emphasis gets the kids looking at their poems and their peers' poems with very open eyes. Generally, they don't do a whole lot of thinking about how they use language. Redundancy is a good example, where a student will use a word yet add a word (or more) to the word. That means I see phrases such as *the big fat man* fairly regularly and from students at all levels of academic ability. A number of them seem to feel that if one word is good, two words are much better. When I tell the kids to look their poems over for redundancy and cliché, I can feel their language wheels turning. That's what I want—to get those wheels turning.

I suspect the grades run a little higher on poems, but I think that's because the kids are really working on their poems and deserve the grades. I also have noticed in my classrooms over the years—and I would bet money it applies to most teachers' classrooms—that there are students who flat out excel at writing poetry. These students are by no means students who excel at essays, reports, journal entries, and other forms of analytical writing. Often they are pretty poor at such writing. Often they are very intuitive writers and poetry clicks for them. The chance to write poems and receive grades for them—grades they have earned according to the criteria of the assignment—is validating for them. When I hear that students in some schools write no poems at all, I cringe. A whole dimension of student writing is being overlooked. So is a whole dimension of self-respect. My students understand I am not grading their souls. I am grading a poem and a poem—like any other piece of writing—exists in its own right. As with any piece of writing, if they are not happy with the grade, I offer them the option of doing another draft. Some take me up on the offer.

november 5

bob dylan

Last night Maura, Ben, and I went to hear Bob Dylan. I have been a fan forever. There are two posters of Dylan in my classroom—one is the psychedelic poster of Bob's head from the 1960s; the other is Dylan in concert sometime in the 1980s. He has his harmonica brace on and he's lost in the music and words. From my perspective as an English teacher, Dylan, as much as anyone, is keeping the word alive in our society. If the world of popular culture has produced one true artist, it must be Bob Dylan.

Today seemed like the right time to play a Dylan song in lieu of a poem. I played "Tangled Up in Blue." Most of my students had never heard the song. I handed out copies of the lyrics beforehand so they could follow along. I kept my introduction to a minimum. I've learned over the years that it's silly to expect your students to pitch their enthusiasm to the level of your enthusiasm. If they are moved, then they are moved; if not, then not. Overselling doesn't do anyone any good. I'm not looking for clones.

I began with talking about rhyme. In most of my poetry writing assignments, I don't allow rhyme. It gets student writers tangled up (couldn't resist the pun) in knots. They pay attention to the rhymes rather than what they are writing about. The rhymes wind up governing the poem and I get the likes of "I feel alone / Like Al Capone." Because I have tried to show them how the whole poem is a soundscape, I point out to them that end rhyme easily becomes a fixation and can work to the detriment of the poem.

My students had a lot to say about Dylan's rhymes. They noticed how conversational he was so the rhymes didn't seem that noticeable to them. They felt that his voice conveyed a degree of awareness that he knew rhymes were a little silly but he also knew that rhymes made songs go. Rhymes "focus us" as Jenna Giannola told the class. "Mr. P should let us use more rhymes," she further editorialized. They were fascinated by how Dylan kept finding rhymes for *blue*. They recognized that it's one of the easiest rhymes in the language, but they were impressed at the range of words he came up with. As a student noted, "He isn't just rhyming one syllable words with one syllable words."

We talked about what rhyme does in terms of putting words together that don't go together at first glance. How, I asked them, did that relate to Dylan's song? They looked at the lyrics and asked me to play the song again, which I did. The composite response was that the song "goes all over the place, but the rhymes keep it connected. First, he's with this woman and then they split up and then he's working here and there and then he meets her again and then they split up again and the rhymes keep it together." We talked about what a ballad was and whether the song was a ballad. A few weeks before I had read a traditional English ballad to them and had them write a couple of stanzas down in their poetry journals to get a feel for the ballad form. Accordingly, they consulted their notebooks for guidance.

I was happy with the discussion, but I wanted to press them further. Poetry, I told them, is written to compel people. If it doesn't compel, then it's not doing anything. Does the song compel you? The range of responses was interesting. A few students were left cold by it. "It's just too weird," Scott Blackman said. "And I can't stand his voice." More students, however, enthusiastically defended the song. Maybe the best was Alicia Clark who said: "I like it a lot because he gives me a feeling of how he doesn't want to let go of this woman even though life makes him let go. He has free will—he goes here and there—but there's a sense of fate too. Things happen to people. He doesn't try to tell us too much. In fact he backs off at times. I like that. I get sick of people telling me what they think about the fate of the planet or whatever. I like how he tells a story and lets us draw conclusions." Another student leapt in right at that point and asked her whether there were conclusions that could be drawn. What was the point of the song? Did it have a point?

A number of students wanted to respond to this, but I thought Alicia deserved the first crack since she had stimulated the question. She said that she thought the point of the song was the title. It was a metaphor and you can't sum up a metaphor. It just is what it is. It's meant to give us a feeling and the song definitely, in her words, "gives me a strong feeling. I can't say though exactly what the feeling is. It's a feeling." She looked around her as if searching for something and the class laughed. "Happy you have a feeling, Licia," the guy next to her cracked.

Maybe this is what frustrates people about poetry. You can only go so far in talking about it. Then there's bound to be some serious inarticulateness as you cross into the world of sheer feeling. Dylan himself has been aware of this and so have many artists who have refrained from interpreting their works. In interviews, Dylan often goes into what my wife calls "Bob talk," a sort of generalizing, beats-me-what-it's-all-about attitude that can waylay the most intense questioner. Robert Frost was famous for making fun of professors and their notions of what his poems were about. He wasn't anti-intellectual; he was wary. A work of art is bigger than our notions of it; that's why it is a work of art. We can't pin it down. Frost said that poetry was a sort of thinking through metaphors. It can be very serious and profound thinking, but it is not anything like syllogistic reason. We'd be poorer as creatures without the insights of metaphorical wondering.

I tell them by way of winding up the discussion that I heard Dylan last night. Given the poster and the song I have played, this comes as no surprise. It turns out one of my students was there. It's a guy who hasn't said anything during the course of our discussion, Todd Spencer. He's a very sharp kid who only speaks when he feels he has something to say. I ask him what he thought of the show and he gives it the thumbs up. "Any words?" I ask him. "Yeah," he says, "Positively Fourth Street." I nod and he smiles slightly. "Maybe some more of you will be there next time." "Maybe," someone in the first row says. "If he takes some voice lessons."

november 9

tell the truth

Year in, year out, one thing that strikes me about my work with young people is how much they want adults to tell them the truth. As they try to make their way in life and begin to find out who they are—emotionally, intellectually, spiritually, sexually—they need all the truth they can get their hands on. Because what they get tends to be lies, evasions, platitudes, and outright rejections of their largely reasonable questions, I can understand their hunger very well. I had the same hunger myself. School did not do a whole lot for that hunger, at least in terms of formal instruction. In terms of what I learned in the boys' locker room, that's another story.

Poetry is all the stories—in school and out—and poetry has a hankering for truth. Not truth with a capital *T*. Not the one, overall Truth that blinds people to other people's viewpoints. Rather poetry pursues all the little truths, the small *t*s that emerge from life as people live it. In that sense, poetry reminds me of what people used to holler at soul music concerts my older sister took me to. When a performer was at one of those slow, heartbreaking, down-in-the-gut-bucket moments of a ballad—typically about a lover who was no longer a lover—members of the audience would yell, "Tell the truth! Tell the truth!" Amen.

The poem I read today is by an African-American poet named

Cornelius Eady. The poem is entitled "Almost Grown" and comes from a book called *The Autobiography of a Jukebox*.

> My father loves my sister so much, he has to strike her. He cares for her so deeply that he has crossed, for the first and only time, into my mother's domain.
>
> He has caught his daughter red-handed at the front door, trying to sneak home late from her boyfriend's house.
>
> And my father, poor ghost, knows too much. Without ever leaving the house, he has overheard every sweet thing this man, an old buddy of his, has whispered to her in bed.
>
> Tonight, my sister discovers her only power. As she tussles with him on the front porch, she is all heat and righteous passion.
>
> He will never try this hard again to tell anyone how much he loves them. With his belt, my father tries to tell my sister what he knows a man is capable of, but all he does is tell her fortune.

Sometimes when I ask a question about a poem, I first have my students write their response to that question in their poetry journals. I want them to do some writing before they start talking. The question I am asking, as a way into the poem, is the big question I like to ask once in a while: What makes this a poem? I think it's an important question to ask. Schools tend to act as if they have all the definitive answers. Art insists we don't have all the answers. That's one reason why we keep making art: Our feelings run ahead of our concepts. And modern art, in particular, is dedicated to scrutinizing, if not subverting, any and all concepts as to what art should be. So what, after the teacher has given you various definitions and signposts, is a poem?

The class and I listen to a number of written responses. I asked each student to write a paragraph or two that buttresses the student's contentions about the poem with references to the poem. Because it wasn't a long poem, I dictated the poem to them so everyone had the text to consult.

I get a number of thoughtful responses. My favorite one is from a kid named Everett McAllister who has been known to make faces when he is bored with what is going on in the classroom. He told me the second day of school that he knew some poetry: "A C / Is good enough for me." He's what they used to call a "shop kid," which is to say he prefers engines to poems. You get the picture about Everett. Everett says that the poem is a poem because it is "a word event." I ask him what that means and he tells me that nowadays the weather forecasters don't talk about rain or snow. Instead they talk about a precipitation event. "That's what I mean," Everett says with something like enthusiasm in his voice. "This is a poem because the words take over. It's not just a story. A story would tell all the details and ins and outs. But that's not necessary. This poem is like a trash compactor." Everett pauses and studies his metaphor. "I mean it just takes a lot of stuff, you know, feeling, and it presses it into a couple of paragraphs. I mean—what do you call 'em?—stanzas, Mr. P. And there it is. It's a poem." Everett is pretty tired from talking. It's more than he's said in the whole last week. Everett doesn't believe in pushing himself, so the poem must have pushed him some.

The class agrees with Everett. Students point out how each sentence is a world in itself. That, to them, is one thing that defines a poem. Also, students point out how words echo more in a poem. *Father*, for instance, "gets under your skin," as one student puts it. "It's more than just a detail. It's about what a father is and what a daughter is and what their whole lives are like as a man and a woman. It's the past of their lives and the present and the future of their lives." She read that verbatim from her journal, which is one reason I have them do it. I think that paper often makes them more articulate.

We talk about specific words, the way we always wind up talking about specific words. A number of students focus on the poem's final word. I have told them that the final word of a poem is like a final note. It's what you leave your reader with and you better think a while about what you want to leave your reader with. The students agree that the word hits them hard. "It's scary," one student says. "It has a couple of different meanings and they both come into play. It's her fate and it's her good luck. It's not the best good luck though." She pauses. "It's scary and sad and it's real because he hits her but she is already lost to him." Another student jumps in: "It's the man-woman thing. Once you get into it, you never get out." There is some laughter, easy and uneasy. The student, Jeb, goes on. "I mean when you read the word *man* in the next to last line you are face to face with it. Guys do what they do and women do what they do. Everyone is caught. But it feels pretty good sometimes." Quite a bit of laughter.

From my observation, I don't have to ask them whether the poem is speaking the truth because they have told me already what they think. They think the poem is telling some very important truths on both sides of the situation. Some know that situation firsthand, some know it secondhand, but to see someone attending to it with the care a poet gives is exciting to them. Even when it's "scary," it's a help to them because honesty, in the sense of staying with an emotional situation and not letting go, doesn't happen everyday—unless you read poetry.

november 12

shakespeare

A number of us in the department teach Shakespeare. We teach his plays at all grade levels and to a wide range of students. We feel strongly that Shakespeare is our heritage and that it is our job to help impart that heritage to our students. That said, we feel as years go by that we are not so much teaching Shakespeare as, in the words of one department member, "leading a guided tour." What she means is something along the lines of: "This is language no one uses any more. Once a year we visit this language. We work and work to understand these words. I mean, the teacher works and works and the kids trail along. Then we're done. We have 'read' Shakespeare. Better something than nothing." We go on, to paraphrase a later playwright.

We have talked about this in department meetings and one thing we have come up with is a way to keep Shakespeare in our students' lives. What we have done is to take a page from my book—we read and dictate passages of Shakespeare throughout the year. To say there is a lot of Shakespeare that we never touch in high school would be an understatement. We simply go into the room and say the word, "Shakespeare" and everyone understands. We are about to get some of the language. Because our focus is language (as opposed to titles in the bookroom), this attitude makes sense to our students.

I like this approach because any given day I can drop a bit of the master in their laps. I provide a context for whatever I am reading them, but they are writing the words down. That physical act of writing the words down is very important to me. If they write it out, the language is a little less strange. If they have to puzzle over spellings and forms and contractions, that's okay. They are encountering the language directly. Because it happens to them regularly, Shakespeare is not an annual advent but a classroom presence. He even starts to have a certain familiarity to some of the kids. (We have our sophomores see Al Pacino's movie about *Richard III* also. That creates familiarity, too.)

Today I read Ulysses' famous speech about time from *Troilus and Cressida*. I first handed out the speech in a photocopy so they could follow it as I read it (I do make use of the photocopier occasionally). Then I had them put it away and dictated the first sentence to them. Then we went after the sentence. The book I took the passage from is a very handy volume entitled *The Essential Shakespeare* by Ted Hughes. It's a bit eccentric in that the citations indicating where the selections come from are all printed in the back of the book rather than underneath the passages so you don't know right away where the passage is from unless you look. I have grown to like this because it jogs me to remember plays and sonnets I more or less had forgotten.

The sentence I dictated is this:

> Time hath, my lord, a wallet at his back,
> Wherein he puts alms for oblivion,
> A great siz'd monster of ingratitudes:
> Those scraps are good deeds past; which are devour'd
> As fast as they are made, forgot as soon
> As done: perseverance, dear my lord,
> Keeps honour bright: to have done, is to hang
> Quite out of fashion, like a rusty mail
> In monumental mockery.

I have my students write down a list of their questions about the sentence. Then we discuss their questions. This defuses the ignorance factor because I want them to have questions. If they have no questions, I am liable to ask them questions—so they have questions. Their questions today were (among others): What is *hath*? Were they really lords? What are *alms*? And what is an example of *oblivion*? How come he spells *honor* with a *u*? Is it the same word? What is *rusty mail*? Ditto *monumental mockery*?

Words, words, words, as someone else said in a play. The value of looking closely at a sentence seems evident: It's not overwhelming and we can focus closely. We can talk about alms and wallets and oblivion. We can talk about how he builds a long sentence. We can talk about how he likes to alliterate at times. We can talk about parallelism. We can talk about how he takes an abstraction and makes it tangible. We can talk about tone: What is with that "my lord"? Is that for real?

Then I do some small group work with them. I break them into groups of four or five and ask the groups to come up with two more questions about the rest of the passage. Once we have questions, we pass them on to another group. That group's assignment is to answer the questions. They have dictionaries to use. Otherwise, they talk among themselves and see what they come up with. I have done a number of variations on this, but I like this one because I like the kids talking about Shakespeare with each other. It takes away some of the passivity of the teacher leading the guided tour. I'm not so much worried about the exactness of their answers as I am pleased that they are talking about Shakespeare's language with each other. That seems precious. It's not artificial either because they have generated the questions. There's a fair amount of teasing one another about the questions and that's good. It's a living exercise rather than a look-it-up and write-it-down.

One of the other teachers in the department, a guy who served in the Naval Air Force, likens our Shakespeare passages to calls for everyone to be out on the flight deck. It's a sort of semi-mad scramble, as they know the Bard is coming after them. It's good-natured, however. They are all in it together. Along the way we talk about different plays and I use snippets of the sonnets, too. Eventually I use a whole sonnet or two toward the end of the year.

All of us in the department feel that when we do a Shakespearean play, it's easier. It's not that there is a big leap in students' initial comprehension. There isn't. What there is, however, is a leap in their willingness to engage the text. It's not so much of "Oh yeah, it's Shakespeare time" and more of "Shakespeare. I know who the guy is. Let's go." When we combine this attitude with speaking the plays aloud, we find our students welcoming rather than fearing the assignment of a Shakespearean play. He starts to become a presence in their lives. For my part, because I am doing something with poetry every day, I can always point to echoes in other poets and ask them if they hear them. Is there Shakespeare in Frost or Dickinson, for instance? I let them decide. They can look up the passages they have in their notebooks. They start to sense what tradition might be and how Shakespeare is crucial to that tradition. That is, to use one of those old words, a *gladsome* event.

november 16

words talking to words

A poem is a choir. All the words are harmonized with the other words. At the same time, every word in the poem is a voice in its own right. In that sense (to change the metaphor a bit) each word is an actor. It has its role and that role interacts with all the other word roles in the poem. Each word is embedded in a grammatical phrase of some sort, in a line, in a stanza, in a rhythmic context, in a soundscape, and in the poem as a whole. This is one reason why talking about poems can get quite complex. Even in a modest lyric, a lot is going on.

Words talk to other words in the poem. There is no exhausting how one word may intersect with another. When we talk about poems, I want my students to be alive to how words can talk to each other. A poem isn't a linear structure. Although we read the poem in a linear fashion, a poem is always producing echoes. Words echo words in our minds. Feeling accrues as one reads the poem and that feeling resounds ("re-sounds").

Periodically, we focus on words talking to other words. Today I chose a poem by the American poet Thomas McGrath. The poem is called "Memorial" and it is dedicated to the poet's brother, Jimmy, who was killed in World War II:

> Nothing prolongs. Neither the bronze plaque
> Of graveyard splendor, nor public memorial. Even
> The watery eye of memory, weeping its darlings back

Fails them. Flung like leaves on the cold heaven
In Time's own season, that Always when totals are taken,
   And the mortal tree is shaken,
      So, from its riven,
   Blood-branched and bony haven,
The soul is blown toward that South where only the dead awaken.

Nothing arouses. Shrouded in marble snow
He enters the house of his fatal opposite, under
His careless star, and the statues. The bedded seeds outgrow
Their sleepy winter, but now there is no Spring thunder
Can shock him awake, who, lying companioned and lonely
   In his small house, can only—
      Against Time's yonder—
   Live nigh as a bloodless wonder
In the chinese box of the mind, a mummied guest in
   that haunted and homely

Dark where nothing endures. Though the heart entomb
And hold that weakling ghost for a season, the altering
Cold years like snow blindfold our love, as time
Darks a stone angel. So does memory, faltering,
Kill you again—your stillness is whirled and hurried
   To nature's wilder order.
      It is the faulting
   Heart in that bloody welter
Fails you and fails. Forgive this second murder.

There are a lot of ways to approach the choir aspect of the poem.
Here are some of the questions and procedures I addressed today:

- Does the first sentence of the poem have anything in common with the final sentence of the poem?
- Do the words that are capitalized have anything in common?
- Are there sound devices that knit the poem together?
- Are there sensory aspects that are repeated from one stanza to another?
- What happens to the *he* in the poem?
- Are words repeated?
- What word surprises you the most in each of the three stanzas?
- Do those three words have anything in common?
- What to you is the most important word in each stanza?
- Again, what do those three words have in common?

The answers were illuminating to all of us. At first students felt the poem seemed "remote," but as we talked they became very involved in it. They noted, for instance, how cold the poem is. We literally are given the word *cold* in the first stanza, then the second stanza speaks of *winter,* and the third of *snow*. That seemed just in that the poem was about death. A student remarked that if she weren't looking carefully she wouldn't have noticed how carefully the words are "tuned." Similarly, students noted how *bronze* and *memorial* are echoed by *stone angel*. Or how *mummied* in stanza two leads to *entomb* in stanza three. Or how *kill* in stanza three is taken up and quickened at the end of the poem by *bloody* and *murder*. Or how *bloodless* precedes *bloody* in the poem. Or how the structure of the *nothing* sentences at the beginnings of the first two stanzas changes in the third stanza.

All these remarks lead to a profile of how the choir works. I am not concerned about an overarching statement of what the poem is about. The connections my students trace dwarf any abstraction. I encourage them to draw lines among the words in the poem so that their copy of the poem becomes a map of sorts. Today's discussion led to some strong feelings about loss and memory. The students discussed how inevitable McGrath made the process of forgetting seem and how he used a variety of words to make that happen. The last stanza, in the words of Tammy Wells, "made me dizzy. I mean the way the 'stillness is whirled.' I can feel that. I can feel the brother being lost. So sad." We talked further about what seems a basic truth about poetry— that it is deeply physical and affects our bodies. It is bred in our breath and nerves.

McGrath's poem, of course, is a classical piece of English poetry. Later in the year when I do poems by the likes of Donne and Yeats, we refer to McGrath's poem. I don't use the words-talking-to-words approach with every poem. I could just as easily have focused on rhymes or the stanzaic structure McGrath uses. Still, it does represent an important model for approaching poems. What I like about this approach is that the kids become detectives. They pursue the words in the poem to see where they go. They wonder what one word has to do with another. Why is *winter* not capitalized but *Spring* is? One student said because *winter* is earth time but *Spring* is a revelation that is now outside of time because death is outside of time. As another student put it, "The energy between the two is different." I remember that one reason I teach is that I am moved by what young people have to say.

november 18

read me a poem

Sometimes my wife asks me to read her a poem. She is a physician's assistant and often the world is too much with her. She gets weary. When she asks me to read her a poem, I know that what she wants to hear is what she calls "one of the old poems." She often likes poetry that is written in our own day, but she loves best the poems that represent poetry with a capital P.

We have had talks about what that capital P stands for. Maura feels that it is the spirit world. In the old poetry there is, for her, a sense of magic. This sense of magic is quite literal. One of her favorite poems is "La Belle Dame Sans Merci" by John Keats. She never tires of it nor do I, for that matter. She likes legends and tales that indicate there are spirits among us and that we ourselves are spirits.

We have talked about where poetry comes from. It's a mystery, of course, and our world is not very graceful at abiding mystery. We have to know and explain. For our parts, I think I can say that we are comfortable with the mysterious origins of poems because the mystery is a gift. It can't be accounted for and it can't be willed. It tells us how little our minds are and how vast is the world of feelings and beings. We find that comforting. The old poems are signs and portents. They wonder and muse. Rarely do they stem from the everyday, embroiled, declarative self. They come from what is haunting.

I think it's good to be haunted. That may seem very odd, but I mean that living with poems gives one a sense that we feel life very deeply and we do our feelings a serious disservice when we discount them. I have nothing against our famous pragmatism. I only object when it sets itself up as the only way to go about life. How often do our minds go back to some scene that haunts us? It happens to me some time or other on most days. I am held captive for some seconds by a sense of sitting under an oak tree in the backyard when I was a boy or seeing a face in a crowd or remembering someone I once knew. I hear a voice; I see a summer afternoon long ago. Sometimes I literally feel a shiver at these moments.

Poetry enters into such moments and fleshes them out. It explores what is there and it bears witness to the testimony of all our senses. Accordingly, the poem I read tonight to Maura was "The Scholar-Gipsy" by Matthew Arnold. It's based on a story about a man who abandoned what we would call these days an academic career and went to live with gypsies. In Arnold's words "he roam'd the world with that wild brotherhood."

It's a famous poem, not only because it's a very well-written poem, but because it speaks to what Arnold calls "this strange disease of modern life / with its sick hurry, its divided aims. . . ." One is inclined to say that Arnold only knew the half of it, dying as he did in 1888. It may be, however, that our world is only an intensification of Arnold's in terms of technological progress and its relentless cadences. Precisely because the world into which Arnold was born was less complicated, he may have felt the changes all the more acutely.

In any case, Maura's favorite stanza wasn't one of the later ones about the "infection of our mental strife," but a stanza midway through the poem that summons up a vision of the scholar-gipsy:

> And once, in winter, on the causeway chill
>   Where home through flooded fields foot-travellers go,
>   Have I not pass'd thee on the wooden bridge,
>   Wrapt in thy cloak and battling with the snow,
>   Thy face tow'rd Hinksey and its wintry ridge?
>   And thou hast climb'd the hill,
>   And gain'd the white brow of the Cumner range;
>   Turn'd once to watch, while thick the snowflakes fall,
>   The line of festal light in Christ-Church hall—
>   Then sought thy straw in some sequester'd grange.

After I read her the whole poem she wanted me to read the "snowflakes" stanza again. And again. I asked her about it and she said that it put her somewhere else and that she loved that. She felt she was there with him and that was special. She wasn't in her own life anymore. The proper nouns gave her the feel of places on earth and that was all she needed. She said she didn't want any more detail than Arnold gave. "It would just be clutter," in her words.

We talked about the word *festal* and how one never hears that word. It wasn't only that it was an old word. It was that it called up all sorts of associations about human beings gathering to feast and celebrate and be together. Whatever else it may be, it is hard to see electric light as *festal*. The image of light being termed *festal* conjures up a whole world of warmth and cheer. And then there is the scholar-gipsy who is by himself and who has forsaken that world.

There is such a premium on coping and getting along in our world that poetry's visions may seem archaic and nostalgic. It seems the opposite to me. Our world of *repeated shocks* (in Arnold's phrase) needs time out. It needs to acknowledge that there is more to life than hurry and that what is sweet and precious about being alive is individual and poignant and barely communicable. Perhaps that galls us. I don't know. I know that we sat there after we talked and let the poem linger. There was no hurry to leave that place and it did our souls good to be there.

november 20

personae

My students tend to assume that the *I* in any given poem is equivalent to the flesh-and-blood person who wrote the poem. It's an understandable enough assumption. We go through life saying *I* to other people and we are referring to ourselves. Why should poetry be any different? Of course, it is different because a poem, no matter how natural its diction may be, is not the same thing as a person talking about him or herself.

To be sure, there are many poets who invite an equivalence between the person and the *I* in the poem. The thrust of Romantic poetry, be it in Wordsworth or Allen Ginsberg (I wonder what Wordsworth would have made of Allen Ginsberg), is the poet's life. In the poem we see William rowing across a lake or Allen hanging out with his cronies in Tangier. For all practical purposes we are there with the flesh-and-blood poet as he or she recalls his or her adventures and misadventures. The poet is testifying to his or her life force.

But one can't be sure. A poet may write a poem about piano lessons and never have taken them in his or her life. A poet may write about growing up in France and never have left Des Moines, Iowa. There is something called *imagination* at the core of poetry and it is unwise to forget that factor. This imagining is one of poetry's chief graces for it enables the poet to go anywhere and become anyone. Many poets have remarked upon the poet's lack of self: no-self becomes all-selves as the poet constructs lives and situations. Shakespeare seems the most remarkable version of this proclivity.

> There is something called *imagination* at the core of poetry and it is unwise to forget that factor.

Consequently in the classroom I try to suggest that we not jump in too quickly to say that the poet and the narrator of the poem are one and the same. By using the term *narrator* in regards to the poem we leave our options open. If we feel that "Yes, this is Allen Ginsberg,"—so be it. But it may not be the poet. As Emily Dickinson noted, "When I state myself, as the Representative of the Verse—it does not mean—me—but a supposed person." Poets construct all manner of personae and the persona who appears in the poem as the *I* may be as much a creation as what that *I* is talking about.

This may all seem somewhat academic, but it matters very much in that I want my students to feel the genuine freedom that poetry affords. You can write about other people's lives from the insides. You can try to imagine what it is like to be another person and try to convey that experience. Poetry really can be an exercise in compassion and empathy as one tries to imagine what another life is like from that life's point of view.

My students tend to worship at the altar of self-expression. I understand this impulse very well. I too live in declarative, talkshow America—the land of mass individualism. What I try to examine is the assumption that poetry is a form of therapy in which one unburdens one's present self by writing about one's past. "Me, me, me," as one of my students once put it. I have nothing against my students writing about their lives. Often I encourage them to do that. I want them to go there, as I like to say. But I want them to be aware that poetry is an avenue into other lives as it offers the opportunity to become other people. Poetry offers them latitude and I want them to feel that. There's a world out there beyond the demonstrative ego.

In that vein I offer the following poem by Karen Fiser to my students. I came across it in the anthology *I Feel a Little Jumpy Around You.* It is entitled "Wheelchairs That Kneel Down Like Elephants."

Last night I rode a tightrope
with my wheelchair. No net.
The night before, I left my body
on the steep ground with its pain.
I walked again by leaning,
elbows careless on the wind,
hitching myself along in light surprise.
Days I am heavy,
a clumsy bear on wheels,
bumping into things
and smiling, smiling. Nights
I invent new means of locomotion:
flying velocipedes, sailcars,
wheelchairs that kneel down
like elephants, carry me carefully
up the long stairs. Intricate
engines of need and night and air.

Whenever I show this poem to my students, they immediately go after the word choices because they are so acute and deft. They notice that even the little words convey a lot—that *light*, for instance, in *light surprise.* They talk about a phrase such as *intricate engines* and how much feeling there is in those two words, how the first word shows a wanting and an appreciation and a sort of genius and how the second word shows power and mechanical force. They talk about the simile that is the title of the poem and how much grace and strength there is in the notion of a huge creature such as an elephant being joined to a relatively small thing like a wheelchair. The poem fills them with feeling.

Because they go right away to the poem, the issue of the *I* is negligible for them. What matters are the words and the experience that the words convey. I like to use the poem as a model for a writing assignment. What I ask of them is to become another person and give me a sense of what that person's life is like. Specifically I want

> What I ask of them is to become another person and give me a sense of what that person's life is like.

them to focus on someone who faces a real challenge in life and how the person feels about that challenge. The poem has to be written in first person and has to convey through detail and metaphor a sense of what the person's life is like and what the person's feelings and wishes are about that life.

Over the years the work my students have done has astonished me. I always know that there is much more in any human being than I can see in day-to-day communication, but this assignment really brings home how much is there. My students range widely in terms of who they become. One favorite is to imagine what it is like to be old. Consequently, they often write about their grandparents. They are often the proudest of these poems because they feel they have connected with something amazing —what it is like to be someone else.

Typically these poems go through a couple rounds of revision because they are imaginative leaps. It isn't easy to see through someone else's eyes and make it convincing. In this case my students are eager to do the revisions because they are fascinated with getting it right. They want it to be convincing because they want it to be "Gramma Alice" or "Grampa Ted."

Later in the year, they take their skills in poetry writing and apply them to history. A history teacher who is simpatico with poetry has her students do persona poems. Specifically, they do two poems and my students model their poems to show them what they did and help them get going. We meet together over the course of a few days for this to happen. The history students write one poem about a famous person from that person's viewpoint. In that poem the student "becomes" Abraham Lincoln or Susan B. Anthony. In the other poem, the student "becomes" someone who isn't famous—a woman homesteader, a laborer on the railroad, a mill hand, a fugitive slave, a soldier in the Civil War. Again, the poem must be from that person's viewpoint.

> Later in the year, they take their skills in poetry writing and apply them to history.

It's a big challenge but the kids are up to it. It gives them a chance to use their historical knowledge for the purposes of making art. It gives them a chance to actualize what often seems theoretical. It gives them a chance to imagine themselves back in time.

In the first poem, it gives them a chance to imagine what it was like to be so-and-so; while in the second poem, it gives them a chance to imagine a particular, anonymous life and what it felt like.

Poetry doesn't tend to be at the top of the list when interdisciplinary connections are being discussed. It's too bad because the likes of persona poems offer extraordinary opportunities to students. The history teacher has been deeply touched by what her students have written. It has been affirming for her in that her students have taken the knowledge she has given them and done something tangible and imaginative with it. For her students, it has shown that they can make history come to life. To hear a kid in a contemporary American high school who is sitting there in baggy pants, a T-shirt, and who is festooned with various rings, read a poem in which he becomes a Confederate soldier who has been wounded at the Battle of Gettysburg is a strange and moving experience.

December and January

We had Thanksgiving at Maura's parents' house in a suburb outside of Boston. Her dad and mom are both retired professors. How
their daughter married someone who isn't a professor still mysti-
fies them. Sometimes I can feel a twinge on their part when I walk
in and there I am—still a high school English teacher in an old
denim jacket. Because we are happily married and because they
adore Ben, they have learned to live with it. For my part, I have
learned only to discuss my in-laws when my wife brings up the
subject. I love their daughter so they are okay with me. Plus
Maura's mom is a great cook and her dad is a basketball fan so all
is not lost.

On Friday everyone is pretty quiet. It's a lot of food that
Maura's mom brings out. I lost track of the number of courses this
year. She doesn't just put it all out on the table and holler "Come
and get it," the way my mom used to do. She's classy and I have
learned to pace myself because that's how she does it. Actually, she
paces you whether you want to be paced or not. Anyhow after my
post-Thanksgiving run in the morning and my meditation about
what the houses in their neighborhood cost (more than I can
imagine), I head in to the city to a favorite bookstore. Maura is
happy to hang out with her mom. Maura's dad and Ben are audio-
philes and will spend the afternoon in stores talking with sales
people about amps and watts and channels and that sort of stuff.
Ben will get some piece of gear for Christmas. There's something
to be said for being an only child.

I go to one of the bookstores that stocks a lot of poetry. Sitting
in a chair and leafing through books is my idea of a vacation.
When you work in a school, you get awfully used to living your
life in segments of so many minutes and then a bell rings. I keep
looking up at the clock until I realize there is no bell here. It's sad

how regimented you get. I breathe out deeply. I have hours without bells, intercom announcements, requests for a bathroom pass, or faux farting sounds.

Typically I wander around in the past and the present. There are two new translations of Dante. We do a bit of Dante in World Lit. The kids like him—hell gets their attention. I make a mental note to ask the school librarian to buy one of the translations. I like to have the kids compare passages and discuss the differences. I know enough Italian to have a notion about the original. We have a good time.

I wind up spending a long time with a book called *The Homeplace* by an African American poet named Marilyn Nelson. One poem that grabs me is called "Star-Fix." It's dedicated to Melvin M. Nelson, Captain USAF (ret.) (1917–1966):

> At his cramped desk
> under the astrodome,
> the navigator looks
> thousands of light-years
> everywhere but down.
> He gets a celestial fix,
> measuring head winds;
> checking the log;
> plotting wind-speed,
> altitude, drift
> in a circle of protractors,
> slide-rules, and pencils.
>
> He charts in his Howgozit
> the points of no alternate
> and of no return.
> He keeps his eyes on the compass,
> the two altimeters, the map.
> He thinks, *Do we have enough fuel?*
> *What if my radio fails?*
>
> He is the only Negro in the crew,
> the only black flyer on the whole base,
> for that matter. Not that it does:
> this crew is a team.
> Bob and Al, Les, Smitty, Nelson.
>
> Smitty, who said once
> after a poker game,

I love you, Nelson.
I never thought I could love
a colored man.
When we get out of this man's Air Force,
if you ever come down to Tuscaloosa,
look me up and come to dinner.
You can come in the front door, too;
hell, you can stay overnight!
Of course, as soon as you leave,
I'll have to burn down my house.
Because if I don't
my neighbors will.

The navigator knows where he is
because he knows where he's been
and where he's going.
At night, since he can't fly
by dead-reckoning,
he calculates his position
by shooting a star.

The octant tells him
the angle of a fixed star
over the artificial horizon.
His position in that angle
is absolute and true:
Alioth, in the Big Dipper,
Regulus, Antares, in Scorpio.

He plots their lines
of position on the chart,
gets his radio bearing,
corrects for lost time.

Bob, Al, Les, and Smitty
are counting on their navigator.
If he sleeps,
they all sleep.
If he fails
they fall.

The navigator keeps watch
over the night and the instruments,
going hungry for five or six hours
to give his flight-lunch
to his two little girls.

There are a lot of things I like about this poem. I like the tone enormously. It's such a quiet poem. To my mind it suits the descriptions of all the aeronautical instruments perfectly. They are performing quietly, the way they are supposed to perform. And the stars in the sky are performing according to their set courses. When the poem is louder, when some human detail pops up as when Smitty talks, it's all the more effective. There I am with a white Southerner. I like how the poet just lets this happen and moves on. The white Southerner owes his life to the black airman and he knows it. There it is.

Of course the ironies pull me in also. The navigator knows who he is very well. He is an African American in an air force that has next to no place for African Americans. But he is there and doing his job very well. You can feel his patience in the short lines that give the reader only a certain amount of information. Every little thing matters very much. The reading eye is greedy but the eye is held captive to the brevity of the lines. You have to slow down to take in those short lines.

The ending surprised me. I was so focused on the world of the war and of race and then here is this little, deeply human gesture at the end of the poem. All this history is going on but the navigator is still a father with a family and he is making a sacrifice that is very real. Hunger is hunger. The navigator knows who he is and what he is up against and I feel he is someone who is capable of making measurements not just about a plane, but about many things in life. He is a hero and the poem feels like an act of homage.

People come and go in the bookstore and it's fair to say they are not buying many poetry books. Practicality calls or information calls or theory calls or celebrity calls or scandal calls but poetry is calling too. Its voice is often quiet and maybe that's why it can't be heard over the commercial hullabaloo. Too bad, I think. To learn of this world in this poem is a gift and I feel it quite distinctly. I can feel this man's life and I can feel a bit of what it must have been like to be up there in that plane. I buy the book.

As is the case with all English teachers, I teach a lot of fiction. One thing that intrigues me is the difference between how narrative works in a short story or novel and how it works in a poem. In prose, the writer can build a situation gradually as incidents and descriptions and conversations are conveyed. We are aware that the author is selecting what gets said but it doesn't feel ultra-selective. Fiction is roomy. There's time to look out a window and see what's out there. There's time to walk down a street and register all the impressions you want to register. The sentences build a sense of a world.

Poetry, to my mind (and I'd be the first to say this is all personal), is tighter when it comes to narrative. That doesn't mean that you can't look out a window in a poem. Sure you can. But in a poem narrative lies in the words themselves. The words are characters in the narrative, whereas in fiction the words point to realities beyond themselves. A simple way of saying this is that poetry tends to the connotative and fiction to the denotative. Poetry is pledged to metaphor. In a poem a wall can be as important as the human being leaning against the wall. Maybe more so. Poetry is inherently animistic.

What I tell my students is that a poetic narrative can focus on anything. You can tell a narrative about a flower, for instance. Nothing is happening to the eye, but there is a world of existence in the flower in terms of description and ambience and that can be a narrative. As far as poetry is concerned, nothing has to happen in the sense that someone does something for there to be a narrative. Being is action. After all, at any given moment for us human beings there is a body, a spirit/mind/imagination, the multifarious earth we live on, and the language (or languages) we speak. That's a lot and it makes poetry an art of simultaneity.

What this means in terms of narrative is that poetry provides a good deal of freedom in telling a story. Poetry instinctively leaps between every sentence and stanza because notions of linear sequence don't govern poetry. Poetry is inspired in the sense that it hops from one moment to another. Its energy resides in its abil-

ity to make these leaps and that energy is its logic. As my students
have put it: fiction is more lifelike in that it gives you a sense of
how someone lives in the world; poetry is more lifelike in that it
gives you a sense of how fragmentary yet coherent our experiences are. Our sense of self, as the self journeys through time, is
the original narrative, so to speak, and poetry emanates from that
powerful instinct. The great challenge is how to use the energy to
convey whatever narrative is at stake. The choices are endless:
from relentless ballads to modern bits and pieces.

The poem we looked at today is by a contemporary American
poet who lives in Georgia. Her name is Billie Bolton and the poem
is entitled "Sunday Drive":

> You can go with me he announces suddenly.
> His teasing blue eyes smile at me from under the curved brim of
>   his hat—
> a tall white one like the cowboys wear—
> You mean it? I jump up from my Uncle Wiggly picture puzzle
> and grab him by his stiff pant leg,
> Wait, I'll need my dolly.
> The front seat of the Oldsmobile is wide as our neighbor's front
>   porch
> where wrinkled Mr. Mathis looks at his gold pocket watch as we
>   pass by.
> Restless behind the wheel Daddy unwraps a cigar,
> clamps it in the corner of his mouth, chews hungrily.
>
> I stand at attention near the open window,
> wind bangs in my ears and balloons my dress.
> My doll wears a soft cotton dress with a petticoat too.
> Red ribbons on her braids tickle my arms.
> I don't ask questions about Mama's headaches
> or where Daddy throws his money away.
> (He gives me silver dollars and tells me to save them.)
> I try to hold still so he won't mind we're along
> and watch as the cement sidewalks of town disappear into bumpy
>   pastures,
> wilted row crops and tired farmhouses where even the dogs are
>   too hot to bark.
>
> I think maybe the wind and speed will please Daddy on this
>   sunny afternoon.
> It is hard to know. Sometimes he smiles when I scold Dolly,

but then he's mad if I make too much commotion.
Pointing to a smudge in the distance,
he shouts that we're heading for the Blue Ridge.
Torn strips of tar paper hanging from chicken houses
are waving to us. A milk cow munching weeds near a wire fence
is a reddish blur. He laughs to see the road retreating in the
    rearview mirror,
lights his El Producto and lets out puffs like white blossoms.

Wind chases the smoke, tugs at my baby doll and makes me
    dizzy.
It seems as if we're flying and home is far away,
still, he knows the way I tell dolly, so we can't get lost.
I clutch her tightly to my chest edging closer to him, but not too
    close.
I'm along for the ride wherever it takes me.

I ask my students how this poem is a narrative. They start with
the obvious: It's about a Sunday drive. It tells what happens. Does
it matter then that we aren't told about whether they get to the
Blue Ridge Mountains? The kids are on me right away for asking
such an obtuse question. LaFrayne Smith shakes her head in pity.
"Mr. P, the narrative is her being with her father. Look at what she
says in the last line. It's about her sense of being with her father.
It's about 'wherever.' She's just a little girl but she wants to be with
her Daddy." LaFrayne stops and looks at me, hoping I'll get it.

Then, I ask, what do the details do in the poem? Are they necessary? What do they indicate? Again, the kids are right on me. I
let LaFrayne keep talking. She's wound up in a good way. "All that
stuff about chicken houses and a cow and stuff like that—that's to
put you there. If you aren't there, you can't experience it. And a
poem is an experience. That's what you've taught us." She pauses.
"In case you don't remember." Giggles. So, I ask, do you need
more details? No, according to the class. More details would make
the poem into a travelogue. The poem is about the little girl and
her Daddy. It's not a "word show" (who said that?—what a good
phrase!) about the rural South.

Why, I ask, is the poem in present tense? Jon Higgins in the
next to the last row is all over this. "When you are in present
tense, you are right there," he says. "I mean, to say the obvious,
we live in the present tense. That's what being alive is. And that

means we don't know what's going to happen next. I mean, I know I'm going to lunch, but I could trip on the way down the stairs—because some idiot is pushing me who is dying to eat his Sloppy Joe—and I will be in a hospital not in the lunchroom. Hospital food is even worse though." Pause to receive a couple of smiles, then he goes on. "She isn't sure about her Daddy and I can feel that she's not sure because the poem is in present tense. If it were in the past tense, I would feel this is all over and done with. But it's not over and done with. She's in the car and she doesn't know where she is exactly. I mean on the road and with her father, too. She's unsure. She's trying to be sure but she's unsure. She's experiencing the drive and that's a lot, just to experience it." He breathes out deeply. He's done.

With one of my classes I use the poem as a model for a writing assignment. I tell them to write a poem about a drive. I tell them to begin before you get in the car, then describe the drive. I want to know what happens inside the car and what is going on outside the car, too. Don't get to your destination in the poem. I see the kids nodding as I talk to them and I can feel that they have connected with the poem. I look forward to what they write. They spend a fair amount of their lives in automobiles. I know they have material to make narratives.

> I tell them to begin before you get in the car, then describe the drive.

december 9

place

We all live somewhere on earth. Some days, however, my students don't seem aware of that. They live in their heads; they live in cyberspace; they live in video games. The attention they pay to where they are growing up seems minimal. It's just where it is and you don't think much about it. Maybe you are going to leave because it bores you or you just want to see what other places are like. No one asks you about it because they live there, too.

I understand their attitudes. It seems second nature to take the place where you are growing up for granted. Because poetry is devoted to asking the "What is that?" question, poetry does pay attention to place. It does more than pay attention. Poems are investigations and confirmations of the power and poignancy of our living on earth. City, country, or suburb—it doesn't matter. They are particular places and in that particularity a world of feeling resides.

My students instinctively feel that life is elsewhere. On the Internet, in movies and television, and magazines, they are looking at images of other places incessantly. Hollywood, that endless purveyor of other places, is a very long way from where they live. They are often cut off from older people who have memories about the town in which they are growing up. Local history seems, at best, quaint to them. As for the conjunction of time with place, it is opaque to them. It's not only that they are young. It's that they live in a world that is obsessed with now. The "then" of the past holds little attraction for them.

For all the excitement that glowing screens convey, I feel there is a real poverty in not engaging the actual, reverberating world one lives in. It too will become the past. This is hard for young people to believe because they are young. Poetry, however, offers endless opportunities to feel what place (and, inevitably, time) has felt like to all manner of people. Poems offer analogies about living on some place on earth. They offer paths of feeling that others can walk down.

Today we looked at one of Donald Justice's poems from a series of poems entitled "My South." I like the title because I want my students to feel how we are bound to personalize where we live. We are living there, why shouldn't we personalize it? The specific poem I used with them is entitled "On the Porch" and is the first poem in the series.

> There used to be a way the sunlight caught
> The cocoons of caterpillars in the pecans.
> A boy's shadow would lengthen to a man's
> Across the yard then, slowly. And if you thought
> Some sleepy god had dreamed it all up—well,
> There was my grandfather, Lincoln-tall and solemn,
> Tapping his pipe out on a white-flaked column,
> Carefully, carefully, as though it were his job.
> (And we would watch the pipe-stars as they fell.)

As for the quiet, the same train always broke it.
Then the great silver watch rose from his pocket
For us to check the hour, the dark fob
Dangling the watch between us like a moon.
It would be evening soon then, very soon.

I have been a fan of Justice's work for a while. One thing that moves me about his work is how quiet his poems can be. This quiet doesn't put you to sleep; on the contrary, it enlivens you as it lets you be still and attend to what is there.

What I tell my students about this poem is that a poem is a lens. How close or far away one wants to make the lens is up to the poet. The poem can be right up close or mid-range or, at times, distant. I ask my students what the lens feels like in Justice's poem. They feel that he is up close but it makes "you feel sort of distant." We talk about what makes them feel "sort of distant" and decide it has to do, in part, with the poem being in third person. The narrator is involved in what is happening, but there is no *I* in the poem. It isn't personalized. It doesn't say *my shadow*. It says *A boy's shadow*.

I go back to the lens and ask what is close up in the poem. Tracy Briggs says the first lines are "real close up. It puts you right there. It feels very exact. It feels like he really watched this happen." Then I ask them if they have observed anything that closely in the world around them. Have they noticed cocoons? Have they observed particular trees? What, lately, have they noticed that is taking place on earth?

At first, there is very distinct silence in the room. There almost always is when I ask such a question. Like just about everyone in the United States my students are busy and noticing cocoons is not on their minds. Sometimes to break the ice I'll joke and ask them if they know what a cocoon is. Usually they remember something they did in the third grade for a science project. Today, I wait (I'm a good waiter and the kids know it) and then Ronnie Battle raises his hand. He's not a talker. His hand doesn't go up much.

"Well," he says. "I live in an apartment building with my mom and my mom is not much of a housekeeper because she is always working and I'm not much for housekeeping." He pauses. You can feel him thinking. "What I notice are spider webs. I mean, it sounds sort of stupid, but I really sit and look at them sometimes.

They aren't the same. I mean there are all different kinds of spiders." Pause again. "I know that sounds stupid because of course there are all different kinds of spiders. I mean, 'Wise up, Ronnie.' But there really are different spiders because the webs are different. And not just the webs, the same kinds of spiders are different because they are, you know, different spiders." Pause again. "This sounds stupid doesn't it?"

I tell him it's the most intelligent talk I've heard in days and to keep at it. He relaxes a bit and goes on. "So I look at these webs that are over the sink or in hall corners and I wonder what spiders live on. I mean I don't see a juicy fly or a moth in them. What are they doing, the spiders? Do they die of starvation? Where do they come from?" He's just staring into space with his questions. Then he comes back. "Well, that's what I've been noticing lately."

There's some laughter and when I ask for more, they start talking about whatever little things they have noticed. Sometimes I give them an assignment to put into their poetry journals three little things they have noticed in the physical world around them. I tell them I want the description to be as exact as they can make it. I'm not looking for a poem. I want some description. Sometimes I tell them to put on their jackets and we walk outside and I tell them to look at the grass and then come in and write about it. The grass? You've got to be kidding, they say. They know I'm not.

I ask them what this sort of observation has to do with a sense of place. Why does Justice begin a series of poems called "My South" with an image of how "sunlight caught / The cocoons of caterpillars in the pecans?" Why doesn't he start talking about the South as the South? The kids know my leading questions and they go right to it: The South is cocoons and pecans. That is the poet's ,South. Without that basis there is no poem. They feel the same way about the "watch business," as Cassie Burlington puts it. We talk about what a *fob* is and the action of checking the hour according to a train. It's not a way of life with which they are even remotely familiar.

So where do you live? I ask them. They look around at one another. They know it's another of those Mr. P questions in which the obvious and the not so obvious are joined. One kid says the name of our town and I say, "What is that?" Another kid says the approximate population and I ask, "Who lives there?" A few more answers and questions and we start to get to some specifics. Are there alleys in this town? What is in the alleys? Do people walk in them? What sorts of houses are there? Are they all the same? How are they different? What sorts of trees are there? It's like the old game of Twenty Questions. I do this sort of questioning all the time because I want them to focus on what they take for granted. I want them to start to see and feel what is there.

How many pizza places are there in this town? How do they differ from one another? "Pizza places!" they exclaim. "You want us to write about pizza places?" "Is it part of where you live?" "You better believe it, Mr. P.," says Tony Benoit. "I can tell you about every one of them. I'm a serious student of pizza places. Like do they have the parm in those shakers or do you have to ask them? Not like the parm is that great anyway. I mean it's like wood shavings mostly." "Simile," I say and then repeat, "the dark fob / Dangling the watch between us like a moon."

december 11

a parent

I had a meeting today with a parent who, as she put it, was "concerned about all the poetry my daughter's class is doing." She told me on the phone that it "didn't seem like the sort of work that was going to help my daughter get into the college of her choice." She paused on the phone for a second and then said, "Poetry is a frill, isn't it? No one in the real world takes poetry seriously." She took it back in the next second when she told me how much she liked Robert Frost and that she herself didn't have anything against poetry. She was concerned about her daughter. I told her that I welcome all parental calls and would be glad to talk with her in person.

Mrs. Jackson wasn't loaded for bear, as they say where I live. She was cordial but she was clearly concerned. I asked her what her perceptions were in terms of what her daughter was telling her.

She didn't look straight at me when she responded. "Well," she said, "some of the poems seem disturbing to me. There was a poem with a suicide in it, for instance. Karen wasn't upset about it but I worry about putting ideas into children's heads." After she spoke, she looked at me straightforwardly.

I agreed with her. I worry, too, and I told her so. It's not worry though that comes from reading poems. I feel that poems counter-act some of the dangers that exist in the lives of young people because they flush various difficulties into the open. When we talk about a poem such as "Richard Cory" by Edwin Arlington Robinson, I can feel how a certain tension is there at the beginning of the discussion and then I can feel how that tension breaks and there is relief. Robinson doesn't portray suicide as a good choice. He does show that this happens. That someone has been there before them is very important for young people to experience. It's one reason to study literature.

What I do worry about is silence and the pain that comes from nothing being said to anyone and the isolation that results from that silence. As I told Mrs. Jackson, I believe in the ability of words to illumine feelings. Those feelings can be hard ones but words can go there. If the words aren't encountered, then all that's there is rumor. As I put, "It's not any one poem that I feel makes a cru-cial difference. It's the environment that poetry creates. It's where young people feel that other people are taking chances and telling people about it. Poets aren't taking chances for the hell of it. They are taking chances in the name of honesty. I think kids respect that. In fact, I know they respect that."

The You-Are-Getting-Preachy-Jim button went off in my head. I know it's hard for a lot of parents to go near a teacher. We are experts and no one likes to tangle with experts. "It's not," I told her, "that I'm out to save the world via poetry. I just think that poetry gets overlooked. Taking care of feelings seems to me as practical as whatever skill you think of as practical. The funny thing is that studying poetry is practical." I smiled a determined smile. I'm sure of myself in terms of my teaching, but I know that parents have their own issues about their children. I know that from my own son and I know that from having been caught more than once over the years in the crossfire between a parent and a child. The reason for the visit sometimes turns out to be more than grammar.

Mrs. Jackson listened to me carefully but I could sense she was at sea. I asked her if she'd like to hear a poem we did that day in class. She shifted in her seat (those perennially uncomfortable stu-dent desks) and seemed a bit anxious but she smiled and said, "Sure." It wasn't, after all, that her daughter was flunking or anything. Actually, Karen had told me that she liked the class. It was parental worry and poetry worry, too.

I read her a poem from a recent book by an American poet named Ted Kooser. The book is called *Winter Morning Walks*. The poems are quite short and were sent on postcards to another writer, Jim Harrison. Kooser composed the poems every day and they each have a header that tells something about the day's weather. I explained to Mrs. Jackson that he took the walks as part of his recovery from a siege of cancer. I read her the poem for December 27. The weather note at the beginning of the poem says "Twenty degrees":

> For the past two years there's been
> a white chenille bedspread
> caught up in a barbed wire fence
> along the road to the quarry.
> For a while it looked like a man
> who had fallen asleep on a sofa,
> sad bachelor uncle of a man,
> the soft ball of his bald head fallen,
> long thin arms stretched out
> along the back and trembling.
> But today that was gone, torn away
> by the wind, and there was no one
> but me on the road. My heart
> flapped like a rag in my ears.

She asked me immediately if she could see the poem and I showed it to her. She read it over for a while moving a finger to follow the lines. When she looked up at me, she seemed a bit saddened.

"It's a fine little poem. I guess it's a poem. It doesn't rhyme but I know poems don't have to rhyme. But tell me, what do the children learn about English from such a poem? It seems as though anyone could write it." She blushed a bit. "I don't mean disrespect. You understand me. It's not at all complicated."

"And complicated is better," I inserted.

We both laughed.

"No, complicated isn't better but it's what the world wants. It's what the tests are about. I know that from my older children. Those tests are hard."

I told her what I truly believe, that the word choices in so-called simple poems are not simple. "How about *flapped* in the last line? What do you think about that word?"

"What do you mean—'What do I think about it?'—It's a word. Isn't that good enough?"

"Well, to be honest, no. It isn't good enough. It's a specific word in a very specific situation. What do you say?"

She blushed again but seemed determined to hold up her end of things. "Well," she said and stopped for a few seconds, "it's a word that comes from the fence. I think a bedspread would flap in the wind. It would, wouldn't it?"

I agreed. "How about the description of the bedspread? Does he use any verbs to describe the movement of the bedspread?"

We looked at the poem and found the phrase *caught up*. Then there was the word for the uncle—*trembling*.

"Well, no, there isn't a word he uses definitely to describe the bedspread moving in the wind. There isn't any wind. The bedspread is *caught* and *asleep*. Those are the words the poet uses." There was more confidence in her voice.

"So," I said, "where does *flapped* come from?"

"Ah," she said and looked slyly at me. "I see where you are going. He saves that word. Anyone could use that word to describe it earlier in the poem, but he saves the word and when it occurs there in the last line he's found a whole other way to use it. I like that."

"And, Mrs. Jackson, we talked about parts of speech, word choices, and tone among other things and we read very carefully."

I paused. "What I think is that a poem is a sharp pencil. It hones students' sense of language. They need all the honing they can get and they need it daily because, as you probably know, they tend to forget. When they see how carefully poems are wrought, they start to feel some respect for language and that respect, I think, carries over into all areas of language use. I'm sharpening them. I'm sharpening them for the real world as much as anything. The more alert they are to how language is used, the better." I waited for another question or comment. For my part, I always learn something when I talk about a poem. Or talk to a parent.

> "What I think is that a poem is a sharp pencil. It hones students' sense of language."

"Mr. P., may I borrow that book?" she asked me.

december 12

crucial words

There are a number of small words that make poetry what it is. They aren't crucial words in the sense of being particularly poetic words. They are crucial in the sense that they make poems happen. By that I mean they either initiate energy or direct it. The first category contains words, such as *when* and *if*. If (there it is) you think about those words, they are amazing forces. *When* is the spark of narrative: "When Alice walked into the room . . ." or "When General Sherman reached Atlanta. . . ." Right away we have a presence and we have a sense of actions that are going to occur. Similarly, *if* posits the possibility of anything happening and then acts on that possibility, "If I were only a year older . . ." or "If I lived in Paris. . . ." *If* opens the door to wherever imagination wants to go.

Other words turn the direction of the poem. Probably the strongest and most indispensable one in this category is *but*. Where would we be without *but*? The word enables us to take the other side and since there invariably is another side to any situation it is crucial. One reason we write poems is that we have feelings that are conflicted. *But* honors that mingled impulse. Many a Shakespearean sonnet turns on that word. I'd bet that *but* is in most of the sonnets.

The impulse is understandable when one thinks about it. Poetry is obsessed with careful articulation and usually (though by no means always) that means there needs to be qualification. Things aren't just this way; they are that way, too. The poet I did in class the other day, Donald Justice, is a great qualifier. When the reader encounters a *perhaps* or *almost*, you feel the presence of the meticulous poet brooding and discriminating and relishing the materials of the poem. The presence isn't oppressive. It's comforting because you can feel the artist's caring and the refusal to be glib. You can feel that the poem is something that is made up and that the making is, at once, inspired and deliberate.

I try to get my students to focus on the crucial little words in a poem, the words that initiate, turn, and refine the action of the poem. It's a way of orienting oneself within the boundaries of the poem. What direction do we have here in the poem? What changes in direction do we experience? How many qualifications do we encounter? How much do they matter? As I noted, I like to use Shakespeare's sonnets as embodiments of these concerns. By focusing on them, students are able to start to read Shakespeare in a practical, focused manner. They can see how powerful *when* is in Sonnet 64, which repeats that word at the beginning of lines one, five, and nine. "No *when*, no poem," as one student concisely put it.

A poet who tangibly is connected with the Shakespearean tradition and a poet for whom my students have expressed genuine liking is Edwin Arlington Robinson. I do a variety of Robinson's short poems with my students. Today we looked at "The Tavern":

> Whenever I go by there nowadays
> And look at the rank weeds and the strange grass,
> The torn blue curtains and the broken glass,
> I seem to be afraid of the old place;
> And something stiffens up and down my face,
> For all the world as if I saw the ghost
> Of old Ham Amory, the murdered host,
> With his dead eyes turned on me all aglaze.
>
> The Tavern has a story, but no man
> Can tell us what it is. We only know
> That once long after midnight, years ago,
> A stranger galloped up from Tilbury Town,
> Who brushed, and scared, and all but overran
> That skirt-crazed reprobate, John Evereldown.

Although there are plenty of poetic words to engage the reader (to say nothing of the very engaging, if less than poetic, *skirt-crazed*), I like to have my students focus on the little words and how they work in the poem. Accordingly we look at the very first word in the poem—*whenever*. It launches the action of the poem. Beyond that crucial word my students note others. *Seem* is important because it allows feeling to happen, but it makes a distinction between actuality and subjectivity. *Something* is crucial because it is general. We know the speaker is a very articulate person. The generality of *something* is all the more unsettling for that knowledge. Then there's *as if*. It mirrors the direction of *seem*. We are there but not there.

> I like to have my students focus on the little words and how they work in the poem.

Perhaps most crucially there is the *but* at the beginning of the sestet of the sonnet. Sometimes my students are frustrated by it. "Why bother to write the poem, if no one knows?" they ask. It's a sensible question, but one that draws immediate answers. "Crimes," as Janice Tomlinson put it today, "don't all get solved. They still are crimes and they still can spook us because we are never going to know what happened. Maybe we know a piece of the story from someone. Maybe we don't." Janice went on to point out that *but* connects with another unobtrusive word, *only*. We don't know much and the poet makes us aware of that with the *only*. That makes the whole thing "all the spookier," as she put it. "It makes me feel how weird and crazy and awful murder is." She ended her comments with the always-expressive word, "Yuck!" A lot of heads nodded in vigorous agreement.

Once upon a time, students were instructed in the ways of *rhetoric*. I mean that word in the sense of persuasion. Certain terms insinuated a sense of persuasion. Certain terms created order. Certain terms allowed for the direction of the argument to change. I think of *yet, but, however, although, indeed, since, because, if*—all the little logicians. Although (couldn't avoid it) the term rhetoric has passed largely into abeyance, the words are still there for students to discover and ponder. They are the inherent thinkers in the language. A poem is a small piece of work; the force of such words is all the stronger because of that.

I ended on a totally different tack. "Where," I asked, "do the accents go in the name that ends the poem?" We agreed on the second and fourth syllables. We also agreed that the last line was somewhat irregular compared to the rhythmic pattern of the poem. "And what effect does that have?" I always seem to have one more question.

december 17

occasions

I want my students to have a sense of how poetry is part of people's lives. That's to say that I want them to perceive some of the emotional reasons why poems get written in the first place. Too often their sense of a poem comes from a textbook—great words that have been buried in a weighty, corporate-issued sepulcher. The emotional occasion behind the poem, how the poem connected with some people in some place on earth, is often left out.

That's why I stress the connection between occasions and poems. Poems celebrate and mourn and commemorate and mock and salute. I could write down many more verbs that all have to do with poetry's social functions. Love poetry is perhaps the most famous instance of poetry that is brought into being by a definite occasion—falling in love. How many poems have been written to a loved one praising the loved one's charms? I know firsthand that high school students are still writing them. Some are sentimental and some are wildly metaphorical and some are just plain obscene (I picked up a piece of paper in the hall one day and was taken aback by the salacious rhymes).

Our feelings connect with all sorts of public occasions. Poets have written poems about every conceivable event—assassinations, births, coronations, revolutions, wars, baseball games—you name it. Since it is December I like to focus on a few poems about the holiday that, along with New Year's, closes the schools for a week and a half—Christmas. I usually do a reading of the "Night Before Christmas" if the kids are up for it. Most classes have had enough of it and tell me to save it. This year I started with the first section of John Milton's "On the Morning of Christ's Nativity." The poem was written in 1629 when Milton was twenty-one years old.

> This is the Month, and this the happy morn
> Wherein the Son of Heav'ns eternal King,
> Of wedded Maid, and Virgin Mother born,
> Our great Redemption from above did bring;
> For so the holy Sages once did sing,
>> That he our deadly forfeit should release,
> And with his Father work us a perpetual peace.

> That glorious Form, that Light unsufferable,
> And that far-beaming blaze of Majesty,
> Wherewith he wont at Heav'ns high Councel-Table,
> To sit the midst of Trinal Unity,
> He laid aside; and here with us to be,
>> Forsook the Courts of everlasting Day,
> And chose with us a darksom House of mortal Clay.

Say Heav'nly Muse, shall not thy sacred vein
Afford a Present to the Infant God?
Hast thou no verse, no hymn, or solemn strein,
To welcome him to this his new abode,
Now while the Heav'n by the Suns team untrod,
    Hath took no print of the approaching light,
And all the spangled host keep watch in squadrons bright?

See how from far upon the Eastern rode
The Star-led Wizards haste with odours sweet,
O run, prevent them with thy humble ode,
And lay it lowly at his blessed feet;
Have thou the honour first, thy Lord to greet,
    And joyn thy voice unto the Angel Quire,
From out his secret Altar toucht with hallow'd fire.

I read the poem once, hand out a copy, then read it two more times. Then I break the class into four groups. Each group has a stanza to deal with. "Deal with," means they have to go over the language in their stanza with the rest of the class. Everyone in the room has access to a dictionary. I tell them that in essence they are detectives. The language is old. The spellings of some of the words have changed over centuries. If, however, they know the story of Christmas, they can follow the poem. I

> Each group has a stanza to deal with. "Deal with," means they have to go over the language in their stanza with the rest of the class.

give each group a grade for their presentation, but am careful to go around the room and monitor what is going on. I don't go out in the hall and catch up on the weather report with another teacher. Group work can easily become one person's effort. They know that I know that.

    The kids like the detective challenge. I picked up the notion from a grade school teacher but high school students are just as eager to show they can sleuth. A stanza is not overwhelming. Plus they are curious to see how the other groups do. We hit, as a class, some snags—*deadly forfeit*, for instance—and I am glad to be the court of last resort. Mostly they manage their way through it. Then I ask them individually for the word or words that intrigue them most. I get all sorts of answers. A couple of students are keen on *Wizards*. As one of them puts it, "It makes me feel the word. It's not a word that you hear in our world. It's magic. I can feel a little of the magic." Another student, Tina Berry, votes for *darksom House*. She says that it makes her feel what a body is, how it is, in a way, a house. I end up with a sort of choral reading. One person from each group reads a stanza. I write the poet's name and date on the blackboard. I like the kids to feel what time is, how old a poem can be.

I move on to a contemporary poem. It's about Christmas also, but it's written from the point of view of an outsider. The title is "Christmas."

> The quietest day. Even when we spoke in
> Ordinary tones to say we wanted jam not butter
> On our toast, it sounded muffled and distant.
> We stayed inside and avoided each other,
>
> Not from dislike but wariness, as if
> Our guarded faces might dissolve and confess.
> We must have read a lot—Dickens for
> My mother, military history for Dad,
>
> Adventures and fantasies for us kids.
> I always seemed to be reading Jack London.
> Now and then, I'd look up from my book and listen.
> What did I expect to hear? Exclamations,
>
> Carols, prayers, supernal sleighs? And my own voice,
> Certain yet misbegotten, chosen yet left out?

Because my students have nothing to go on beyond the text (I dictated the poem and did not give the poet's name), I ask them whose point of view this is. They scrutinize the language (*supernal* means?) and talk. What they decide is that this is a family that doesn't celebrate Christmas. Everyone agrees that for people who celebrate the holiday, it is not a quiet day. The poet is clueing in readers right away. "My uncles come over," says Tisha Jarvis. "Do you know what my uncles are like? They could be asking you who your English teacher is this year and it's like they are cheering at a football game. Loud. They are loud."

Who is telling the poem? After some lively discussion, the class feels that it is someone "who knows who he or she is but isn't Christian." Many students feel that it doesn't matter a whole lot who the speaker is. What matters is the feeling of not celebrating Christmas, of not being part of things. Kenny Christopher says

that he never thought about it really. "I mean I know people who have different religious backgrounds but I never thought about it. Our family is big on Christmas and the world is so big on Christmas, I just never thought about it." There is a lot of agreement about this, how pervasive Christmas is and how it feels as though everyone must be going ho-ho-ho throughout the day. "But not everyone is," says Kenny. "Not everyone is."

january 5

fishing

Over Christmas vacation I have a chance when I'm not shoveling snow (amazing how it snows on vacations and weekends) to catch up on the literary journals to which I subscribe. I don't have a lot of money or a lot of time, but I have enough of both to subscribe to five or six journals. As I tell my students, it's a form of fishing for me: fishing for a poem I like. I'll start a poem and if it doesn't grab me, I'll turn the page and start another. It's not an ordeal. The journals are full of poems by contemporary poets and I like to see what they are writing. It matters enormously to me to know that people are out there writing poems. I like to hear what strangers have to say. I like to feel how enormous human experience is.

I bring the journals into the classroom after I am done with them. It's safe to say that I have never had a student who saw a literary journal before he or she encountered one in my room. I have a couple of bookshelves in the room and in the beginning of the year I explain they are there for my students. One shelf is filled with journals I have collected over the years. When we have quiet reading time, the shelves are ransacked. Also, when I tell the kids to bring in a poem that they would like to present to the class, the journals are consulted.

After a while, they get used to the presence of the journals. Some kids will pick up a new one when I bring it in. They are, like me, curious. What might be in there? I think this curiosity is precious. What is the point of an education if you don't connect with what is being done around you? Is connection defined totally by popular, commercial culture? For the overwhelming number of my students it very definitely is. As for education, it is about what is known, "what's dead," as students have put it. The notion of having a sense that culture continues in one's own world and that, as a student, one can interact with that culture is foreign.

One thing I want my students to wake up to is taste. Specifically I want them to feel that they have aesthetic taste. Sensibility belongs to every human being. How many opportunities are presented in the classroom to explore that sensibility? The usual route is: "Here is the poem. It's famous. Whatever you feel about it is irrelevant because you are here to explicate it not respond to it aesthetically." When I bring in journals full of poems that are written by people who are trying to make art right now, I give my students a chance to exercise their taste. I am not up in front of the room telling them this poem is really great and they better listen up. Rather, I am showing them a poem and asking them what they think about it. Is it a keeper? What do you think? What strikes you? What leaves you cold? How does the language work?

One of my assignments later in the year is to hand out literary journals to students and ask them to find a poem they like and write about why they like it. I do this right in class as an exam. I am not interested in their explaining what the poem "means." I am interested in their responding to the poem and pointing out what in the text made them respond. It isn't easy to be articulate when talking about art and I take that into account. They have, however, been working on it all year. They do start to become comfortable. Most importantly, they start to become aware that they have taste, that they prefer one poem to another and can say why. They start to perceive literature as something people continue to make. It isn't an over-and-done-with, textbook monolith, but a continuous human endeavor. They can see themselves as consumers of literature and they can feel how a poem can speak to them. Not to read any contemporary poems is to be cut off from a huge source of feeling. The music they listen to, however vital it is, is not the same thing.

Today I bring in a poem from *The Manhattan Review*. It's a poetry journal that a friend gave me a subscription to and that I

have kept on renewing. In every issue I seem to find poems that grab me one way or another. Some poems are by Americans, but many are translations of foreign poets. The one today is by a contemporary American poet named Jeanne Marie Beaumont and is called "Afraid So."

> Is it starting to rain?
> Did the check bounce?
> Are we out of coffee?
> Is this going to hurt?
> Could you lose your job?
> Did the glass break?
> Was the baggage misrouted?
> Will this go on my record?
> Are you missing much money?
> Was anyone injured?
> Is the traffic heavy?
> Do I have to remove my clothes?
> Will it leave a scar?
> Must you go?
> Will this be in the papers?
> Is my time up already?
> Are we seeing the understudy?
> Will it affect my eyesight?
> Did all the books burn?
> Are you still smoking?
> Is the bone broken?
> Will I have to put him to sleep?
> Was the car totaled?
> Am I responsible for these charges?
> Are you contagious?
> Will we have to wait long?
> Is the runway icy?
> Was the gun loaded?
> Could this cause side effects?
> Do you know who betrayed you?
> Is the wound infected?
> Are we lost?
> Will it get any worse?

I read the poem twice and ask them if they need to hear it again to be ready to start talking about it. They want to hear it once more and I read it. I'm feeling a little cocky so I put the big question to them, "So, guys, what makes this a poem?" I can feel them shifting in their seats—not nervous but getting ready to go after the question. The first one out of the gate is Merry Taylor, a spry kid who sprints on the track team and talks just as fast.

"Now, Mr. P.," she says, "You've told us a poem can be most anything. Well, this poem is a bunch of questions. That's all, just a bunch of questions." Merry is thinking to herself (furrowed brow), but also making motions to Joey Espinoza that she has the floor and he has to keep quiet until she's done. Merry is not one to back down. She continues, "The questions seem at first kind of random and dumb, but then you realize that all the questions we ask about everything are kind of random and dumb. But they aren't random and dumb." Merry is smiling now. She's got solid braces—top and bottom. "They're human questions and we worry and there are no answers. There are no answers in this poem. That's what it's about, Mr. P. No answers. But a lot of worried questions."

Joey smiles and I notice he's got braces too. I start to think how well the orthodontists in this town must be doing, but Joey interrupts my idle thoughts with a "Well said, Merry." I wonder where Joey got "well said." Has he been watching old movies?

We talk about writing a poem in just one mode, such as a string of questions. Merry feels that "it takes guts. It's easy to be boring. But she's not boring." She pauses. "Maybe I'll write her, Mr. P., about her poem." I'm always glad to hear that because I encourage my students to write to poets. Because poets aren't rock stars, they often write back. A student a few years ago wound up becoming friends with a poet who lived 1500 miles away. I can't say how much that contact meant to her. She never would have known such people existed or that one of them could become her friend. It opened up a world to her, a living world.

Where we wind up today is using the poem as a writing prompt. What I ask the students is to write a poem in one mode—in this case the mode is back and forth between things they are told to do and things they are told not to do, as in "Clean up your room." and "Don't do drugs." This is Merry's poem. It's called "What Girls Hear."

Do the dishes.
Don't throw your clothes around.
Be nice to guys.
Don't come on strong.
Give out compliments.
Don't talk behind people's backs.
Do your schoolwork so you can go to college.
Don't stay out too late.
Be who you are.
Don't step out of line.
Smile.
Don't you dare get pregnant.

january 9

department meeting

We try to meet as a department every six weeks or so. School being what it is, this sometimes turns into two months and leaves us with some fairly substantial agendas. We meet after school. For a time, we tried to do the meeting before school, but it just didn't leave us enough time to talk. Plus, more than half of us were virtually incoherent until our morning coffee had kicked in.

This afternoon we have the usual on the docket—upcoming state tests, curriculum for next year, budget, student–teacher assignments, bulletins from the guidance office. There's the usual jockeying about courses and grade levels. Some teachers covet the higher end students and make some fairly ingenious arguments as to why they should have those students. Our department chair, Susan Paresi, is a remarkably impartial soul who goes by a number of factors in making assignments. People complain but if they didn't complain I'd worry something was wrong with life on earth.

At the end of the meeting we hear a poem and talk about it— if we want to talk about it. Originally, this was my idea although a couple of other members in the department immediately picked up on it. We are English teachers and, however much we feel put upon, it's a sad commentary on us if we don't have any time for the content we teach. At workshop days, we almost invariably are presented with some expert in technology, methodology, or some other "ology" who regales us with tales about what is going on in the big world and should be happening in our classrooms. Or we learn about new standards from the State Department of Education—as if we didn't have standards before in our classrooms. I can't remember the last time we had a real workshop in our content area.

We bring in a poem to read of our own choosing and rotate the person from meeting to meeting. One little rule we have is that the person who is reading can't tell the others beforehand what he or she is going to read. As in my classroom, it's always a surprise. While there is some looking at the clock, everyone agrees that a poem doesn't take a long time. If a teacher needs to excuse him or herself to pick up a child or whatever, that's fine—after the poem is read.

Today it's Susan's turn to read. She has been teaching for the better part of thirty years and is a very solid teacher. I don't mean that only in the sense that she knows her subject matter and knows how to get it across to kids. I mean she is always thinking about what she is doing in her classroom. She is always eager to talk about how a classroom runs. She uses all of her minutes with the kids and she is constantly evaluating what she is doing with those minutes. It's awfully easy to teach the same books each year and make a virtue of one's habits. It's awfully easy to pull a folder out of one's file and start to do the same old, same old. Susan has never done that.

Susan has observed me many times. I respect her feedback a great deal. Some days are better than others are, and I know that sometimes I'm asking for more than the kids reasonably can give me. One thing Susan has picked up on is how much the so-called "low end" kids glom on to poetry. I felt this instinctively but we have talked about it and it has changed her classroom practice a lot. The kids who are programmed to succeed often balk at poetry. They want to know what hoops to jump through, but in going over a poem there really are no hoops. Emotional responsiveness is crucial to poetry and the kids who are SAT-obsessed (or who have parents who are SAT-obsessed) often just want to know what I want them to say. Many of them get frustrated with poetry because there is no right answer. They like hierarchies but poetry isn't at all hierarchical. It bugs them.

The kids who are not SAT-obsessed, which is to say the larger number of kids in our school, respond, by and large, very strongly to poetry. Their feelings tend to be closer to the surface because (to my mind) they are not as inclined to conceptualize. It's not that they are "dumb" (though a lot of them perceive themselves that way). Far from it. They simply are more inclined to call them as they see them. Once they understand that I value their responsiveness—as long as they stay focused on the poem—they are off to the races. They like the actuality of focusing on words and how those words trigger feelings. I have made a point in this journal not to label kids in terms of how they are tracked. I couldn't count the perceptive remarks that have been made by kids whose grades and overall attitudes are less than sterling. They have written some tremendous poems also.

I haven't forgotten our meeting and the poem. Susan tells us the title of the poem she is going to read is "Women" by a nineteenth-century poet named Lizette Woodworth Reese.

> Some women herd such little things—a box
> Oval and glossy, in its gilt and red,
> Or squares of stain, or a high, dark bed—
> But when love comes, they drive to it all their flocks;
> Yield up their crooks; take little; gain for fold
> And pasture each a small, forgotten grave.
> When they are gone, then lesser women crave
> And squander their sad hoards; their shepherds' gold.
> Some gather life like faggots in a wood,
> And crouch its blaze, without a thought at all
> Past warming their pinched selves to the last spark.
> And women as a whole are swift and good,
> In humor scarce, their measure being small;
> They plunge and leap, yet somehow miss the dark.

For me it's been a stinker of a day. A kid in my first period class announced to the other kids that he was "sick of all this poetry shit" and proceeded to walk out of the room. In my fourth period class an assignment about metaphor that I had worked hard on was plainly too ambitious and I watched my students try and flounder. Plus, I managed to spill ketchup on a shirt I got from Maura for Christmas. So I'm full of my own woe but there it is— that poetry silence. We sit there and don't move or say anything. Then simultaneously Ed Ottinger, who's a pretty crusty guy, and Emma Terzio, who's a young, ebullient feminist, both say, "Read it again." They look at each other—and believe me they are not keen on each other—and they nod with conviction to one another. The poem's gotten under their skins and mine too. Susan reads the poem again and we talk for a good ten minutes. No one looks at the clock or coughs out of boredom or complains. We talk about women's lives and how fierce and tender a poem can be at the same time and how astonishing the last line is and how none of us particularly knew who this poet was. On the way out of the room Ed and Emma talk to each other—animatedly.

january 12

emily dickinson

I read Emily Dickinson the way my older sister consults the *I Ching*. I mean I just open the *Collected Poems* to a random page and read a poem. I sit with it, read it again, sit with it, read it, speak it aloud, sit with it. It's hard to put into words what this process is like for me, but when I read Dickinson I feel I am touching something so deeply original that I am touching a source of life itself. Because her poems represent a veritable ocean, I feel I will never exhaust her. And I won't.

Dickinson can be a very hard poet to get across to the kids. Typically she has been handicapped by an enormous emphasis on how hard she is to understand. That's not a happy way to go into a poem. For my part, I foremost want my students to have the experience of engaging Dickinson. If they don't experience her, what do they have? Reading a poem while worrying about what it may mean is not a good way to engage Dickinson or anyone else for that matter. There's worry enough in the world already.

By experiencing Dickinson I mean that I dictate her poems a line at a time. We stop after each line and talk about it. There's no hurry. We don't gobble up the poem, the way one does when one reads a poem. As I noted earlier, eyes are greedy. I want the kids to experience how much happens from one line to another in her poetry. Dickinson is surely one of the greatest leapers from line to line in English-language poetry.

> By experiencing Dickinson I mean that I dictate her poems a line at a time. We stop after each line and talk about it. There's no hurry.

Her famous dashes signal a propensity for making associations that are lightning quick and that span all manner of chasms. It's been said that a poem is, in part, a conversation with oneself. Dickinson made a superlative art of that propensity.

Today I read "#613" to them. I had never encountered the poem and the first line alone threw me over a rainbow.

> They shut me up in Prose—
> As when a little Girl
> They put me in the Closet—
> Because they liked me "still"—
>
> Still! Could themself have peeped—
> And seen my Brain—go round—
> They might as wise have lodged a Bird
> For Treason—in the Pound—
>
> Himself has but to will
> And easy as a Star
> Abolish his Captivity—
> And laugh—No more have I

As I noted, we go through the poem a line at a time. Here are my notes of the poem on a line-by-line basis:

Line One: Who is *they*? Does it matter? What about the word *Prose*? How can someone be *shut . . . up in Prose*?

Line Two: Starts an action. Feels straightforward.

Line Three: There's the *they* again. *Closet* is what? Punishment?

Line Four: Why is she being punished? How she quotes them directly. What feelings do you have at the end of the first stanza? Where do you think the poem is going? (Kids have strong noses for "abuse" issues. Emily meets Oprah.)

Line Five: What about the repetition of *Still* with the exclamation mark? What sort of sentence does *Could* begin? What sort of word is *peeped*?

Line Six: What does *Brain* connote? What motion does she ascribe to her brain?

Line Seven: Connection of this to what begins in line five.

Line Eight: I tell the kids that the line is going to end with a direct rhyme on *round* that was in line six. What might the rhyming word be? They enjoy guessing—a lot! It gets them to create senses of where the poem might go that are intriguing and gets them to look carefully at where the poem has been. What about the word *Treason*? How does that fit in the poem?

Line Nine: Where did *Himself* come from? What does it have to do with *They*? Anything? What about *will*? How is that word being used? What happens in lines where Dickinson doesn't use a dash?

Line Ten: How does this simile feel to you? What sort of easiness do we have here?

Line Eleven: What does the word *Captivity* mean? How is Dickinson using it? Does it relate to other words in the poem?

Line Twelve: How does *laugh* fit in with other words in the poem? How do you read the last phrase? For example, "No more than this behavior (that the rest of the stanza is occupied with) have I available to me." Or can we read it in other ways?

Dickinson is all about resisting, being pinned down to one meaning. In her sublimely gawky way she is a dancer. I always picture her lines as the leaps across a stage that a modern dancer makes. What the discussion does is get the kids very involved in pursuing the poem. That's different from unraveling the poem. When they are pursuing it, they don't know where they are headed, but they are curious to see what develops. They are paying careful attention as they move through the poem rather than reading the poem backwards. (A reading teacher I know calls this "looking for clues.") They have time to ask questions before they move on. They develop a feeling for Dickinson's energy: how she moves from short line to short line. They experience her dashes as the physical phenomena they are. They feel how the poem is a jumpy journey.

What we wind up with is a strong feeling for the poem that is based on a pretty thorough profile of the poem. To say they find Dickinson intriguing is an understatement. A lot of them flat out love her. Why wouldn't they? She's a rebel and her attitudes are appealing to adolescents who have had their fill of bogus authority. She's sly and they love that, how she wheedles and digs and protests and exclaims. They love how shrewd she is.

For some people it's disconcerting that the father and mother of American poetry are a homosexual declaimer who loved crowds and a woman who kept to herself and published next to nothing in her lifetime. Not two prime-time human beings. If I do nothing more than get the kids to perceive what great soul mates Whitman and Dickinson can be to them, I think I have earned my salary. They are the yin and yang of poetry and you could fill up a page describing their differences. To my mind, it's beautiful how different they are because together they add up to a large sum of human experience. Every time I open Dickinson's *Collected Poems* I get excited. I am holding genius in my hands. It's not a burden. It's a scintillating pleasure.

january 17

parts of speech

Like most people in the United States, for me the word *grammar* means a set of exercises from a textbook. I don't know how many of those exercises I did. I don't want to know. I have a reasonable sense of the difference between *who* and *whom*, although I notice that it is mangled in the media fairly often and those who are doing the mangling don't seem to be getting their pay docked. Probably I could walk around feeling superior and thankful about all those exercises.

I can't say that I do. The price I paid was some serious boredom. I did the work because I had to do the work, but it meant nothing to me. As someone who grew up to become an English teacher, I find that I don't want to put my students in that place. What I want to give my students is a sense of how grammar is lodged in writing. It isn't some separate world where one does exercises and then forgets about them as soon as one is done with them. Grammar is intrinsic. Grammar is always there.

One benefit of studying poetry steadily is that we are always focusing on sentences. Prose, as it takes up much more room, is nowhere near as amenable to minute considerations as poetry is. With poetry we are always scrutinizing the medium of language and grammar is part of that medium.

In particular I find that poetry is the best way to teach parts of speech. When I was a student in school, I wondered what was the point of knowing parts of speech. Who cared? What poetry has taught me is that poets care mightily about parts of speech. Poets are people who think about whether a noun wants an adjective before it or wants to be by itself. Poets are people who think about whether a verb wants to take an adverb. Poets are people who think about the quality of the verbs in a given poem.

Consequently we do a fair amount of talking in class just about parts of speech. At first, students find the emphasis fairly comical. Someone is thinking about adjectives? Whatever. With time, however, they start to see how focusing on parts of speech is crucial to what poets do. They start to appreciate how much focus and care goes into making a poem in terms of those verbs, adjectives, nouns, adverbs, and, even, prepositions.

Today I did a poem by the contemporary African American poet Afaa Michael Weaver. It's a car poem. The title is "The Black and White Galaxie."

> With water warm enough to make me
> feel the gust of spring color,
> I added dish detergent and a rag.
> The rag was soft enough to caress her
> but raise the dirt from her skin.
> The soap was strong yet weak so
> it wouldn't make her complexion crack.
> Then I started at the top of her,
> scrubbing the roof of the Ford Galaxie,
> my uncle Frank's cruising machine.
> When he trusted me, he watched me
> from afar. Then he let me go alone,
> having given me a tenet of his wisdom—
> *a black man gotta make his car shine.*
>
> I knew how to hold the water hose,
> spray it so it came out in a shower.
> I chased the bubbles away and over her,
> until the white was like a star's smile,
> and the black seemed to pull me into it.
> Thru the rolled up windows, I checked
> the preliminaries, the interior,
> an intimate space of hushed conversations,
> smiles, and hands on thighs in corners
> after bars closed, of lipstick,
> of the black woman's accoutrements.

I checked to see if it was clean enough
to hail a woman's aloof eyes and lips.
Uncle Frank told me what women want—
a *black man gotta look like money.*

The tires were the last, but I saved
a tough energy for them. In motion,
a car's wheels are the signals of the way
its soul hisses, sucks in its breath.
It breathes air like that spring air
of purple and yellow when I washed
the first car I ever drove, as Uncle Frank
let me turn it around in the alley.

I dreamed of chasing women with a machine
that could play music and smell like evergreens.
I dreamed of the hunt and being in the cut.
Uncle Frank threw in *men's mother wit*
to keep me out of Baltimore's apocalypse—

a black man gotta wear suits and ties,
a black man gotta have a private world.

As Timmy Pace, a definite joker, put it today, "Where else can I talk about something like parts of speech and be thinking about sex at the same time? Thank you, Mr. P." Talk about defusing a charged subject. It doesn't defuse it, however. It's just another way into the subject matter, a very important way. The dull neutrality of the phrase "parts of speech" turns out to be neither dull nor neutral.

I started them off today with listing three important adjectives. I asked for a sentence about why each adjective was important. I collect these to see if they can apply their knowledge of what an adjective is. Our discussions, of course, highlight what an adjective is. They can see the part of speech at work and develop a feeling for how it works.

One adjective that comes up a lot is *hushed*. We talk about the word and what it connotes; what it sounds like. A number of students feel that it is an onomatopoetic word, that it sounds like what it is. Some students notice that in the line in which *hushed* occurs Weaver balances the adjective-noun combination with another adjective-noun combination. "It gives you a total feeling," one student says. "You

> I started them off today with listing three important adjectives. I asked for a sentence about why each adjective was important.

feel the scene because he is so complete about what he is describing there."

Aloof is an intriguing adjective to many students. They talk about what the word means. Karen Forbes wants to know where the word came from. "It's like remote and sexy at the same time," she says. I tell her the dictionary is awaiting her. She finds out it comes from ship terminology. "Go figure," she says and puts the dictionary down with a bemused smile.

After the adjectives, I ask them to consider the nouns. Specifically I want to know why many nouns in the poem don't have adjectives. How do they function in their own right as nouns? They really go after this one. Timmy Pace is on it again, "Well, Mr. P., a thigh is a thigh. I mean who needs more description? I don't need more description. I'm there." "You wish," the guy next to him says. Laughter while Tim shakes his head to indicate he can take the laughter because he is the man.

One noun that throws the kids is *apocalypse*. After we consult the dictionary, we talk about the word. Some don't feel that the word belongs in the poem: "It feels like such a big, vocabulary test kind of word. It's not a word you use the way you use *rag* or *lipstick* or *Uncle Frank*." Sherry Nichols says the word does belong in the poem, precisely because it is different. "You are just focused on the car and then this word is there at the end of the poem and you think about where that car is going, what streets that car is driving along. They are bad streets. It changes everything for me. It's not just a car poem, the way you introduced it, Mr. P. It's a poem about being a black man in the city. *Apocalypse* is as heavy a word as there is. Can you drive around *apocalypse*?" She pauses. "I guess you can try, huh?" She looks around at the rest of the class, then at me.

Sometimes I don't know what to say or where to go. "Amen," I say. "Please hand in your parts of speech notes."

january 25

expressive

Poets, I like to tell my students, are *animists*. As the kids say, "Means what?" Means they believe that everything is alive and that everything is expressive. Every picture tells a story; every moment holds feeling; every single detail of life on earth—a table, a dish, a tree, an old green M&M you find in a coat pocket—has something to say about being alive. Another way of putting this is that every detail is metaphorical. The issue is how much the poet allows the detail to speak. There is more feeling in any given moment of life than anyone is ever going to get down on paper.

I work with students to see in their own writing how much is there. When someone asks me what is the point of so much poetry, one thing I tell them is that it makes my students more alert. That seems like a big, improbable statement but over the course of the year, my students start to become aware that writing is a way to access the enormous amount of attentiveness that can go with being a human being. As I like to tell my students, everything is already there. Life is a whole lot bigger than anyone of us is.

Patience is a big part of alertness and my students don't, as young people, tend to be very patient. They are used to pushing buttons and things happening immediately. What they come to feel and to see is how much isn't automatic, how much wants to be considered. They come to feel how poetry's ability to slow down any moment and really look at what is there is a remarkable asset. When I play Twenty Questions with them about any situation, they start to realize how much there is in a bus ride or a walk down the hall or sitting in a classroom daydreaming and looking out a window. Poems epitomize such attention. Poems believe that the expressiveness is always there.

To my mind, it's a very important connection that students are making. They start to see why people make literature. It's not just self-expression or wanting to tell your own story. Lots of poems and books aren't in the least bit autobiographical. The impulse to make literature has a great deal to do with honoring attentiveness and being comfortable with attentiveness. School tends to reward appropriateness but appropriateness isn't at all the same thing as attentiveness. It's one reason that creative people are not necessarily "good" students. In poetry, attentiveness is appropriateness.

I have used an anthology entitled *Real Things: An Anthology of Popular Culture in American Poetry* a lot. The kids live, for better and for worse, in the world of popular culture. For them to see that poets access that world and make engaging poems out of it is important. Students tend to have notions that somehow literature is wandering around on a high, mist-shrouded mountain over-looking what we do in our daily lives. No one drinks Pepsi or watches TV in a work of literature. The anthology shows them that notion isn't true. It challenges them to use the materials of their own day-to-day lives in America to write their own poems. It challenges them to think twice and really notice what they tend to take for granted.

The poem I chose from the anthology today is by Tino Villaneuva and is called "Scene from the Movie *GIANT*." When I ask if anyone has seen the movie, I get no response. No one has even heard of the movie. "All the better," I say and plow ahead:

> What I have from 1956 is one instant at the Holiday
> Theater, where a small dimension of a film, as in
> A dream, became the feature of the whole. It
> Comes toward the end . . . the café scene, which
> Reels off a slow spread of light, a stark desire
>
> To see itself once more, though there is, at times,
> No joy in old time movies. It begins with the
> Jingling of bells and the plainer truth of it:
> That the front door to a roadside café opens and
> Shuts as the Benedicts (Rock Hudson and Elizabeth
>
> Taylor), their daughter Luz, and daughter-in-law
> Juana and grandson Jordy, pass through it not
> Unobserved. Nothing sweeps up into an actual act
> Of kindness into the eyes of Sarge, who owns this
> Joint and has it out for dark-eyed Juana, weary
>
> Of too much longing that comes with rejection.
> Juana, from barely inside the door, and Sarge,
> Stout and unpleased from behind his counter, clash
> Eye-to-eye, as time stands like heat. Silence is
> Everywhere, acquiring the name of hatred and Juana
>
> Cannot bear the dread—the dark-jowl gaze of Sarge
> Against her skin. Suddenly: bells go off again.
> By the quiet effort of walking, three Mexican-
> Types step in, whom Sarge refuses to serve . . .
> Those gestures of his, those looks that could kill
>
> A heart you carry in memory for years. A scene from
> The past has caught me in the act of living: even
> To myself I cannot say except with worried phrases

Upon a paper, how I withstood arrogance in a gruff
Voice coming with the deep-dyed colors of the screen;

How in the beginning I experienced almost nothing to
Say and now wonder if I can ever live enough to tell
The after-tale. I remember this and I remember myself
Locked into a back-row seat—I am a thin, flickering,
Helpless light, local-looking, unthought of at fourteen.

I'm fond of this poem for many reasons, not the least of which is that it is a very fine piece of writing. For my purposes, I like how it focuses on a scene in a movie. Movies are deeply ingrained in my students' minds. You would have to say that the dominant art form of the twentieth century is the cinema and it shows no signs of abating at the beginning of the twenty-first century. Many (it may be most) of my students have seen more movies than they have finished reading whole books.

I ask students to choose a detail that is crucial to the poem and write a sentence or two about why it is crucial. The open-endedness of the assignment allows them to do the choosing and shows us some very different perceptions. For instance, I have one student who feels right away that the phrase *Holiday Theater* is expressive. As she puts it, "The poem focuses on prejudice and its consequences. Yet the prejudice is being encountered at the *Holiday Theater*. It's ironic. That's the word isn't it? Ironic? When things don't fit together and you notice how they don't fit together, how one thing is making fun of another thing, that's ironic, right, Mr. P.?" We go on to talk about how the metaphor is right there in the name of the theater and how much metaphor is there in daily language, particularly in things people name.

> I ask students to choose a detail that is crucial to the poem and write a sentence or two about why it is crucial.

Another student focuses on the phrase *By the quiet effort of walking*. She says that she can't believe it, that you can pay attention to walking, that walking matters. "They didn't drive in there in some big car the way I bet Elizabeth Taylor drove in there," she says. "They walked and it was an effort and it was quiet. They weren't making a big deal about it. They were just walking. They weren't out to bother anyone. Just the way they just want to eat and not bother anyone." It's Kari Gunnelson who is talking. She is an intense, wound-up-tight kind of kid. "It was an *effort* for them to walk. It didn't just happen because they got into a machine and it took them there. That matters a lot, I think." She pauses and then just says, "Wow! I get it."

We talk further about the details. I have them go back to their poetry journals and write a response piece about the poem based on our discussion of the poem. The topic is "How Details Matter in a Poem." One of my favorite moments in the classroom is when the students are really engaged in writing and it's utterly quiet. I can feel their energy, how focused it is. It feels as though it could move mountains.

> I have them go back to their poetry journals and write a response piece about the poem based on our discussion of the poem. The topic is "How Details Matter in a Poem."

january 29

william blake

This is William Blake week. All week I do poems by Blake—lyrics from the *Songs of Innocence* and *Songs of Experience*. For me, Blake's lyrics personify how poetry speaks for the spirit and to the spirit. I realize that *spirit* is a slippery word that does not figure into the world of norms and medians and raw scores. I am not so much interested in defining the word as looking at Blake's little poems and how they go to the heart of what it means to be alive. What are we doing on earth? That's the question Blake asks over and over.

Initially, my students find Blake unbelievable. As one student once put it, "Do they let him into the textbooks?" Good question. Blake was one of the great influences on the Beats and there is an outlaw side to him. It's not really outlaw, of course. It's so pure and intense and aware that it seems outlaw because Blake believed in the holy dignity of human beings. Ginsberg (more about him later in the year) and Corso and others translated, so to speak, Blake into America. The Beats sought vision and Blake had a great deal of that commodity.

It's the vision aspect that throws my students. They simply aren't used to someone who literally presents visions. They are used to descriptions, anecdotes, and poems that rely on some degree of personal actuality and comment on it. Blake isn't really like that. Blake is making it up and the lyrics are little worlds unto themselves. To be sure, they speak for the world at large: One of the poems we do is "London." Yet they create senses of life that are utterly primary.

Today I paired a poem from the *Songs of Innocence* with a poem from the *Songs of Experience*. I do a fair amount of this pairing during the year, as I like to get my students to compare and contrast poems. It's a fine way to promote higher order thinking skills as they also exercise their tastes. I do it in genres (two villanelles), subject matter (two poems about rock 'n' roll), and within eras and across time. Sometimes, as with Blake, we look at two poems by the same poet to get a better sense of that poet.

I used "Holy Thursday." I'm fond of this pairing because one doesn't find that many occasions where two different poems by one poet have the same title. Before dictating the opening stanzas of the poems, I wrote the words *innocence* and *experience* on the blackboard. Then I asked for responses to those words. What's in those words? What do they stand for and mean to you? We made lists and I had the kids write down what got said. I told them that I wanted them to refer to the words after we looked at the Blake poems to see if Blake corroborated (did I use that word with them?) what they had to say.

Also, I told them what Holy Thursday was. I asked first but no one knew. For the record, it is known also as Ascension Day and is the Thursday forty days after Easter that is observed in commemoration of Christ's ascension into heaven. I told them too about the custom in London where children from charity schools (I told them what that was) went to St. Paul's Church (I assigned students in different classes to tell us tomorrow about St. Paul's) to hear a sermon and sing before their patrons (I told them what that was). We talked some, in addition, about the Christian church calendar in general and how Blake lived in a Christian society. Sometimes when you're teaching it seems as though all you do is warm up and never get into the game.

I did do the poems. I am putting down "Innocence" first and then the "Experience" poem.

'Twas on a Holy Thursday, their innocent faces clean,
The children walking two & two, in red and blue and green,
Grey-headed beadles walk'd before, with wands as white as snow,
Till into the high dome of Paul's they like Thames' waters flow.

O what a multitude they seem'd, these flowers of London town!
Seated in companies they sit with radiance all their own.
The hum of multitudes was there, but multitudes of lambs,
Thousands of little boys & girls raising their innocent hands.

Now like a mighty wind they raise to heaven the voice of song,
Or like harmonious thunderings the seats of Heaven among.
Beneath them sit the aged men, wise guardians of the poor;
Then cherish pity, lest you drive an angel from your door.

And then the other, "Holy Thursday."

Is this a holy thing to see
In a rich and fruitful land,
Babes reduc'd to misery,
Fed with cold and usurous hand?

Is that trembling cry a song?
Can it be a song of joy?
And so many children poor?
It is a land of poverty!

And their sun does never shine,
And their fields are bleak & bare,
And their ways are fill'd with thorns;
It is eternal winter there.

For where-e'er the sun does shine,
And where-e'er the rain does fall,
Babe can never hunger there,
Nor poverty the mind appall.

On the wow-ometer, Blake is way up there. It's not just that the kids are very quiet after hearing the poems. I sense that they feel something like amazement. I'm quiet too for a while and just let the silence be. I want the silence to be there. It's healthy.

When I do go to the poems, I ask my students first about the words that are new to them. We talk about *beadles* and *usurous*.

We do this by having students look up the words in the dictionary and tell their fellow students the words' meanings. Then I ask the students to look carefully at the poems and see if they have any words in common beyond their titles. The kids fasten on the word *children*. Are they the same *children* in the two poems?

> When I do go to the poems, I ask my students first about the words that are new to them.

"Yes, Mr. P., they are the same children. It's not about this child and that child. It's about all the children who are poor children. That's another word the poems share—*poor*." And "What," I ask, "is *poor*?"

We talk. We talk about the different forms the poems take. We talk about rhymes. We talk about what pity is. We talk about what holy is. We talk about the last stanza of the "Experience" poem and how Blake is praising the natural world while criticizing the world of human relations (*usurous*). We talk about the metaphors that are used in reference to the children. Do children use those metaphors about themselves? We go back to the list of words about innocence and experience that we generated before we started talking and talk about how many of those words apply to Blake's poems.

One thing that stays with me is when Sharon Walker says that innocence is simple and that experience is complicated. "When we're little we see things just the way they are because we only know so much. But as we get older we know too much. You know what I mean? I mean we get complicated, like we make excuses for everything that it shouldn't be the way it is. We think that's smart but it's dumb. When we're little kids we take in life more because we're little and life is big. We just drink it in when we're little. When we're big," and she pauses as if she is surprised at herself, "we start choking." I nod and a lot of other people in the room nod.

On the way home from school I find myself thinking about how we all use the word *kids* for *children*. Blake would never use that word. It's easygoing but after reading Blake it feels degraded. It's more of an animal word than a human word. I use it everyday many times. I understand why I use it but I think about how being familiar and democratic can take away the dignity that Blake tried to make us aware of. I know we don't live in poems. But I know that poems can make us think about how we do live. It's not that I'll give the word up. It's that I'll be more aware of it. Somehow that matters.

February and March

Oftentimes it seems that a student has more feeling for some celebrity whom that student has never met than the person sitting next to him or her. It feels to them that the basketball player or movie actress or rock 'n' roller is utterly known to them. They have seen the person countless times on screens. They have read about the person so that they know about love lives, family tiffs, and vacations. They don't typically know all these things about the person next to them in second period English. Nor do they want to. That person isn't famous.

I'm never sure what to make of the obsession with celebrity. Part of it is based on inspiration and that seems healthy. My students really like the great basketball player and admire his prowess. They think the actress is superbly talented. They buy the rock 'n' roller's CDs because they like the lyrics and the music. I tend to tell myself that there have always been kings and queens and that the glamour that is attached to such celebrities is perfectly healthy. These people have earned the adulation that comes their way. It's one way for young people to orient themselves. It's a sort of currency among people in a mass society. We may not know one another, but we know who Michael Jordan is and we can use that as some sort of starting point for knowing one another.

But what, I ask them, do they really know? Do they know, for instance, that Elvis Presley was an intensely spiritual person who meditated? Does that fit the vision that the tabloids portray? Does that fit the movie roles he was given to play? Does that fit with the lounges where he performed in Las Vegas? This leads us to talk about the prices that people pay for stardom. I find the kids are sensitive to this issue. They know that today's star is tomorrow's nobody. It's one of the lessons that pop culture imparts to them. They sense that losing a piece of your private life is a big price to pay.

Accordingly, I like to do some poems with them over the course of the year that are about famous people. How famous is up to me and leads us to talk about that word. Given the fleetingness of media attention and given that my students are young, fame appears all the more transient. Many a celebrity would blanch if he or she could hear me say that person's name and hear my students respond, "Who?"

One poem along these lines that I like to do is "Say Good-bye to Big Daddy" by Randall Jarrell. *Big Daddy* was Big Daddy Lipscomb, a defensive lineman for the great Baltimore Colt football teams in the late 1950s and 1960s. Here is the poem:

Big Daddy Lipscomb, who used to help them up
After he'd pulled them down, so that "the children
Won't think Big Daddy's mean"; Big Daddy Lipscomb,
Who stood unmoved among the blockers, like the Rock
Of Gibraltar in a life insurance ad,
Until the ball carrier came, and Big Daddy got him;
Big Daddy Lipscomb, being carried down an aisle
Of women by Night Train Lane, John Henry Johnson,
And Lenny Moore; Big Daddy, his three ex-wives,
His fiancee, and the grandfather who raised him
Going to his grave in five big Cadillacs;
Big Daddy, who found football easy enough, life hard enough
To—after his last night cruising Baltimore
In his yellow Cadillac—to die of heroin;
Big Daddy, who was scared, he said: "I've been scared
Most of my life. You wouldn't think so to look at me.
It gets so bad I cry myself to sleep—"his size
Embarrassed him, so that he was helped by smaller men
And hurt by smaller men; Big Daddy Lipscomb
Has helped to his feet the last ball carrier, Death.

The big black man in the television set
Whom the viewers stared at—sometimes, almost were—
Is a blur now; when we get up to adjust the set,
It's not the set, but a NETWORK DIFFICULTY.
The world won't be the same without Big Daddy.
Or else it will be.

We start talking about the poem in terms of syntax. It may seem a curious way of initiating a discussion about a poem about a football player, but we always keep our eyes on how the poem in front

We start talking about the poem in terms of syntax. It may seem a curious way of initiating a discussion about a poem about a football player, but we always keep our eyes on how the poem in front of us works.

of us works. I ask my students about the first stanza: how many sentences? Three. Then comes the why: Why did Jarrell write such a long beginning sentence? What does that long sentence do? How does that long sentence work? Where is the verb that hooks up with the opening proper noun? Ah, grammar, it never goes away.

Sentence structure often seems like the weather to my students. They notice what the sentences say, but they don't pay much attention to how the sentences are constructed. Poetry asks for that sort of attention and I find it carries over to prose—both in their reading of prose and their writing it. Today they say that Jarrell's long beginning sentence is a perfect way to present the character. They note that Jarrell builds up an enormous amount of feeling by not letting go of the sentence. "Even if you want to give up, he won't let you. He makes you be with the guy." And when the sentence does end, you are right there staring at the awful, capitalized "Death." When I ask a student about the word, she says, "I don't know. I mean he's dead and what can we say about that? There it is. It hurts. To see that last word in the stanza, it hurts. You feel how he was alive and how he was afraid and that word hurts."

So what about the second stanza? Why do we need it? Why couldn't the poem end with the first stanza? Jarrell was under no obligation to write the second stanza. What does it do? Some students feel it does nothing; the poem doesn't need it. "It loses the feeling," Kip Nicholson says. But a lot of students don't agree. Darnell Hanson is vehement. Darnell is a pretty big kid himself, not huge like Big Daddy, but a good way over 200 pounds. He says to Kip, "You don't get it, man. It says that the people watching the game *almost were Big Daddy*. That's what it feels like sometimes when you are watching TV. Like you are the person. You can feel what's happening. But it's not true. You hear me, Kip, it's not true." Darnell stops and smiles. "I'm not on your case, Kip, believe me, man. But it's not true. There's all kind of stuff in between the person and you watching the game. I mean there's the TV and the camera and the wires and all that stuff. You don't know. So when he talks about the world at the end and it sort of sounds like the poet guy is copping out, well, he isn't. Because both things are true: Big Daddy is dead but someone else will play Big Daddy's position and life will go on. And we still won't really know because there's all this stuff in between. And that stuff is the world, too." This is more than Darnell has said in weeks. I remember that he plays ball, too. I remember that he wrote in a paper that "people think if you are big, you are dumb."

We keep talking about the ending. It seems sad to just about everyone in the room. Sadder than if the poem ended with the first stanza. As Darnell says, "These poet guys tend to know what they're doing. I'm learning that, Mr. P."

We talk about motive. Do we need to know more about what drove Big Daddy to heroin? The kids decide it's another one of my superfluous questions. Darnell, whose voice is very focused, says, "We know everything we need to know. It's not the poet's job to spell it out. The poet makes us feel it. I mean he quotes Big Daddy. You get Big Daddy's own words. There it is and that's enough. How much can you know, Mr. P., about what makes someone do what he did? How much can you know?" The question hangs in the air.

I use the poem as a model for a student poem. I ask them to write about someone who is famous and try to make the reader feel what that person's life is like from the inside. I want them to try to give a sense of what really is going on with the person. Not the media hype but the person inside. If they want to construct a narrative, that's fine. If they want to tell the poem from the person's point of view, that's fine, too. If they want to refer to pop tunes such as Elton John and Bernie Taupin's "Candle in the Wind," which is about Marilyn Monroe, that's all the better. I tell them I want enough details to give me a sense of the person. They didn't know Big Daddy Lipscomb before they read the poem, but now they do. That's what I want their poems to do.

Emulation should never be underestimated. The poems they encounter fire the kids up. They want to write that. And in their ways they do. I got the poem below a number of years ago after Kurt Cobain died. It's named after him:

> Can you sell your anger?
> Can you sell your love?
> I'm telling you that my guitar
> is my life.
> I'm telling you that drugs

make a man sick.
I'm telling you that I wanted
to look you in the eye but couldn't.
I'm the guy on the big stage
and the stage is too big.

february 8

found poems

This time of year things get a little blah: It's snowing, the basketball teams don't look as though they are going to make it to the state tournaments, everyone looks as though he or she could stand a week on a Caribbean beach. Two weeks probably. The kids' version of this is "Another poem, Mr. P? Don't you wear out?" Well, no, I don't but I do have some wrinkles in my repertoire. One of them is the found poem.

No less a major poet than W.H. Auden noted many times that poetry is rooted in play. Poetry is a sort of serious fooling around with words. Some of it isn't even very serious—light or comic verse as represented by the likes of the limerick. We do limericks and the kids enjoy it. There's an ingenuity challenge that they revel in. As a student once put it, "I feel like an engineer with words." Because my rule with limericks is no outright obscenities, it challenges my students' inventiveness. Certainly, the limerick is one form of poetry that never seems to go away. Many students can spout them—"My dad told me this one, Mr. P."—although a lot of them (particularly the ones their dads impart) are not great for spouting in a classroom.

The found poem is a poem that is already written. One comes along and looks at a text and turns it into poem. One does this by putting the poem into lines. Accordingly, the found poem is an exercise, in part, in what a line constitutes and how lines make a difference. Accordingly, the found poem is particularly important in considering what makes free verse tick. One thing, for sure, that makes free verse tick is the line.

Some poets are downright mystical about the line. They talk about how they can feel the line, how the line has a life, has physical force and presence, how the line is connected with breath, how the line can surprise and lull the reader. I think all these things are true. Most times when we discuss a free verse poem, the issue of the line comes up. It's understandable because the line is a *sine qua non* of poetry. It's an element that defines poetry.

Line is a mysterious entity. There is no way to add up all the line breaks in a free verse poem and come to some conclusion about the sum of them. They may be unremarkable—breaking the line at the end of a syntactic unit qualifies as unremarkable. They may be unsettling—breaking the line at places where the reader doesn't expect the line to be broken. In any case, the line breaks affect how we read the poem and how the poem is read aloud. It's been said that some of the genius of free verse is its physicality, how it feels its way to whatever degree of conclusion it reaches. The line is part of that feeling—part groping, part assurance. Like freedom.

> I give my students a stack of papers and magazines when they walk into the room. I show them some examples of found poems. We talk about the examples and how the poems are lineated (put into lines). Then I say go to it. I tell them to remember that I expect them to be able to explain why they lineate the text the way they do.

I give my students a stack of papers and magazines when they walk into the room. I show them some examples of found poems. We talk about the examples and how the poems are lineated (put into lines). Then I say go to it. I tell them to remember that I expect them to be able to explain why they lineate the text the way they do. They aren't to change a word from the text they are appropriating. All they are doing is rendering that text into lines.

It's fascinating where they go with this. A lot of students tackle the police report. As in:

    5:13 p.m.,
    police arrested
    Christopher A. Beckwirth
    22,
    North Edgewater,
    on a warrant
    for failure to
    appear,

    operating
    after suspension

and
illegal
attachment
of plates.

The student who did this one explained that she wished to create an imagist poem that focused on words as entities in their own right. She wanted to "isolate language" in her words and "see what's there in the words." There's something unnerving about slowing the flow of prose down. My student clued in on that. In fact, she took great pleasure in it. What one normally would breeze through (unless one were Christopher A. Beckwirth), is suspended in time and left to dangle. The metaphysical undercurrents that lurk in language can be freed in found poems. The notion of failing to appear seems a good deal more sinister and odd in this context. How do you *fail to appear*? Aren't you here already?

We talk about the lineation and I ask for suggestions, how other students might do it. Some students, for instance, wanted to break the lines down even further and isolate *failure* in its own line. I have different students read the poem, too, so they can hear how the lines come out of different mouths.

This is play, for sure, but I know my students are making all kinds of judgments—if not as artists, at least as artisans. They are tackling an aspect of the medium of poetry—the line—from a very different angle. When they write their own poems, I can see how they internalize this work. They start to feel how part of the process of composing a free verse poem isn't just getting the thoughts down and then somehow or other putting them into lines. The line making is part of the creating and is integral to how the poem proceeds.

Here's another one from the local paper:

Earl Wallace
Doesn't know of any secret
That has kept him alive
For 102 years
And says that
If he did,
He wouldn't tell you.

Wallace,
Known by some residents

As "The Duke of Earl,"
Is the kind of man
Who lights up the room
When he walks in.

Wallace grew up
In Old Comstock in the 1900s.
He later joined the Army
And fought in World War I.
When he returned home,
He became a carpenter.

The student who did this one talked about how hard it was to choose just some lines from a whole article and how it made him think about how "you only have so many words to do what you want to do. Putting the words into lines is like framing them in pictures. I'm putting those words on display. So I've got to choose the words that give a sense of the person." He went on to say, "a poem is a little light amid a lot of darkness. You feel that when you do this. You don't feel that with the newspaper because it's a whole article and it's among a bunch of other articles. But a poem is all by itself. It's isolated. A spotlight. It's a kind of spotlight. And you really feel the darkness at the end of the poem. I mean there's so much to be said about a life and this is all you are saying."

February in my classroom doesn't seem quite so draggy. More than one student has said it reminds him or her of taking out scissors in elementary school and cutting up magazines for a scrapbook. It's cozy when the weak but gaining light is coming into the room and my students are poring over all those newspapers and magazines. Let there be lines. Let there be play.

february 13

the test is coming

It's that time of year again. There's no avoiding it. It's one bane of my existence. Not that I mind hanging around and proctoring exams for three days. I get a chance to make up for any deficiencies in my coffee consumption.

After the liveliness of classroom discussion, it is a considerable come down to watch them sit and ponder such questions as "What do the last two lines of the poem mean?" Not that the test is overrun with poems. There is usually one poem on the test. I think this is what used to be called tokenism but there are no poems to go sit up in the front of the bus and protest.

Over the years my students have done well with the test. It's not because I give them a lot of multiple-choice questions to do. I don't. What I do give them every day is a focus on language. My students are used to confronting a text with which they are wholly unfamiliar and dealing with that text. They have definite strategies for doing this.

Whenever they confront a poem in my classroom, they are looking carefully at syntax and grammar and punctuation. They are developing vocabulary each day. I don't mean just learning new words. I mean that they look at the etymologies of words and think about how those words are being used in the poem. When they see new words on a test, they don't panic. They are used to thinking about what a word might mean based on the context of the poem. They are close readers. This habit of close reading applies to prose as much as it applies to poetry. It may be easier for them to tackle prose after a lot of poetry. What is anything compared to Emily Dickinson?

> Whenever they confront a poem in my classroom, they are looking carefully at syntax and grammar and punctuation. They are developing vocabulary each day.

My kids have confidence in their ability to read and master language. They get a chance to do this every day. The range of poems opens my students to the diversity of sentences that can be constructed. That diversity represents an amazing multiplicity of thoughts. When I look back in my journal and think about the range of poems that my students have encountered, I am proud. They are actively dealing with language—William Blake's, Randall Jarrell's, Afaa Michael Weaver's, John Milton's.

The test seems awfully flat to them. It seems a pretty sad notion of how to measure intelligence. All year long they have been rummaging through the connotations and denotations of poems. Now they are confronted with little prose sections that ask them to attribute a one-dimensional answer to what they now know is a multifaceted experience.

Last year 48 percent of what gets called my B-level sophomores passed the state competency exam. The year prior to that
the figure was around 18 percent. The difference in terms of my
teaching is that I did more poetry with those students than the
year before. They became actively engaged in their own learning.
They started to come out of their shells and stopped seeing themselves as stupid, low-level students who are being passed on from
year to year.

There's Jerome Tyler. He's one of those kids in baggy pants
who announces on the first day of school, "I'm totally pissed. I'm
having a bad day." His "don't bother-me-mister" attitude hung in
the air like a cloud in no hurry to move. Jerome was a student who
invariably was told to shut up and sit still. Neither of which he
did. As to how bright he was, no one really knew or particularly
cared. His parents were not his parents. No one showed up on PTA
nights to talk about Jerome.

Because Jerome never stopped talking, I called on him
steadily. At first, he thought I was just going along with whatever
foolishness he was mouthing that day. But I tried to find a thread
of intelligence in whatever comment he would make, probing his
answers and taking him very seriously. Over time, his responses
began to change. As with most of my students, he had done very
little work with poetry. He had no particular train of bad associations with poetry. It was new to him the way it was new to most
of my students.

When I asked that class if anyone else would like to read the
poem aloud, Jerome started raising his hand. I teased him at first,
"Like to hear the sound of your voice?" "You got it, Mr. P." What
the class and I discovered is that Jerome was a superb reader of
poems. He had inflection, voice, and feeling in his readings. He
made you want to hear that poem. It got to the point where kids
would say, "I want to hear how Jerome reads that poem."

It probably goes without saying that Jerome had never performed very well on the state exam. The Jerome's of the world
have no stake in the high stakes testing world. They put up with
it the way they put up with much of school, which is to say they
try, pretend, get frustrated, and give up. I talked to the whole class
about the test. I recited to them what they've done in our class:
They have looked at language carefully; they examined syntax
carefully; they have pondered all manner of images, metaphors,

and thoughts. "This test," I told them, "is little league compared to what you have been doing for me in this classroom." I could see them looking around at one another when I was giving them this speech: "Is he for real?" Which is to say, "Am I for real?"

The day after the test, Jerome came in during lunch when the kids have a free five minutes to talk with me. He told me that the test didn't frighten him. He was a little afraid at first: "You know what those things look like, Mr. P." He went on to tell me that he had read the material carefully and had answered the questions carefully. It was hard for him to concentrate for so long. "But then," he said, "I thought about how we talk about these poems in groups and that's not easy. So I thought if I can talk about this John Milton dude, I can answer a question about the Louisiana Purchase."

In terms of succeeding, not every student I have is a Jerome. Far from it. He is, however, indicative of what I deal with as a teacher. He responds to an active environment. His engagement with poems feels natural because he is talking about words within a defined, artistic context. If you want kids to feel comfortable with language and competent with it, it stands to reason that they need to be talking about language regularly. Poetry provides that field of energy.

A standardized test is small change compared to talking about poems every day. It's the notion of the test that freaks them out. Once they understand that they are in control, they know they have a chance. Poetry is bound to trump any standardized test. Poetry is alive; the test is canned.

My principal called me into the office and asked me about the test and what I was doing. "A lot of careful test prep, Jim?" he asked me. "Well, I said, not really. A lot of poetry actually." He raised the proverbial eyebrow. "Poetry, huh?" he asked. "Every day we look at poems and talk about them. That includes Shakespeare and William Blake." "Shakespeare, huh?" "Shakespeare." He patted me on the back, literally, and said to keep it up. I told him that I intend to.

february 15

memory

I didn't read a new poem today. Instead I asked my students if they knew who the Muses were. After the usual first response—"That's the name of an Eighties rock band"—I heard some answers that pointed to "something about mythology." We looked the word up, as we do in my classes, and read the definition aloud: "any of the nine daughters of Mnemosyne and Zeus, each of whom presided over a different art or science." After we noticed the use of *whom* (my many years in the grammar mines), I asked who Mnemosyne was. I wrote the name on the blackboard—it's not your everyday name. Again we consulted our dictionaries and we learned that Mnemosyne is the mother of memory. As the kids say, "That's cool. I didn't know memory had a mother. It's great we get to come to school and learn these things." I have a number of students who would get an *A* in sarcasm; goes with the adolescent turf, I guess.

Of course I wasn't done with my questions. I don't usually pursue information for the sake of information. My question was "Why is memory the mother of the muses? Why isn't imagination or reason or spirit or pride the mother of the arts and sciences?" I got that I-knew-you-were-going-to-ask-something-like-that stare. It's not the world's happiest stare. Still, a question is a question and I let it sit with them. The kids know I am comfortable with silence. Too comfortable, they have told me on numerous occasions.

"Where are we without memory?" I asked when the silence was starting to cause noticeable twitching. More silence. The world around them runs on novelty: *new* is a very important word in a market economy. Memory is something to associate with grandparents, not young people or the society at large. I got different answers in different classes to this question, but Glenda Merrill's stood out for me. She said, "We're nowhere without memory. We live a lot of days and if we don't remember anything about the days, then what are we? Memory is the mother of the arts and sciences because if nothing is remembered we have to start over again all the time. That would be foolish. We'd never know anything." Glenda is a very serious, straight-shooter kid who wants to go to a serious, straight-shooter college. Some days the kids get annoyed with her and some days they respect her a lot. I could tell they were listening to her. She, after all, took my dare. They respect that.

We talked some about what Glenda said. Students gave examples from various sciences. "And what about poetry and memory?" I asked them. They were warmed up and went right to it. In Glenda's class, the consensus was that memory worked a couple of different ways in poetry. One way was that poets knew the work of other poets and created poetry from that knowledge. Another way was that people knew poems and passed them on to other people. Another way was that memory was personal: You remembered a poem for yourself.

This was all a prelude to my assignment, which was to remember a poem we have done in class so far this year that moved you and write about why it moved you. I told my students they were not to look in their poetry journals. I wanted them to sit and think and try to remember. I wasn't concerned with them quoting exactly. I wanted them to recall the experience of a given poem and what that poem meant to them. Without a doubt, it's hard for a lot of the kids to remember. I tell them to write about yesterday if they can't remember anything else. I can feel the concentration in the room as they try to remember. Some of them look at one another as if by looking at another student, they could focus their thoughts.

> This was all a prelude to my assignment, which was to remember a poem we have done in class so far this year that moved you and write about why it moved you. I told my students they were not to look in their poetry journals. I wanted them to sit and think and try to remember.

Afterwards, I told them I didn't do this to torture them. I just wanted them to think about memory. What about memorizing poems, for instance? What's the point of that? It's a serious question on my part and we write on the blackboard what might be some reasons to memorize poems. Some of the answers we came up with were that it became yours when you memorized it, that it was a neat way to impress people, that it was a sort of companion, that it kept your mind alert, that it could be handy. How, I asked, could it be handy?

Jason Liu told me that he had learned English as a second language and that memorizing little poems helped him a lot. "It gave me confidence. Sort of like a lucky penny in your pocket. They weren't poems you would consider great poems, Mr. P., but they helped me. Nursery rhymes a lot. And stuff like 'I've got a rocket / In my pocket; / I cannot stop to play. / Away it goes! / I've burned my toes. / It's Independence Day.' You can see what I mean about great literature. But it helped me. I've got lots of them inside me. No one made me do it. I just felt it was a good thing for me. A handy thing for me." He smiled a shy, strong smile. The other kids looked at him with what I would call "new found respect."

Other students chimed in. Some said that they had a hard time memorizing a poem. It wasn't natural to them. I know that for some children memorizing a poem can be hellish. Various learning and personal disabilities can get in the way. That's one reason why I try to approach the issue of memory casually and as an exploration as to what memory constitutes. Too many students have been turned off to poetry by having to memorize poems that made no sense to them. As adults, they can repeat the poem to this day and it becomes a sort of unhappy totem to them: "I know this one and I don't know any others because I know this one." They may know a Robert Frost poem by heart but they don't read Robert Frost any more. Why would they?

I gradually encourage memorizing over the course of the year. The poems they choose are based on their poetry journals. We start small—literally a line or two. It opens up the process. I build from there. If a student is having problems, I ask him or her to talk with me and I will come up with an alternative written assignment (the sort of thing I did with my classes today).

By the end of the year we have worked up to whole poems. The capacity varies greatly among my students. I'm not interested so much in how many lines they commit to memory as that they see the possibilities that are in them in terms of making poems their own. Some of them, to use a cliché, take to it like ducks to water. You never know which students will take to it. And you can never predict what poems they will gravitate to.

Sometimes I worry about how much of the work we do in the classroom seems to fall into oblivion. The school year goes by and how often do we look backward? How often do we sit down and consciously try to recall what we have done? To a degree, this seems natural. Important as it is, we don't, for instance, remember much of our talk. It falls like leaves to the ground. Memory seems important to me because, as we invest it in poems, it is a memento. That we can share these mementos seems very important. It forms a common ground for a classroom and for society. We may treasure different poems but poetry remains a central presence—one of those arts and sciences of which memory is the mother.

february 20

haiku

When, during the course of the school year, I raise the topic of haiku, I usually encounter some serious groans. "We did that in the fifth grade, Mr. P. It's kiddy stuff. Five—seven—five. See, we remember." I smile tolerantly and proceed. What I tell them is a story.

Once there was a famous African American writer who wrote books that laid bare the terrible racism of the world he lived in. His work is full of violence—people habitually do awful things to one another. He got tired of dealing with the racism in his native country and moved to Europe. He lived there for the rest of his life. It wasn't a long life; he died when he was fifty-two.

Toward the end of his life—the last eighteen months—this writer started writing haiku like crazy. He wrote hundreds and hundreds and hundreds of them. He seems to have known that he was dying—certainly he knew he was sick—and somehow he felt the desire, the need, and the inspiration to write many haiku.

No one could have predicted from the man's prose work that he would end his life as a writer devoting himself to a sort of writing that is so spare and delicate. He achieved his fame as a novelist. He covered page after page with words. A haiku is an awfully little thing. It's a little thing compared to prose and it's a little thing compared to the death that the writer seemed to know he was facing.

"What," I ask my students, "do you know about the history of haiku?" Usually someone remembers being told that the form comes from Japan. "Is it," I ask, "associated with any religious traditions in Japan?" Usually I get no takers on this although sometimes a brave soul will say, "Buddhism." Sometimes that brave soul says, "Zen Buddhism."

I don't try to explain Zen Buddhism in five minutes to my class. What I talk about is how writing poems can be a sort of spiritual practice—a form of meditation. Invariably I address a talkative student at this point: "You know what meditation is, right? It's when you are utterly quiet and stay quiet for many minutes." I get some amused nods from the unquiet.

"What happens when you are quiet?" I ask. It's a curious question but they are used to my curious questions. They know I am serious. What usually gets pointed out is that when you are quiet you start to look around you and see and hear what is there around you. You stop obsessing, as the kids say. You stop putting yourself at the center of everything. You just let life be.

"And what," I ask, "is the question that poems ask?" "What is that?" is the answer I get. Because I ask the question most days, I am reasonably sure we are all on the same page about that point. "So how can a little haiku ask that question? They don't contain many words."

I read them a famous haiku by Bashō:

> Under a *single roof,*
> Prostitutes, too, were sleeping;
> The bush clovers and the moon.

"What?" they ask. "What is this?" I tell them that it was written in the seventeenth century by a famous haiku writer. He is traveling and at night he sleeps in a shelter with some prostitutes who are making a religious pilgrimage. Outside there are plants such as the kind of clover he describes. There is a moon. "So what is this?" I ask.

I know I am throwing a curve at them but I want them to have to grapple. As I noted, many of them have the notion that haiku is for grade school. We talk about the poem, the way we always talk about poems—by looking at the words carefully, every word. We talk about, for instance, *too* and how important it is that *too* is in the poem. It shows, in the words of one student, "that prostitutes are people also. They aren't just sex all the time. There's a world that doesn't care who you are, *too.* There are plants and the moon and they don't care. It all just is." We talk about contrast and how much can happen in a little space. We talk about how poems bring together different realities, different aspects of being under the "single roof" of the poem.

There are many reasons to spend some serious time with haiku. One reason is certainly the "What is that?" question. I want my students to slow down and notice life. The haiku form is perfect for that. It doesn't care for the intellection that many of my students figure is the essence of school. It cares for attention and alert feeling. It cares for suddenness and patience. It is exciting and humbling. Writing, after all, is about making choices. You can't put everything in. Haiku pushes the choice process to the limit—three lines to say something.

Economy of language is something I preach and the haiku exemplifies it. "If you can say it in fewer words, then say it in fewer words." The kids know that mantra and gradually it starts to take. They are trained to think that words are like the mashed potatoes in the cafeteria: Glop them up into a big ball and sling them. Something is bound to stick. The haiku shows them a whole other way of looking at writing: the less is more approach. Each word is like a tile in a mosaic and you only have a few tiles to work with. You can't waste any of them.

> Economy of language is something I preach and the haiku exemplifies it. "If you can say it in fewer words, then say it in fewer words."

I also like the haiku form because it makes students pay very careful attention to syntax. How you construct that opening line is going to have a huge effect on your two other lines. We look at a lot of haiku in terms of structure only. These are some of the structures we have noted: The first line is a prepositional phrase that the rest of the haiku completes—*Inside the dark room.* . . . The first line is a noun phrase—*A young mechanic.* . . . The first line is an adjective/noun phrase and a verb—*A yellow bird flits.* . . . The first word in the first line is a participle followed by a prepositional phrase—*Lying in his bed.* . . . The first line is an address to someone—*Hey, girl with the perm.* . . . The possibilities are endless.

This sort of consideration redeems for me some of the tortures that I endured while diagramming sentences many years ago. Somehow it was deemed important that I know the taxonomy of clauses and phrases. I have forgotten all those terms as I suspect my classmates have because we never used them beyond the confines of our classroom. When I look at the syntax of haiku, I feel we are looking at sentence structures from a point of view that makes sense: This is a work of art and how the sentences are constructed makes a huge difference in saying what you want to say. Syntax matters. It isn't an exercise.

Another aspect we look at is what the three lines have to do with one another. One approach is to simply write one sentence that takes up all three lines. Students, however, quickly start to see that the possibilities go well beyond that format. The genius of the haiku is what it brings together and how it does it. My students come to see that if they want, each line can be a separate world. Or two lines can be about one thing and another line about something else. Of course, the lines are always related somehow but the somehow is enticingly elastic. Here is one that typifies the different worlds/one world approach. It's by a student.

> No dogs are howling.
> The leaves are still as mountains.
> Ice cream is melting.

"Very Zen," as the kids say, but also very fascinating in terms of how the lines hold so much and how they work with one another despite the lack of syntactic continuity.

We write haiku many days and we listen to haiku many days. I don't tackle a long poem every day. I don't need to. One haiku can be a big experience. Over the year the kids adapt haiku to their own uses and write about anything that they want to write about. They enjoy the challenge of the format very much.

And I tell them the famous African American writer was named Richard Wright. "The guy who wrote *Native Son?*" "Yes, that guy." I read them the homage that a student wrote one year to Wright:

> On a street in France
> A man sighs deeply, then smiles.
> The wind salutes him

february 26

long poem: walt whitman

A short poem such as the haiku lends itself very well to the confines of the daily school schedule where time is at a premium. It would be a serious omission on my part, however, if I made no mention to my students of the world of the long poem. Because my students are used to looking at a poem that is a page or two, the long poem that takes up a whole book or the better part of a book comes as something of a shock. "You mean it goes on like that?"

It's not only that I want them to know the form exists. It's also that the long poem has a lot to do with the character of poetry in the United States and seems particularly expressive of the expansiveness of our country. If Emily Dickinson is the genius of liberation within seeming constriction, then Walt Whitman is the genius of locating deeply felt moments within the overwhelming breadth and vitality of the United States. Expansiveness, which often seems in our nation's political history to be little more than self-serving rhetoric, becomes in Whitman's hands a principle of generosity and fellow feeling. It's crucial to me that my students know who Walt Whitman is because he shows us a United States of America that is deeply human. His vision remains very important.

And his vision needs the long poem to realize itself. If you are going to portray breadth, then you need the many pages the long poem allows you. "Song of Myself" is more than fifty pages long. Because no one is ever going to exhaust that poem, I have no compunctions about treating a poem my students may have encountered in their American literature class. Indeed, the compartmentalization of writers in high school curricula tends to be absurd. When my students say, "We already had Walt Whitman,"—as if they had crossed him off their list forever—I play the Zen master with them and ask them what it means to already have had Walt Whitman. Have you memorized him completely? Can you quote from his work? Can you give an extemporaneous talk about him? Can you tell me about the differences between the early and late versions of *Leaves of Grass*? It's overkill but my questions make the point.

Facing as I do the usual constraints in terms of time and attention, I am not interested in marathon sessions in the classroom. (We have had marathon readings outside of the classroom. A couple years we have celebrated Walt Whitman Day by having students take turns reading "Song of Myself." To walk into the cafeteria and see and hear someone reading "Song of Myself" is a unique experience for everyone.) I pick a section of the poem that seems representative to me and read it to my students a number of times. Then I ask them to extrapolate from the section I read in terms of the qualities that they notice about the poem. Then we talk.

Today I took a section from the 1855 version of *Leaves of Grass* that begins "The pure contralto sings in the organloft. . . ." The section goes on for four pages listing different occupations and sorts of people. Most lines begin with *The*, which my students can tell you, based on their experience of Whitman, is a technique

called *anaphora*, which means the repetition of a word or phrase
in successive lines of poetry. Although the kids complain sometimes about the words they learn about poetry, I think they really
like learning these words. As a student once said to me, "It's sort
of a secret vocabulary. I feel like I'm a member of some secret
group that really knows these words." The Anaphora Society.

I read the section twice—once without the pages in front of
them and then once with a photocopy in front of them. I gave
them time to read the section over for themselves. We talked, as
always, about the unfamiliar words. Today they came up (from my
notes) with the following observations:

It's overwhelming.

It's like a catalog.

It's the equal of America.

It doesn't get tiresome—which is surprising. Instead it carries you along.

It is rhythm and you give yourself up to the rhythm.

It's very precise and careful, not general—even though it
seems general.

It honors people.

It moves at the end (I quote exactly) "to sort of ultimate
things."

It's enchanting because you know something is going to
occur next, but you don't know what it will be.

It makes me proud.

It's very physical.

It shows that you can't pin America down, that any idea of
America is too small.

It suspends your sense of time and puts you in a long
moment.

It talks about work, what people do.

It has (I quote) "a million verbs."

There were a couple of remarks I couldn't read because my
handwriting is less than great. Still, I was delighted at how much
we turned up. We also talked about what our favorite description

was and why. A number of students called attention to the lines about the prostitute and Whitman's response:

> The prostitute draggles her shawl, her bonnet bobs on her
>   tipsy and pimpled neck,
> The crowd laugh at her blackguard oaths, the men jeer and
>   wink to each other,
> (Miserable! I do not laugh at your oaths nor jeer you.)

They were plainly moved and surprised, I think, that he put himself in the poem at that point. A couple of students said that they thought his exclamation mark was "awesome."

What I felt is that through the passage we examined, my students were getting a sense of who Whitman was as a poet. High school, after all, isn't about exhausting knowledge; it's about getting a sense of what is there to encounter. If you graduate from high school and don't have a sense of Walt Whitman as a poet, that's sad. There's no guarantee that anything else in life is going to give that to you.

I've had a few foreign exchange students and they are very enthusiastic about Whitman. One year I had a student from Brazil who had a sweatshirt with Walt Whitman on the front. Whitman's America is the America they want to encounter—the marvelously open, diverse, vast, and feeling America. They ask the other students if Whitman is our national poet and if we all memorize him. It's a rather awkward moment for my American students. "National poet?" I want to say, "We're about standardized tests not national poets." I don't say that of course. I just let the kids say what they say, which is "Well, he's not exactly our national poet like Shakespeare or something, but we like him a lot. He's the man. Right, Mr. P.?" I imagine that Walt would understand the American phrase, "He's the man" very well.

march 1

long poem: allen ginsberg

Once my students have spent some time with Whitman, they are curious about whether there are sons and daughters of Walt. They start to perceive, as the year goes by, how poets connect with other poets. They start to perceive how poetry is a conversation that's held over the course of generations. I value this insight because it's often quite difficult to see what one generation has to do with another in the United States. If you are old in this country, it means you are outdated and quaint. For my students to feel that poetry doesn't become outdated and quaint is a learning that is as important as any test score. More important, really.

Accordingly we spend some time with, arguably, the most prominent *scion* (what's that word, Mr. P.?) of Walt Whitman— Allen Ginsberg. I like to focus on his poem "Kaddish" because students find it accessible and very moving. Amazingly enough, few of them have ever heard of Allen Ginsberg. He's dead and gone now and it seems all the more important to help my students realize that he may be dead, but as an artist he is not gone.

First we talk about the word, *Kaddish*. I tell them about the Jewish prayer for the dead and the commitment that prayer entails. Then, we talk about mourning—what it is and how different people mourn. We talk about rituals in other religions that relate to mourning. Then I show them the opening page of the poem and read it to them.

As with Whitman, they pick up on the rhythm immediately. They tend to be intrigued by what the poem looks like on the page—all the dashes and fragments. I ask them to describe the rhythm using some word from their feelings and we talk about those words. As you might expect, I get a big range of words. Rhythm is hard to talk about, but the words—such as *pushy, edgy, meditative, jazzy*—move us toward the energy of the poem.

They are intrigued by the syntax, too. It doesn't look quite like anything they have ever seen. We talk about how the syntax, with its bursts of words, its run-on's, its pauses, affects the reader. The kids recognize that Ginsberg is presenting something like a speaking voice. "Like someone talking to himself" is what they often say. "Like someone trying to make sense of things."

We talk about what an elegy is, too, and they look through their journals to see if they have encountered any during the course of the year. Actually some of the kids remembered the poem by Thomas McGrath right off. They looked at the poem and marveled at how different the poems looked on the page and how different their sentences were. Threading the poems.

By this time, they just want to hear more of the poem and I oblige them. I read the entire first section. It's five pages. It's hard to put into words what it's like when they are listening to a poem that goes on for so long. I have the feeling that they are there, that their minds are not wandering. Indeed, afterwards we talk about the listening and what it was like.

A number of students liken it to listening to music. "You just sort of take it in. It goes by but that's okay." Another student says that you hear certain words being repeated and that "sort of keeps you focused—like the word *forever*." I'm proud of how my students can listen. Inattentiveness and distraction often seem like the sum of contemporary life. For my kids to just sit and listen feels like an achievement. After all, the material is remote to them—a Jewish immigrant woman who loses her mind. And the world of the poem—Manhattan—is far away from them. Still, when they listen they are with the world in the poem.

Over the course of the following days I read them more of the poem. The poem is available in the library if they want to read all of it and I have copies in my room. I let them know up front that Ginsberg was gay and that he wasn't bashful about letting the world know it. Far from it. For my part, I always give my students a choice when I am making assignments. There are enough poems to go around. A few years ago I had a student whose parents were incensed that I was using Allen Ginsberg in my classroom. The mother called me up to tell me I was promoting "godless homosexuality." I told her I was reading Allen Ginsberg and that the only thing I was promoting was poetry. We read *Romeo and Juliet* and I am not promoting suicide. She sputtered at me and threatened me with someone on the school board that, in her words, "knew what I was up to." I said I would be glad to talk further with her if she wanted to. It ended there.

I don't claim to be someone who is fighting battles. I do claim to be someone who feels that young people need honesty. I am always thinking about what is appropriate—which is to say not sensationalistic. When I see the sensationalism that is routine in our society and that bombards my students daily, I have to laugh a little at the concern about the classroom.

It's ironic about her using the word *godless*. I like to read to my students a passage from "Kaddish" that is actually about God. In it Naomi, Ginsberg's mentally disturbed mother, talks about her vision of God. Naomi sees God as being *a lonely old man.* It's deeply affecting as we are made to feel the sadness and beauty of Naomi's being. We are also made to feel the foolishness of trying to define the indefinable: Who can say what God is?

I would have liked to read this passage to the mother. Maybe she might have talked with me about it, maybe not. I wonder exactly how she learned about Ginsberg's godlessness. As for my students, I know that it is important for many of them to know that Allen Ginsberg wrote such a poem.

march 7

what a poem can be

When I reach the world of contemporary long poems, I realize that the question I am posing to my students is a basic one: What can a poem be? At first glance, it may seem a curious question. Poems in their perennial concerns—love, loss, dwelling on the earth—seem on the immutable side of the street. However, because they exist in time they are anything but immutable. Nothing is written in cement as to what makes a poem a poem. The most notorious example, and one we talk about all year, is free verse. When it started to gain some notoriety at the beginning of the twentieth century, there were many anguished howls that traditional poetry was under attack.

In a sense it was. Many poets felt that meter had done all it could do for the time being and that the world around them called for something new. Gradually the anguished howls diminished in the face of much exhilarating art. To my students, free verse makes very good sense. It isn't at all foreign or strange or threatening. Times change.

In terms of the long poem, the notion of the poem as a series of consecutive lines that focus on one subject is only one among many notions in our world. To show students what the long poem can be, I use a range of different poems. This year I focused on Campbell McGrath's "The Bob Hope Poem" and C.D. Wright's book length poem *Deepstep Come Shining.*

McGrath's poem is a sort of inspired grab bag. Nominally he is writing about Bob Hope. ("Bob Who?" my students ask. How humbling.) The real topic is the United States of America as it variously stumbled and soared during the lifetime of Bob Hope. When we looked at the poem, we identified a number of aspects that constituted the poem: lists of places, quotes, questions, pieces of mail the poet receives, historical lore, personal narrative, addresses to the reader, comments about anything the poet wants to comment on (I like how the kids put that), observation, poetic descriptions, not-so-poetic descriptions, semi-haiku (three-line poems), various remarks people make to the poet, assertions, metaphors, and fooling around with words (I like that one, too.). A pretty full plate, as they say.

"So," my question goes, "how is this *amalgam* (look that word up) a poem?" I have them write a formal response to this question. It's a grade. We have looked at enough of the poem in class for them to get some handle on it. Now what do you think?

What they think is fairly fascinating. There are students who think it isn't a poem. As long as they can defend their point of view, that's fine with me. One student felt the poem was a "hamper into which the poet threw a couple centuries of laundry." He went on to write that he felt the poet was trying to evoke how vast and mind-boggling America was, but the only mind that was boggled was the poet's. "I like Walt Whitman better," this student opined. My students don't lack for critical instincts.

Plenty of students thought the poem was very much a poem. They noted that the poem was like a recipe—some of this and some of that. They noted that form and content were combined—the various-ness of America with the various-ness of modes in the poem. They noted that the poem was a meditation and that when you meditate all sorts of things go through your mind. They liked how they never knew what was going to happen next in the poem but "you trusted the poet. He was keeping it all together." All the students who supported the poem felt it opened their minds up to what a poem can be. "It's a big world. How do you get that into a poem?" I have to remember that one.

We also looked at C.D. Wright's poem. Wright's poem has the feel of some people talking. She proceeds down the page with a series of what seem like random remarks. Gradually as you read the poem, they don't seem so random at all. They seem brilliantly concerted and that they feel somewhat random is part of their brilliance.

What interests me in terms of my students is how Wright gets speech onto the page. I want my students to listen to what comes out of people's mouths. I want them to notice speech and hear what's there. (I ask them at various times to record verbatim what they hear in the school halls. The words have to be exact. No obscenities allowed, however.) Many passages in Wright's poem have the feel of people driving along in a car and making observations and comments. They look around at what is going by them and talk about it or they talk about personal history. The kids find her entrancing:

> What does she look like, the handsome young blind man asked his pretty, freckled girl at the festival.
>
> She has black hair. Strange, he said. I pictured her blond.
>
> The rain would let up and then it would start up. Some brought umbrellas. Some brought garbage bags turned into ponchos.
>
> The refrain to the rain would be a movement up and down the clefs of light.
>
> The boats in the bay took in the festival from the water.
>
> Blur in. Blur out.
>
> The darkness will eat you.
>
> A bullet don't have nobody's name on it.
>
> HAIR TODAY. GONE TOMORROW (sign at the electrolysis center) Dontouchmymustache. That's all the Japanese I can say.
>
> They didn't have a metal detector. So you know folks were packing. Club Paradise. Saturday night. Bowlegs Miller led the house band.

The kids like Wright enormously. I'm pleased with this because if I show the poem to people at large (other members of the English department) they tend to scratch their heads and start talking about the meaning. By and large, my students have come to realize that a poem is an experience and that first of all you have to feel the experience. They can talk about what the poem is about, but they know there's only so much to be gained from such talk. It's like driving somewhere. You can say you drove from Baton Rouge to Biloxi. So what does that tell you? What was it like? What did you feel? How much mystery is in any given moment of existence? Especially when that moment is looking dully at a billboard or tearing at a hangnail or yawning. What do you see when you are in a speeding car?

I have my students write a poem in which two people in a car talk (and I refer them to the earlier car poem they wrote in case they have forgotten, which some of them definitely have). It's one of the best poems of the year that they do. They get excited. They have been in plenty of cars on plenty of drives and heard plenty of people. They themselves have talked plenty. Now they can put it onto the page and see what happens: We write to find out what is inside us. Because some of America's energy is, for better and for worse, about people driving around in cars and talking, it seems an appropriate assignment. What can a poem be?

Here is one by a student named Schuyler Leeds. It's called "On the Road."

> I talk to God at night before I go to sleep.
> If Wal-Mart doesn't do something about that parking lot, I'm going
>   to move to outer space.
> God's not real happy with people.
> You hungry?
> God's voice isn't as deep as you think. It's kind of high pitched.
> You see what that guy just did? Cut me off. You really have to
>   watch it these days.
> Anyhow, God reads the Bible and he was talking to me about Noah.
> There used to be a vacant lot over there. I'm pretty sure.
> Maybe something bad is going to happen.
> It's a hassle getting here but a two for one sale is always worth it.

march 10

personal ache

After school today a student named Jason Smith stopped by. He had a piece of paper in his hand. It was the sheet that a teacher signs off on to show that a student doesn't owe anything. It's the sheet that a kid hands you when he or she is leaving school. Most of the time they are transferring from one school to another school. In Jason's case he is dropping out.

Jason wasn't flunking my class, but I wouldn't say he was very interested. I wouldn't say he was here every day either. He was drifting. I saw it and spoke to him about it and he kept drifting.

I used to think that dropping out of school was the end of the world. It seems natural from a teacher's point of view. You invest all this energy in school and then a sixteen-year-old tells you he or she has better things to do with his or her daylight hours. You think your classroom is a real haven for them. They don't think so.

I've learned it's not the end of the world. Kids have all kinds of forces operating on them and inside them. Some get their GED and move on. Some don't. I know of some cases where some pretty bad things have happened in those daylight hours. Still, I try to be hopeful whenever a kid comes along with that particular piece of paper.

I can tell Jason doesn't want to talk. He's not looking at me. He just thrusts the paper forward and doesn't say a word. I make some small talk about textbooks, but I can feel that a lot more is going on inside Jason than I'm going to hear at this moment. I wish him "good luck." He looks at me and says, "Yeah, no hard feelings. I gotta do what I gotta do." Then he's out the door.

I sit there by myself—just me and the empty desks. What I am feeling is how alone so many kids are. I mean it in the sense of their inner lives, how much their lives are ruled by the terms of popular culture. Jason had some fairly serious gear on. Something exciting is happening on the screens and in the ads, but for a number of them what is happening is trouble at home, someone using way more of a substance than that person should be using, and a sense that school just gets in the way. The discrepancy between what they have and what the world seems to offer could eat a person up.

Every year you get very involved with more than 100 young lives. You pay as much as attention as you can pay, but it never feels like enough. You know so much is going on. Mostly the kids are okay; they stay in their lane. School works for them one way or another. Jason wrote in his journal that he thought poetry was a "good thing but not for people like me." I asked him what that meant and he was cryptic. "If you have to ask, you'll never know." He smiled that bewildering, maddening smile adolescent boys often give you—knowing beyond their years and utterly unknowing, at the same time. Jason was a secretive kid rather than one who acted out. There are a lot of years between us and sometimes those years feel like chasms.

I did a James Wright poem with my students today. Actually I just read the poem and moved on. I do that a certain number of days. We don't always talk or write. Some days the poem is all I want to do. Some days a kid won't let you move on, however. Today that happened in my second period class when I read the poem.

The poem is short. It's called "Autumn Begins in Martins Ferry, Ohio."

> In the Shreve High football stadium,
> I think of Polacks nursing long beers in Tiltonsville,
> And gray faces of Negroes in the blast furnace at Benwood,
> And the ruptured night watchman of Wheeling Steel,
> Dreaming of heroes.
>
> All the proud fathers are ashamed to go home.
> Their women cluck like starved pullets,
> Dying for love.
>
> Therefore,
> Their sons grow suicidally beautiful
> At the beginning of each October,
> And gallop terribly against each other's bodies.

What happened is Trevor Schneider raised his hand and said, "I got a question, Mr. P." The question was "Why are poems so sad?" Trevor went on, "I just don't get it Mr. P. I mean we're alive and everything and that seems pretty good but these poems are always looking for what's wrong. You know what I mean? What's wrong with a football game? I don't play football myself, but what's wrong with a football game?" I can see by the look on his face that there's nothing smart-alecky in his question. It's plain that he's been thinking. The class around him is quiet.

I tell him that it's a genuine question and one I have asked myself more than once. I also tell him that I'm going to let the rest of the class answer that question also, but first I want to say a few words. "Just a few words, Mr. P.," Trevor says to me. "You've been known to go on."

What I say (approximately) is that there is a personal ache inside each of us and poetry speaks to that ache. It's the ache of being alive and knowing you are mortal. It's the ache of not having people understand you. It's the ache of wanting things you'll never have. It's the ache of regret. It's the ache of confusion. It's the ache of love that goes wrong, that burns up, that forgets what love is. It's the ache of loss. It's the ache of frustration.

"I hear you, Mr. P., but football? Give me a break. It's just a game. Coach Richmond would not post this poem in the locker room, I can tell you."

I look around and Melissa Kennedy has her hand up. She says, "No, Trevor. The poets do love life. That's why the poems are sad so much. They feel how much is there and if you feel how much is there, then maybe you have to be sad." She pauses; there's a bit of a throb in her voice. "Look at the poem. The men work too hard and their wives don't get the love they crave and so their sons— look at the words—*gallop terribly*. It's violent. It's approved violence, but it's violent and it comes from people's lives. We can't help being sad. It's part of who we are." The throb in her voice has gotten a little stronger.

Trevor turns to her and says that he hears her. "You buy Mr. P.'s ache thing, huh?"

Melissa laughs one of those sudden clouds-breaking-up laughs that kids are full of. "I like stuff like this poem. Don't you think, Trevor, that we feel more than we can say? Don't you think so?"

"Yeah," he says. "I do."

As a writer once observed, happiness "writes white."

march 13
the lens

There are a lot of metaphors used to talk about what poems do. One that makes sense to me is that a poem is a lens. That lens allows us to look very closely at any moment of existence and see what's there. That lens is still and is in no hurry. How could a lens be in a hurry?

For the poet the great question is how closely you focus that lens. If you get real close, do you lose your perspective and get bogged down in trivial details? Do you lose the outline of what you are looking at? If you choose a middle ground, is it clear enough what you are focusing on? And a distant shot can be just that—too far away to matter. It's tricky.

It's also tricky because the lens is alive. A poem is not passive.

It's imagined and that imagining is a form of exploring. If you know ahead of time where you are going, then it makes no sense to go there. When you focus the lens, when you try to see and hear and feel and touch a moment of life, you don't know what the results are going to be.

Nor do you know ahead of time exactly what the lens is going to focus on. If, for instance, you walk into a living room, in most houses there are many objects in that room. Which ones do you focus on? The ones that somehow speak to you would be my answer. There's a lot going on in that *somehow*. When I do prewriting work with my students, I often ask them to just pick one detail from a room and describe it in great detail. It's not that the detail is representative, it's that careful description gives the detail a life of its own.

How the details that come into focus are going to relate to one another is another mystery. I think of the details in a still-life painting and how all our attention goes to whatever the painter has elected to paint. In a painting we can talk about how shapes and colors relate, but the details that come from life and that the lens reveals—who can say? The poem, in that sense, is a gist, a suggestion. It's one reason I tend to tire of the thumping, rhythmic, rhymed certainty of the nineteenth century. They wanted the poem to nail down the subject with a series of hearty swings. I go to a poem for what can't be nailed down.

The question I ask my students is "Where is the lens in this poem?" In, for instance, the James Wright poem I read the other day the lens seems mid-ground. He tells you a lot in a few, careful details and he doesn't want to get any closer than that. He wants the feelings that the details evoke to be foremost.

It's, of course, a lens that uses all our senses as it focuses on a specific moment or object or event. It's a lens that listens and feels and smells and sometimes even tastes. The poem I did today by the contemporary American poet Debra Marquart shows how persistent the lens can be and where it can take you. It's titled "Hearing My Mother's Voice":

> The blinking telephone reminds me
> to unwind the tape, let loose
>
> the voices that have called me.
> I unbutton my blouse, pull on

a sweatshirt. Time to let go
of the meetings, the commute,

what my boss said in passing.
I recognize her voice even from

the other room, anxious breath
on the line, the ends of words

clamped tight. Her voice rises
at the end of each sentence,

as if forever asking. The one time
she visited, she quizzed me again

and again. *Now, to get back on
the freeway, do I go right and follow*

*the loop, or go under the highway
and turn left?* In her small town

there's not even a yellow light
flashing caution. Beside the phone

now I rewind the tape, listen again
for the details, the heavy breath,

the vowels that refuse to sing. I find
it's me, calling home earlier in the day

telling whoever gets this message
to pick up some bread, some milk,

and asking, in a small voice,
what we will be doing tonight?

In the words of Kayla Murray, "The lens is right there, Mr. P. She's almost in the phone it's so close. She goes other places in the poem like where her mom lives, but she never leaves the message tape." I follow up what she says by asking what words are repeated. One word the kids glom on to is *voice*.

We have talked a lot this year about how little things make a poem, how important it is, for instance, to pay attention to how someone speaks, that a world of feeling resides in the human voice. The close attention that Marquart pays to the particular qualities of what she takes to be her mother's voice convinces the reader how well she knows that voice. Then at the end, it's *a small voice*. Kayla picked up on how much work that one adjective does: "After she says a lot about the voice, when she says *small* you feel so much about who she is. It's like she's still a child. A child has a small voice. She has that stuff in there about her boss and everything to show us how grown up she is. But her voice is small."

One thing my students have told me that they like about poetry is that poets are willing to show how the joke can be on them. They aren't trying to impress the reader. What they are doing is much more important than that. Given that my students live in a world in which image and public relations seem to dictate every square inch of public space, the candor of poetry seems an important alternative. After all, one thing poems do is assert how much the inner life matters. A number of students said today that they respected the poet for being so honest about herself. To find out that we do not know everything, that we are blindly and deeply human is comforting.

Kayla is one of those young women who has every hair very neatly in place. Maybe the control that she exudes comes naturally, maybe not. I do know that she has made contact with a living poem today that spoke to her. I do know that she understands how it's worth the time to consider where the lens is and what the poet does with that lens. In a way, the poems are parables to my students. They show them ways of being. They aren't so much studying poems as starting to live with them and to see what the poems have to say to them.

march 16
physicality

During the school year I run and I walk a lot—around the neighborhood, dirt roads, trails. It's not just about being fit. It's that I like to be outside and feel that I'm on the earth. I spend enough time already under fluorescent lights. Some days I feel like a mothball in a button down shirt. I need the feeling of my feet on the earth, of looking around, of pausing and being still. To me, being on the earth seems the most amazing thing about being alive. I'm still full of naïve awe.

My students, as befits their age, are busy being cool. Naïve awe is not high on their list of priorities. They are happy to leave it to me, as in "Mr. P. is a nature type." I'm okay with that, but some days when I ask them about the name of a tree or a bird or a plant and they stare at me as if I were asking them about the lineage of Ostrogoth kings, I'm not so okay. Some days it feels like *robin* and *pigeon* are the extent of what they know about the natural world.

I am well aware that a lecture about the joys of observation and nomenclature is less than worthless. As a student once said to me, "I know what a tree is. I'm not going to marry one." Touché, P. Still, I want my students to get a sense of how the earth figures so enormously in poetry. Poets are celebrators of the earth—including the dark, feral aspects.

What I try to get across to my students is how ineluctably physical poetry is. That's why I keep talking about sound and rhythm during the year. It's why I insist on poems being read aloud. We even make a list up about all the physical and environmental factors that come into play when you read a poem aloud: voice box, throat, tongue, mouth, diaphragm, and so on. The biology teachers love it as an interdisciplinary exercise. The kids are not so excited about it, but they tend to like the challenge of applying their biology to such a foreign clime as the English classroom.

> Sometimes I will isolate a sentence in a poem and simply ask what words seem appropriate to describe how the sentence is constructed.

Syntax is another aspect of physicality I stress. Sometimes I will isolate a sentence in a poem and simply ask what words seem appropriate to describe how the sentence is constructed. Is it laborious? Conjured? Tacked together? Balanced? Made by hand? Serpentine? Slow? Fast? This talking about sentences is important work. I don't expect to be hatching great stylists, but I like my students to think about how sentences are put together. Because a poem puts relatively few sentences on a pedestal, it seems natural to look very carefully at those sentences as sentences. I'm not so much concerned about the world of labeling clauses as I am concerned about feeling how sentences can be fashioned in different ways. Although I would never use the phrase with them, I want them to take note of the physical glory of sentences.

> This talking about sentences is important work.

I used a poem today I haven't taught before. It's by Margaret

Gibson, a poet who lives in Connecticut. It's called "Collect" and I had my students go to the dictionary to check the meaning of the word. They were surprised to learn there is a whole other word meaning a whole other thing: *collect*, according to the *American Heritage Dictionary of the English Language,* is "A brief formal prayer that is used in various Western liturgies before the epistle and that varies with the day." We discussed what that meant (*liturgies?*) both before and after experiencing the poem:

Just now in the living room of rafters and secluded summer light a wren
      is hurling itself, body and breath,

against the stubborn, self-watchful, hard transparency we call window,
      and it can't break through, nor avoid

its own desire, nor land there on the branch of shagbark just out of reach,
      nor be flung into the accustomed avenue

between the oaks, nor dip to the distant blur of brown mirage the pond is,
      never mind that I have opened

fully two doors and all the windows and stripped them of their screens.
      It doesn't realize its freedom.

I am its harrier, encouraging—if it's courage—with whispered cries:
      Go *on,* go *on,* go . . .

as it nears, then veers from its own release, retreating to a high rafter,
                      huddled
      now into the pitiless solitude

that hasn't name nor motive, cause nor certitude nor solace. Who can
                      praise
      enough—if it's praise—this last,

if it's last, sufficient and humble refusal? As surprising as the gathered
      urgency that lifts it, and soundlessly

takes it beyond *inside* or *outside, free* or *not free,* unevenly straight
                      through
      the door of whirling depth and wind

the wren in its lonely and passionate passage just now is.

Sometimes when I read a poem the physicality is so strong, it feels as though all the air has gone out of the room. That's how it felt after Gibson's poem. The physical engagement was so powerful that my students were spent. I know I was from reading the poem. Once our breath came back—and it took a minute—I asked about the poet's sentences. How many were there and what did they do?

One thing I love about looking at sentences is the scrutiny that punctuation receives. We talked about the first sentence, how it began with a run of language, then went through a spate of commas, then extended itself again, finally ending with a long skein of uninterrupted words. And then there is a short sentence that as one student put it, "Sounds like a judge or a teacher or even a policeman, someone just saying something very directly." Then a long sentence with a sort of shimmy in the early part where the ellipses appear. Then a question that has some pauses in it. Then the last sentence with a few commas and then the unpunctuated flight of words.

The sentences make the poem possible. I want my students to see and feel that simple fact. Too often sentences are cardboard to them. A sentence in a poem has torque and you can feel that in Gibson's poem. It moves in a certain way and how it moves is intimately connected with what is being written about. The form of the sentences is as much the subject as the wren. When I hand the poem out, after I have read it, the students immediately talk about the way the poem looks on the page, how it expands and contracts, expands and contracts, how long those long lines are. They know by now that the look of the poem is the poem.

"And what is a wren?" my largely indifferent-to-nature students asked. I passed a bird guide around the room. We talked about birds, about our feelings about birds. It turns out that my students do have some very strong feelings about the unnamed creatures around them. It's just that those creatures don't come into their focus very often.

We talked more. We talked about the amazing language of the poem, about how the poet keeps questioning her language and pushing her language at the same time. We talked about the occasion, how someone would say, "There was a bird in the house" and how a whole world of feeling and occurrence resided in that statement, a world that a poem was made from. We talked about religion, about the poem being a prayer and the sort of prayer the poem was and what a prayer was. Ashley O'Donnell said that she thought a prayer was about asking for something or trying to get God to protect something. "The bird itself is a prayer," she said. She said that and we all listened.

march 22

attention

We talk in class about writing and words, but we also talk about what it means to pay attention. I emphasize that good writing uses all our senses—including our emotions. Consequently I do a fair amount of prewriting or just exercises to get my students to focus their attention on an experience and generate details from that experience. A poem is an experience in its own right and I want my students to give me an experience.

> I emphasize that good writing uses all our senses—including our emotions. Consequently I do a fair amount of prewriting or just exercises to get my students to focus their attention on an experience and generate details from that experience.

Recently we worked on the experience of coming to school in the morning. We divided up among students who rode the bus, who got a car ride, or who walked to school. Then I asked them for five details from each sense and from their feelings about the experience of coming to school that morning.

I have found the kids like the challenge of doing this. At first, they just sit there and stare into space. No one is asking them to pay close attention to what is going on in their lives. School asks them to learn new things rather than scrutinize their daily existence. Because they do have lives, however, and because I want them to link experience with language, I ask them to generate lists of details for me. I have learned that they can do it and they can do it well.

Here, for instance, is what came from one student about taking the bus.

Hearing: Crinkly rustle of potato chip bag being opened behind me—Snippets of tunes on various Walkmen—Whispers (must be gossip)—Sheer yelling ("Gimme that!")—Teasing ("I know you like her!")

Sight: Kids' clothes (Abercrombie and Fitch sweatshirts, for instance)—Graffiti on the back of the seat in front of me ("T.K. is a geek")—Haircuts (Joe DeStefanis has a new buzz cut)—Little trails of gravel and dirt on the aisle floor—The lunchboxes of the elementary school kids on the bus (I think I had a Power Ranger lunch box once).

Smell: Perfume (heavy smell, cloying)—Hair cream our bus driver uses (smells weirdly chemical)—A fart (nasty)—Post-shower body smells (some clean and some starting to become body odor)—Bus smell (hard to describe—sweat plus vinyl plus metal plus bad air—smells like old cardboard)

Taste: Greasy but agreeable taste of some potato chips I bum from the kid behind me (not my favorite brand of chip, but I never met a potato chip I didn't like)—Can you taste the air? I think it's heavy and sort of rancid—That's all my tongue got a hold of

Touch: Reassuring softness of my old sweatshirt—Run fingers through my hair (clean!)—Clammy feeling of metal top of seat in front of me—Drumming fingers on the top of my algebra book (feels solid, but not hard like wood or metal)—My skin feels sort of heavy (I didn't get enough sleep last night)

Feelings: Anxiety (algebra test second period)—Tedium (how many bus rides have I been on?)—Hunger (those potato chips got my stomach going)—Gladness (I sit next to my friend)—A little ashamed (my mind goes back to a scene between my mom and me this morning)—Wow! I have all those feelings at the same time!

We go different places with this material. Sometimes we do list poems in which students string together their details to construct a narrative poem. I want them to be faithful to the original material and think about how the details cohere and in what order the details want to be. We talk about how details need to be modulated in terms of their length—all one length tends to become boring. We talk about the syntax of the phrases that constitute the details. Again, the same syntactic order can become boring. We talk about point of view. How much of yourself do you want to put into the poem? Can the point of view get in the way of the expressiveness of the details? How can the point of view aid the expressiveness? ("Treat yourself like a detail," as a student once put it. I have students do one piece a year in which they write about themselves in the third person.)

Sometimes I have the students peer edit their lists. I ask them to tell their partner which phrases work and which can be improved. Then they work on them and go back to their partner. As always with peer editing, I create definite tasks—for instance, at least three details that might be improved with remarks about how they might be improved. The person who does the peer editing is graded on how thoroughly he or she does the editing. Editing is serious work.

Sometimes I have the students take one detail and expand it. I want them to write a poem that evokes the trip to school through the lens of that one detail. "Really look at and smell and taste those potato chips," I will say to them. I want them to go further in terms of finding out what is there. The poem is typically twenty lines or less. I want them to be explorers and pay even closer attention. Writing is discovery.

In terms of the going-to-school assignment, this is the poem the student wrote when he expanded the sight aspect of the poem. He called it "One More Tee Shirt":

> In front of me
> I've got Abercrombie and Fitch—
> Crimson lettering on gray background.
> Next to A & F,
> There's The Gap.
> Hey, I don't have to go
> To the mall.
> All I have to do is just
> Ride the old yellow bus
> To school in the morning.
> I turn around to check out
> Who's behind me
> And New York Yankees
> Is talking with Dallas Cowboys.
> What am I doing wearing
> A plain blue oxford cloth button down shirt?

In all this, my philosophy is simple: The world is expressive. The more of the world you let into your writing, the more your writing will make the reader feel. My students often come to me with the notion that poetry is all about them telling the world what they think and feel: "I was so heartbroken, etc." Or at the other end of the spectrum they don't know what to write about: "My life is so boring." We notice an enormous amount each day but what do we do with it? Not much of it comes out in language.

No one is asking for it and not that many students keep diaries anymore. (Poetry remains one road into the realm of personal scrutiny.) What I find is that attention exercises wake up students to how much is going on. It's validating work because it shows how alive they are. They aren't sleepwalking. It just seems that way some days.

march 25

biography

I have a colleague who loves to give lectures on poets' backgrounds. You don't touch the poem, until you have made a passing acquaintance with the life and times of the poet. I can understand this approach fairly well. It cradles the poems and when, finally, they are touched they are full of signs that speak to their provenance. It is a help to know something about Irish political history when encountering the likes of "Easter, 1916;" there's no question about it.

The difficulty—to continue my metaphor—is that fairly often the poem is so swaddled in historical and biographical details that it is hard to experience as a poem. It seems more an aspect of the historical spirit than an individual human effort. History has a way of summoning up the powers of inevitability and they are potent powers, indeed. The quirkiness of authoring can get left behind. The poem is full of meaning about Irish history but its life as a poem—the life of stanzas and lines and word choices—may be scanted.

It's not just that, however. What seems to me to be crucial for my students who are very much regular students in a regular American high school is that they do a bit of thinking about what it is like to be a poet in the United States. It's not a topic they have given much thought. Why would they? Part of my job, as I see it, is to humanize the figure of the poet. However modestly, I want to put a face on the poems. I may just identify the poet in terms of where he or she lives. It's not a big thing but it's something. The kids start to develop some curiosity about poets and sometimes go off on their own and look up more information.

In some cases I feel it's very important that I say some words about the poet's career. I mean the word *career* in the sense of what it was like to be that poet over the decades that the poet practiced his or her poetic vocation. What was it like to make poetry in the United States? What has it been like to be a poet in our society? Do, for instance, poets make a living being poets? Do they live off their books in the way that some authors live off the proceeds of their books? And how do they become known as poets?

One poet I make a point of touching on is Robert Frost. His career seems crucial because he is so unique yet he is considered representative. He is America's poet in the sense that he was a popular, financial, and artistic success. What could be better?

So I tell them the story of Robert Frost the artist. That's not the same story as Robert Frost the historical figure or Robert Frost the maker of poems. It's a bit more tangled. You start with someone who has a passion for poetry in an age where poetry is very much a proper and polite endeavor. The poet does not come from particularly well off circumstances—far from it. Although he tries his hand at college, he does not stay with it. In fact, he drops out twice. He keeps alive by some teaching and some farming. The farm is a gift from a relation, for the poet is not much of a money-maker. He spends an appreciable amount of his time writing poems. He believes in his vocation as a poet although there does not seem to be much money to be had writing these poems. His wife believes in his vocation, too. She is a sensitive woman who reads his poems and responds acutely to them.

I spin out the whole story to them: the early oblivion, the leaving America ("Robert Frost left America?" is the scandalized question I often get), publication in England, the runaway success of the first two books, the fame, the public spotlight, the personal grief, the personae the trickster poet favored, how he made his living. I follow the story of the artist to the day he read at John F. Kennedy's inaugural. I show a video of him—*The Ancient Poet*.

It's quite a story and evokes a blizzard of questions: Why did he believe in himself? What would have happened if he weren't taken up in England? Did he cause his sorrows? How did he get along with other poets? What did he think of himself? What place did he believe poetry had in America? Who are the popular poets in America now? Are they like Robert Frost? What is it to be a poet? And what do poets give us? They are bottomless questions.

The more we talk, the more we wonder. I end with a poem by
Frost. I point out to my students that this poem is Frost's first
poem in his first book (not counting a prefatory poem). It is called
"Into My Own":

> One of my wishes is that those dark trees,
> So old and firm they scarcely show the breeze,
> Were not, as 'twere, the merest mask of gloom,
> But stretched away unto the edge of doom.
>
> I should not be withheld but that some day
> Into their vastness I should steal away,
> Fearless of ever finding open land,
> Or highway where the slow wheel pours the sand.
>
> I do not see why I should e'er turn back,
> Or those should not set forth upon my track
> To overtake me, who should miss me here
> And long to know if still I held them dear.
>
> They would not find me changed from him they knew—
> Only more sure of all I thought was true.

I like to dictate this poem line by line. I dictate a line and we pause
and talk about it. It lets my students experience the poem slowly.
They follow it like a scent or a trail. There's time to ponder and
feel how the poem unfolds. We can talk, for instance, about that
should in line five. It's a word that recurs in the poem. More than
one student has said, in effect, "He never really does anything
then, does he? He's just wishing. He's certain of himself but he's
wishing."

We talk about getting your nerve up to say you are a poet.
Who are you saying it to? Your self? America? Who are *they*? The
poet's audience? The poet's friends? Why would they *long to*
know . . . ? Isn't he maybe bluffing?

I ask my students if they know what shadowboxing is. Is the
poet shadowboxing? Is the poet asserting himself? Is the poet
watching himself? In any case, he is certainly aware of himself.
Writing poems isn't like falling out of bed in the morning. For all
the naturalness that Frost projected, he knew he was making art
and he knew that the odds were shaky. Yet he believed in himself and he persevered. Before he became famous more than one
person thought him something of a fool and ne'er do well. He
cheerfully admitted to both descriptions. Yet the speaker of the

poem, who surely feels close to the poet Robert Frost, was *Only more sure. . . .*

At the arbitrary end of this talk (we could talk for days), I ask my students to write a brief response piece about the man at the inaugural. Does he seem to be the same person as the speaker of "Into My Own"? It's an impressionistic question, but I prize my students' impressions; they are, after all, the stuff of poetry.

march 29

margin

Some days I walk in with a question. My question today was "Why do poems keep going back to the margin?" Followed by a post-script to the effect that we had looked at a fair number of poems and most of the time every line went back to the margin. Followed by the repetition of the question, "Why is that?"

I think the kids enjoy the questions because they are genuine thought questions—an artist or a scientist might equally ask such a question. We have a certain behavior and then we ask why that behavior occurs. Some students are happier than others are with such questions. Alas, my so-called "top division" often wants to just give me the answer I want them to give me. It pains some of them that I am not looking for the right answer and that instead I am looking for evidence of thinking. I understand their attitude. It's gotten them this far. Being bright is about knowing the right answers.

I get quite a range of responses. Some focus on the mechanical aspect: Computers are geared to a margin and once upon a time so were typewriters. This leads to a consideration of book margins and writing paper. It's a convention. It's a way of keeping writing orderly. Poetry likes orderliness. It doesn't want you wondering where the margin is going to be on every line.

We talk about the word *verse* and how it has to do with plowing a field and going back to the side of the field and doing another row. We talk about the physicality of the notion: How lines can be likened to rows in a field and how fields tend to have a shape of some sort. They are defined; they have outlines.

We talk about conventions and how writing is a social activity and social activities require conventions. You wear certain clothes to the prom. Even if you don't wear certain clothes to the prom, your wearing jeans would only highlight the conventions. "You can't get around it," more than one student observes, and it's plain that some of them have thought about it. We read *The Catcher in the Rye* in some classes and this is ground we have gone over.

Then we talk about their own poetry and whether they think about the margins. By and large, they don't. It feels natural to go back to the margin to begin a line. Again, there is a feeling that the convention is natural. It's what poems do. The line moves as far along as the poet wants the line to move and then it returns.

This talk is not self-conscious. We are trying to think about art and how it works. My students trust that I would not ask them a question that I wasn't genuinely interested in. They have encountered enough modern literature to know that conventions often wind up being flouted and that art thrives on reconsideration. Doing something because everyone has always done it that way is not much of a reason as far as art is concerned. Artists have to reaffirm conventions and experience them for themselves.

All this is about what I call "thinking like an artist." It's fascinating how much intuition and savvy my students have about artistic issues. Once they get out of the "right answer" mindset, they enjoy contemplating these issues. It's my job to keep them fresh. New poems each day do that, especially because we keep looking at those poems from different angles. Like prisms, poems have endless facets. Each day, if I so choose, I can look at a different facet.

Accordingly, we considered a section from a poem by the West Coast poet Robert Duncan. Duncan was a poet who thought a good deal about margins. I like to show my students that the questions we talk about have been seriously considered by artists in the making of their art. They are not empty questions. Even something as seemingly slight as a margin makes a difference to the artist and the person that comes along and alertly experiences that art.

Duncan was a poet of mystery and romance and magic. He's strange and I have found that my students like the strangeness. They are somewhat amazed when I tell them that Duncan wrote in the latter half of the twentieth century. We looked today at the fourth section of a poem called "Four Songs the Night Nurse Sang":

Let sleep take her, let sleep take her, let sleep
        take her away!
The cold tears of her father
have made a hill of ice.
        Let sleep take her.

Her mother's fear has made a feyrie.
        Let sleep take her.
Now all of the kingdom lies down to die.
        Let sleep take her.

Let dawn wake her, if dawn can find her.
    Let the prince of day take her
from sleep's dominion at the touch of his finger,
    if he can touch her.

The weather will hide her, the spider will bind her

    : so the wind sang.

O, there she lay
in an egg hanging from an invisible thread
spinning out I cannot tell whether

from a grave or a bed, from a grave or a bed.

Sometimes after I read a poem a few times and then show my students the text there is some major blurting aloud about the poem. Today, Gene Garrelsman exclaimed, "It rhymes at the end! I can't believe it. It's sort of all over the place and then it rhymes at the end. See it? *Thread* and *bed*." Some nods, some smiles, some surprise about the poem. Gene has never been reticent about diving into a poem.

I acknowledged that Gene had noticed something important that would probably come up again as we considered the poem. What I wanted to pursue first of all was the business of margins. What about the margins in the poem? What is the poet doing with margins?

I could feel them looking. First, they observed that the poem observed different margins in different places. They counted four different margin positions. We talked about them one by one. What was observed was that the margins were almost like characters in the poem. They noticed that the far margin that is repeated spoke for the refrain. But they noted that the first occasion of the refrain is different from the others. Before I could ask why, they noted that Duncan begins the poem with an exclamation and that the rhythm of the exclamation builds—once, twice, three times! A student observed that it felt like a sudden spell being cast. The refrain needed its own margin to distinguish its role in the poem.

Then there was the indented margin in the third stanza. Again it seemed to my students to have a role to play in the poem. This is where the prince enters the poem and the margin signifies his appearance. He is not asleep though he too is touched by the command "Let . . ."

As for the colon hanging by itself, the kids were fascinated that a poet would take such a liberty. "I guess we won't see this poem on the state test, huh, Mr. P.?" We talked about the why of the line. It wasn't easy. Students aren't used to thinking carefully about punctuation. They take it for granted or ignore it, usually both. Lori Newton, who is in my last period class and who I can honestly say truly loves poetry, said that the colon belonged with who was singing, the wind. A little time passes, she observed, when our eyes travel down to the colon. That time matters because it lets the statement about the weather and the spider have its say without being connected to whoever is saying it. It just happens. The wind is another character and the colon introduces that character. There was some applause after Lori spoke. We were impressed.

We talked more about how the regular margin is such a home in this poem, how it is a place to return to and how the other margins are ventures from that home. And we talked about the rhyme at the end that Gene noticed and how it provides finality. We could have talked more, for instance about how repetition works. As the year goes by, my students feel more and more how much there is to talk about in a poem. Sometimes I round off a discussion with a call for a written response piece about a dimension of the poem we haven't spoken about. It works well because they are so engaged from talking about the poem. I think there is a lot to be said for constant small analytical pieces rather than the glorified term paper. I want them to stay on their toes rather than occasionally ascend to that position.

> Sometimes I round off a discussion with a call for a written response piece about a dimension of the poem we haven't spoken about.

April, May, and June

April Fools' Day is parody day. *Parody* is a form of homage, a mischievous form, to be sure, but still a species of homage. I have my students look through their journals for poems whose style they wish to parody. Before we start writing, we discuss what stands out for them, stylistically, in the poem they have chosen. Students focused, for interest, on Ginsberg's run-on sentences in *Kaddish* or the flat style of the found poems we did, or Whitman's love of lists, or Dickinson's jumpiness from line to line. They showed a good eye and ear for the prominent characteristics of a poet's style.

This year I received numerous zingers. Here is one that is based on Carl Sandburg's well-known poem about the disappearance of the buffalo on the Great Plains of the United States. Sandburg's poem is called "Buffalo Dusk" and repeats lines about the disappearing buffalo herds. The poem is called "Heavy Metal Noise."

> The heavy metal bands are gone
> And those who thrashed in the mosh pits are gone.
> Those who saw the heavy metal bands and how they
>   mutilated chords with their deranged guitars,
>   their greasy heads jerking to great spasms
>   of black noise,
> Those who thrashed in the mosh pits are gone.
> And the heavy metal bands are gone.

Or how about a perennial favorite, a parody of William Carlos Williams' "This Is Just to Say":

> I have eaten
> the canoli
> you were hiding
> in the fridge

behind Mom's
fish oil supplement
and Dad's
mega-vitamins

and which
you were saving
for some
high caloric moment.

Forgive me
I lack self-control.
Lick my
Sugary fingers.

We take turns reading them aloud. The trick is to identify which author is being parodied. It becomes a quiz show of sorts: "Name That Poet." The day has become a school tradition and I save parodies from year to year. Students like to be regaled with parodies from past students: "My sister did that?" It's good clean fun.

april 5
form

The word *form* comes up frequently in our discussions of poetry. We look at the shapes of poems—whether they are in stanzas and what those stanzas are. We listen to poems and then discuss their sounds—regular end rhymes, slant rhymes, assonance, and consonance. We scrutinize line lengths. I want my students to experience the notion of form as a sort of fixed variable in poetry: It's always there, but it changes profoundly from author to author and from poem to poem.

We talk about metaphors for form. One is that form is the skeleton of the poem. It's the organized bones that support the flesh of the words. These skeletons come in all varieties and I challenge my students on any given poem to identify what the formal structure is. What are the bones? What sort of whole do the bones form? I want them to see that the noun *form* emerges from the verb *form*. Form is a making, a fashioning.

That's not the only metaphor we use. Another metaphor concept we use, and one that is closer to the world of modern free verse poems, is the notion of organic form. Here, the poem is organized according to impulses and how those impulses play out in rhythms and lines and sounds. It's more moment by moment and may seem more arbitrary. Typically, though, when we start carefully looking, it doesn't seem arbitrary. We notice that principles are at work in issues such as margins and lines and stanzas. We can see that an informal poem still has formal concerns. It, too, is shaped and how that shaping works is crucial to its form.

The metaphor that applies to organic form is dance. We see the poem as a series of movements—words, lines, stanzas, punctuation—and we ask ourselves how those movements are organized. We study the poem as we would study an organism, although our feelings come into play also. We don't pretend to be "objective."

All this work gives my students an expanded and heightened sense of what form can be. Too often, I have sat in on classes where form is defined as a preconceived mode—sonnet, villanelle—and that is that. Form is presented as a sort of ultimatum. Anything less than a sonnet is dithering. I once sat in a classroom where a teacher grandly pronounced the sonnet to be "the beacon of English poetry." Alas, why and how the sonnet came to be and what people do nowadays with sonnets is ignored by such proclamations.

Which is to say, I do talk about sonnets, but in April rather than September. I want my students to thoroughly experience many notions of what form constitutes before they encounter the seeming rigidities of the classical sonnet. The sonnet is an elegant boot camp. You have to deal with certain inexorable realities and it's work to deal with those realities.

So today we tackled two sonnets—one from the sixteenth century and one that was published in a book in 1989. According to my approximate math, that's 400 years. It's one reason I try hard to pair poems when I am looking at the literature of the past. On one hand, I want my students to feel its past-ness—this is really old. On the other hand, I want them to realize that poetry never dies. It keeps reinventing itself and it often does it within forms that are many hundred years old. The past keeps talking to the present because the present is interested in what the past has to say. Art is never a dead letter. I hope this gets them thinking about what traditions are and why the past matters. At least I am making a practical suggestion that they can experience on their own.

We looked at (we wrote down the opening lines) sonnets of Fulke Greville and Hayden Carruth. Greville's sonnet goes like this:

> You faithless boy, persuade you me to reason?
> With virtue do you answer my affection?
> Virtue, which you with livery and seisin
> Have sold and changed out of your protection.
>
> When you lay flattering in sweet Myra's eyes,
> And played the wanton both with worth and pleasure,
> In beauty's field you told me virtue dies,
> Excess and infinite in love, was measure.
>
> I took your oath of dalliance and desire,
> Myra did so inspire me with her graces,
> But like a wag that sets the straw on fire,
> You running to do harm in other places,
> > Sware what is felt with hand, or seen with eye,
> > As mortal, must feel sickness, age, and die.

We started off by talking about words we did know and I listed them on the blackboard. We discussed such words as *desire, protection,* and *reason* in the context of the poem. Many times I ask for what words the class doesn't understand because I trust they understand most of the words in a given poem. In the case of a sonnet from the sixteenth century, I don't feel that way. I want us to get some ground under our poetic shoes before we go further.

We then worked our way through the poem line by line by talking about the language and the sorts of sentences Greville was writing. Not every poem opens with two questions in the first two lines. We took a good pause after those first two lines and talked about what sorts of questions he was asking and to whom the questions were directed. Cupid, Venus, and Eros are not characters on the tips of my students' tongues.

I have a poster in my room that is billed as "Thirteen Questions Concerning Form." It notes the following:

1. What are the stanzas doing?
2. What do you notice about sound?
3. Why is the poem the length it is?
4. How do the lines work—short, long, mixed?

5. How does rhythm declare itself?
6. Is the poem written in a defined form?
7. At what point in the poem do you first notice its form?
8. What does the end of the poem have to do with the beginning?
9. Does the poem have a turning point?
10. If you drew a drawing of the structure of the poem, what would it look like?
11. What sort of energy does the form have?
12. How organic is the form?
13. How does the form help the poet write what the poet writes?

When the kids look at this chart at the beginning of the year, it is largely Greek to them. By this point in time, they are used to consulting it, and, in some cases, have internalized most of the questions on it. Greville's sonnet, although it comes from the very remote sixteenth century, is still approachable because all year my students have been approaching what constitutes form. When I resort to my battery analogy for poetry—the poles of the battery are art and language—I feel reasonably confident. My students are engaging art when they deal with form and they are engaging language when they deal with Greville's actual words. Words such as *wanton* and *dalliance* wake them up quite a bit. They tend to have the notion that sex started three years ago.

A sonnet is a sort of argument. It may be with oneself or another person or an imaginary creature. In a sense, it is an exercise or perhaps more like a geometric proof. By querying and examining propositions the poet comes up with some sort of conclusion. How many turns there are in the argument is crucial to the particular nature of the sonnet and we talked about Greville's sentences quite carefully in terms of what each one of them does. We wound up with a list that went like this:

Question.

Question.

Qualifying sentence.

Action in the past.

Personal narrative and observation.

It's rough but it gives my students a way of considering structure and of getting some strange language and strange thinking in their sights. As with the geometric steps of a proof, they have something to trace and follow.

The Carruth poem comes along 400 years later:

> At the hospital where I had the echocardiogram
> I saw the shuffling troop rescued from death.
> Let one suffice, the old man (my age) with his pajamas
> open (on purpose) to show his wound, his torn chest—
> frightful. I thought of the field of Troy. Not charming,
> not at all. And laboring to catch my breath,
> I of course asked what's the use, this rescuing. Lamb
> or ram, the flock cares nothing. Must we be the shepherds?
> No. Nor do I wish any longer to be accused
> of humanism, that delusion, having in these threescore
> years seen evil, hatred, ugliness, and perhaps more
> than my share.
>   Yet, Cindy, have not these rescued
> a sterner meaning? Maybe that desperate guy
> was Eros grown old and hurt, who cannot die.

After sorting out the language issues (*humanism* anyone?), we talked not about how the poems differ but, rather, what they have in common. I prize this sort of comparative thinking and challenge anyone to tell me that my students aren't doing very substantial higher order thinking when they confront two poems. In this case, we wound up talking about what a sonnet is. One point that my classes focused on was how limited a sonnet was in terms of space. It knows from the beginning that it only has so much space to do what it wants to do. It has to make the most of its space. Yet it has to generate energy within that space.

My students were fascinated by how talky and "regular," as a student put it, Carruth's sonnet was, yet how formal, too. In terms of tone, the ending lines didn't feel very different from Greville's. The kids also were intrigued by Carruth's rhymes. "Is it still a sonnet, if he doesn't use full rhymes?" We looked at how the rhyming words worked and what sorts of words they were. They were impressed by the range of Carruth's vocabulary.

Again we charted the sentences to get a feel for the structure. I imagine teachers have been using such a technique for millennia. I like the feeling of grounding my students in the ways of rhetoric. Poetry has been defined as sincere rhetoric (as opposed, say, to calculating rhetoric). Certainly the sonnet partakes of the rhetorical impulse. Carruth, to my mind, is one of the great arguers in the history of poetry. He has never been a poet to take anything on faith. He likes to tinker, and his tinkering with the sonnet shows my students how a contemporary poet is alive to the challenges of form.

A poet such as Carruth is one of the elders and I want my students to know that elders exist. I want them to know that there are artists they can look to who truly have done the work. They can take pride in living in the same society as such artists. I try to remember each day how important the inspiration factor is in poetry. Not just in the poems themselves, but in the sense of belonging to a community that recognizes poetry and poets. Young people need elders—my students write eloquently about how much their grandparents mean to them. For all their youthful braggadocio (what is that word, Mr. P.?), they don't want to be all on their own. They want to know that elders exist and that they can go to them. That's why empowering students to put poetry in their lives really matters. It's a path they can walk on—if someone takes the time to show them what the path is.

april 8

turns

One reason I like to dictate poems is to give my students a palpable sense of how the poem develops from line to line. When one reads a text, one approaches it as a done deal. Indeed it is, but its movement from line to line is part of the energy of the poem that can get lost in the doneness. Poems are made up and I want my students to experience how they are made up.

Consequently, one activity we pursue is looking at poems in terms of the turns they take: Where do they go from line to line and from sentence to sentence? This pertains especially in narrative poems: Where is the turning point in the poem? If there does seem to be a turning point, how does it function? Is it obvious, understated, dramatic, sudden? Is it the result of a single word— *but*, for instance —, an action, a simile? Is it a shift in tone, a narrative twist, a movement from one verb tense to another? Turns come in many guises, but the bottom line is the feeling that some crucial shift has been encountered. Poems aren't freeways; they thrive on turns that redirect the energy.

Pursuing these issues is not an idle exercise. A poem (yet another metaphor) is like a series of steps. How evenly or unevenly and in what direction those steps proceed is not a preordained affair. Even within the strict form of the sonnet, the poet can vary his or her approach considerably. The sonnet consists of fourteen lines, but how many sentences occur in those lines, is totally up to the poet.

Noting the turns helps students considerably in their own writing of poems. It is easy to take a first draft and consider it the correct version of what one is trying to say. By considering the turns carefully, my students have to confront why they are going wherever they are going in the course of the poem. This leads them to confront, for instance, redundancies that bog the poem down or superfluous details or concerns that do not contribute to the economy of direction the poem seeks. It leads them to think about how poets build poems and how much is enough in making a poem.

My students have a lot of feeling for the darting, leaping, associative energy of poetry. Their own minds take considerable leaps that often leave me saying, "What was that you said?" Looking at the turns is a way of appraising the leaps that the poem makes. The beauty of the approach is that it can apply to any poem. If a poem is more static—an invocation or chant or heavily repetitive poem—then we notice how it stays more or less in the same place. If the poem is a narrative, then we notice the turns that the narrative takes.

I like to do a poem or two each year by the American poet Weldon Kees. He doesn't show up in many anthologies, but that's not because of the quality of his work, I think. It may have more to do with the unsettling circumstances of his life: Kees disappeared in 1955 and no one knows what happened to him. His work, too, is unsettling—quiet yet darkly dramatic. Kees was very aware of how much a poem could say within a small space and how carefully the poet can manage the poem from line to line.

"1926" is a poem that I like and that my students respond strongly to.

The porchlight coming on again,
Early November, the dead leaves
Raked in piles, the wicker swing
Creaking. Across the lots
A phonograph is playing *Ja-Da*.

An orange moon. I see the lives
Of neighbors, mapped and marred
Like all the wars ahead, and R.
Insane, B. with his throat cut,
Fifteen years from now, in Omaha.

I did not know them then.
My airedale scratches at the door.
Am I back from seeing Milton Sills
And Doris Kenyon. Twelve years old.
The porchlight coming on again.

After I dictated the poem, we began our discussion by looking
at how the poem moves from sentence to sentence in terms of
time. We looked at the verb tenses (grammar never goes away nor
is it segregated) and considered how they work. It usually takes a
bit of time (it did today), but we puzzled out where the narrator
is in time. It's interesting that the consideration of verb tenses led
us to noting a dramatic crux in the poem, a turning point. It's the
line—"I did not know them then." Suddenly we are in the past
tense and we feel it very strongly. The briefness of the sentence
makes us feel it. As Cindy Demers in my second period class
noted, "It's the first match we meet in the poem between a sentence and a line. The sentence equals the line. Until then the poem
kind of jags along but then, for a line, everything is in synch."

It's not only that I love it when a student is that attentive (and
I do—very much), it's also stimulating for all of us in the room
because we start to feel how much art has gone into this little
poem. The line jars and yet it fits perfectly into the first line of the
final stanza. There it is—an unassailable fact. Yet we don't stay
there. We go back to the present tense. We wind up at the haunting, simple line the poem began with. We realize we have gone in
a sort of circle. We linger on that word *again*. As a student said, "I
don't know if I can count all the meanings in that word."

When we consider the turns that poems take, it makes my students feel, at once, how free art is and how calculating it is. They
don't articulate that perception to me, but I know from what they are

saying about the poem that they are experiencing that perception. A number of students commented on the weight of the words and how the poem felt much longer than its length. It's as if everything were frozen in time because time is so pervasive in the poem—perennial, past, present, and future. All the senses of time are there.

And who, my students ask, are those names in the poem? We talk about it, how names fade. The fading seems appropriate, we decide. Time is like that.

april 11
national poetry month

Things we have done to celebrate National Poetry Month:

Readings of student poetry. Typically we have one reading in the evening so that parents and community can hear what our students are writing. Also we have readings during the school day that students who are in study hall can attend.

Poetry marathons. We do readings during lunchtime in the cafeteria. We take a long poem and keep reading it—Whitman is a favorite. The poem is listed with the day's menu: Sloppy Joe's and Section 37 of "Song of Myself."

Poetry posters. As I am graphically challenged (stick figures are my limit), I tend to forget visual exercises for my students, but this is one occasion I let them go at it. They do posters to illustrate a favorite poem. Part of the task is to situate the text of the poem within the illustration. The posters go up around the school.

Reading poems on the loudspeaker. We hear a poem each morning on the loudspeaker. The poems are read by students and staff.

Send a poem to your senator. We send poems to our representatives and senators. Poetry is a gift and they deserve something in the mail beside worry, complaint, favors, etc. We try to look for poems we have encountered that have something to say about history and politics, but we have sent Lewis Carroll to them also.

Poetry trivia. What can I say? If you can't beat 'em. . . . The kids like it. Each week during the month we ask a trivia question on the loudspeaker. Correct answers qualify for a gift certificate at a local bookstore. What poet's name spelled backwards. . . ?

Poetry across the curriculum. Foreign language students translate poetry and have a special reading of their translations. Art students do all sorts of projects. My favorite was poetry wrapping paper. The students designed a sheet of paper that featured one line of a favorite poem of theirs. They were sharp looking. Isn't that how a product gets started?

Teachers read poems. We do a reading after school in which teachers read favorite poems. It's open to anyone in the school community.

Teachers sharing poems. This is the put-a-poem-in-a-teacher's-mailbox movement. It's amazing to see responses when a teacher sees a poem rather than a memorandum from the superintendent of schools.

Local cable access channel. Some of my students each year go on the cable access channel to read poems and talk about poems.

Library displays. Lots of books and recordings out for everyone to see and use. Also a sheet for recommendations for new books of poetry the library should get.

Visiting poets. We invite poets to read and discuss poetry with us. It's very important for students to actually spend time with adults who are writing poems. We apply for grants to pay the poets. Also I badger the principal and superintendent.

Chapbooks. In the spring students prepare chapbooks (small personalized books) of their writings. We start to make these available in April. Students have done beautiful jobs and they become cherished keepsakes.

Dress up. One day is poetry dress up day in my classes. Students are invited to dress up as their favorite poet or poetic character. I have poetry postcards all around my room so my students see what Dickinson and Eliot and Yeats looked like. To say nothing of what they think J. Alfred Prufrock looks like.

Read poems in other places. We have students go to other venues, such as senior citizen groups to read poems. It's a good endeavor for both groups—the readers and the listeners.

Act out poems. The drama club has an improv group that takes on poems as fair game. One year they developed a rendition of "The Rime of the Ancient Mariner" that I thought was Broadway worthy. The student acting out the motions of an albatross was not like anything I ever have seen.

April is the you-fill-in-the-blank month parody. We sponsor a competition for who can come up with the best parody of Eliot's "April is the cruelest month." "April is the cuddliest month," a poem written by Ted E. Bear was one of my favorites.

We also include miscellaneous student-initiated activities such as the Guerilla Haiku Front that posted haiku in the boys' and girls' rooms.

The notion behind the activities is simple—to celebrate April as a birthday party for poetry. Buddha has a birthday. Jesus has a birthday. Poetry has a monthlong birthday.

april 12

baseball

It's that time of year—the baseball season has started. Because I want my students to feel that poetry is not an airtight, compartmentalized entity but an accessible part of life, I like to throw (had to use that verb) some poems at them from the world of sports. Their lives, for better and for worse, are saturated with sports at all levels. Some days, given the presence of T-shirts and jerseys with various team logos on them, it looks as though I am teaching in a locker room.

I try to reach all levels. Many of my students are athletes and many simply enjoy playing whatever sports they enjoy playing. They aren't aware—why would they be?—that poets have written many fine poems about what they are doing: learning and practicing and trying to master as best they can one sport or another. Nor do they know how many poems have been written about famous and less-than-famous sporting figures. When I show my students anthologies devoted solely to poems about various sports, they gasp. Poets know what baseball is?

Sport is social in that one does it in front of people and oftentimes one does it as part of a team. The practicing, however, is an
individual matter. I often use comparisons between sports and
poetry. You don't walk up to the free throw line in basketball for
the first time and start making every free throw. There are ways to
shoot the foul shot and you have to make those ways your own. I
talk about this in terms of writing: There are many different
aspects of poetry writing, and a person makes them his or her own
over time. There may be overnight sensations in some fields, but
rarely in sports or poetry. Time is of the essence.

As for baseball, poets are notorious for their love of the game.
Numerous essays by some very distinguished hands have been
written about this affinity. To my mind, the attraction has to do
with the clarity of the game mingled with the complexity of the
game. A lot is going on in any given moment of a baseball game—
that's one reason the managers are sucking on antacids all the
time. Yet the game is utterly simple—a ball and a bat. You can follow the game clearly, the way you can follow a poem from word to
word and line to line, but a lot builds up along the way. This seems
similar to baseball where, as the innings go by, more and more
must be taken into account.

There's the surprise factor, too. You never know how a game
will turn out or exactly where the ball will go. Every pitch in a baseball game is an instance of intention encountering physical actuality. Small acts make a difference and as a writing teacher I am always
talking about how every word makes a difference, how there are no
unimportant words, how no two words are the same. This sense of
consequences keeps players on their toes and can keep writers similarly open. It always has to do with paying attention. Alertness is
crucial for a ball player. Any little quirk in a pitcher's motion signal-
ing which pitch is going to be thrown is important information. Ball
players are watching carefully—just as I want my student writers to
be watching life around them carefully.

There are endless poems to pick from concerning baseball.
One of my favorites is called "The Hummer" and is by William
Matthews:

> First he drew a strike zone
> on the toolshed door, and then
> he battered against it all summer

a balding tennis ball, wetted
in a puddle he tended under
an outdoor faucet: that way
he could see, at first, exactly,
where each pitch struck.
Late in the game the door
was solidly blotched and
calling the corners was fierce
enough moral work for any
man he might grow up to be.
His stark rules made it hard
to win, and made him finish
any game he started, no matter
he'd lost it early.
Some days he pitched
six games, the last in dusk,
in tears, in rage, in the blue
blackening joy of obsession.
If he could have been also
the batter, he would have been,
trying to stay alive. Twenty-
seven deaths a game and all
of them his. For a real game
the time it takes is listed
in the box score, the obituary.
What he loved was mowing
them down. Thwap. Thwap.
Then one thwap low and outside.
And finally the hummer.
It made him grunt to throw it,
as if he'd tried to hold it
back, but it escaped. Thwap.

By this time of year, I am asking my students to tell me what they think are paths into the poem. What are the questions they would ask to start discussing the poem? I asked them to do that with "The Hummer."

Questions centered on a couple of aspects. One was word choice. Students were enthralled by the sounds in the poem, foremost the words *hummer* and *thwap*. Onomatopoeia never tires and my students respond to it. As one student put it, "It's a way to act out in poems and no one can get on your case about it. I like that

about poetry." So I heard some very pronounced pronunciations—
the m in hummer took on a life of its own. As for thwap, we agreed
that more words should begin with thw in the English language.

Other sorts of words surfaced, too. The phrase, "blue / blackening joy of obsession," spoke to many students. It was noted that
it felt strange to encounter a nonphysical word in the poem and
yet that word was crucial to the poem and gained for the physical
words in front of it. Indeed, one student, Jen DiMillo, said that
baseball was "another stupid guy thing" as far as she was concerned, but she liked the poem because it wasn't so much about
baseball for her as it was about practicing something on your own.
"It's like when I'm doing something like baking by myself—I'm
the baker in our family —and I'm really concentrating and I'm
into it. I make up all sorts of things about the way the cookies
have to be. I make it into a game. You know, how many cookies in
this shape, how many cookies in that shape." She paused and
looked around the room a bit warily. She was telling something
about herself, something small but personal. "Anyhow, I get into
it and I'm sort of lost. That's what obsession is isn't it? Being sort
of lost?"

"How come you never bring these cookies to school, Jen?"
Bobby Singh, who sits in back of her, asked her right off.

"I have three little brothers. Do you know what it's like to have
three little brothers? Vacuum cleaners. Their mouths are vacuum
cleaners."

I like this sort of discussion because we move from the subject
of the poem into the deeper waters of the poem, which are human
nature—how people behave. "Give the poem a chance," is what I
say when a student tells me that he or she doesn't like baseball or
Beethoven or New Jersey or whatever a poem might be about. The
poem, I tell them, is a pebble thrown into a pond. The circles keep
moving outward and there's no predicting how those circles of
feeling are going to touch you. Who throws the pebble into the
pond is part of that effect. I remind my students that there have
been some very fine poems about baseball by women.

We also wound up talking about line. A number of students
wondered about the short lines and why Matthews wrote the poem
in that style. Rather than kick it around in a discussion, I had them
write a brief response piece about the short lines in "The Hummer."
Here is part of what one student wrote: "A pitch doesn't take long.

It moves through the air and then hits whatever it hits—a barn door, a catcher's mitt, a bat. A line in a poem is moving, too. It's moving into the next line. It is here and yet as it moves it is disappearing. William Matthews is pitching his lines: they go by and we feel them and then they are gone. . . . When the poem ends with that final sound, it's the line hitting the final moment in the poem."

I have a file full of student responses and I read through it periodically. However I feel before I go into the file—Ben is still touch and go in terms of his passing history, our union contract talks are going nowhere, we need a new car but I don't want to face up to it—I feel better when I look in the file and read what my students have written. *Thwap.*

april 21

blues

I try to make my students aware of how wide poetry's range is. Although I focus on carefully authored texts, I do not want to slight the various oral traditions that have produced very fine poetry. We look, in the course of the year, at gospel songs, cowboy songs, ballads, and work songs, for instance. Many of these pieces are anonymous. My students come to see that relative simplicity of expression can allow for remarkable feeling. The oral tradition comes from some deep wells of human feeling.

Over spring vacation I spent some time listening to various blues recordings. I like to come in after vacation with something that is really fresh and new to my students. That what I am presenting to them is not at all new makes it all the better. In the case of the old blues tunes, my students are ignorant that such music exists. If it isn't on MTV. . . .

When they hear for the first time the often scratchy yet riveting voices on the old recordings, it's a remarkable occasion. One student once said that it was like discovering a new species of life when you thought you knew all the species of life. It startles them in the root sense of that word—the songs kick them.

I played a tune for them today by a bluesman named Robert Wilkins. It's entitled "I'll Go With Her Blues."

I'll go with her, I'll follow her, I will
    To her burying place
I'll go with her, I'll follow her, I will
    To her burying place

Hang my head and cry, friend, I will
    Mmmm as she pass away
Hang my head and cry, friend, I will
    As she pass away

Up a yonder she go, friend, please run
    Try to call her back
Up a yonder she go, friend, please run
    Try to call her back

'Cause that sure is one woman I do
    Mmmm love and like
'Cause that sure is one woman I do
    I did love and like

I b'lieve I'll go home, friend, and do this:
    Dress myself in black
I b'lieve I'll go home, friend, and do this:
    Dress myself in back

Show to the world I wants her but I can't
    Mmmm get her back
Show to the world I wants her
    I can't get her back

Every time I hear that lonesome
    Mmmm church bell ring
Every time I hear that
    Lonesome church bell ring

Makes me think about that song my
    Baby used to sing
Makes me think about that song my
    Baby used to sing

    Mmmmmm mmmm, Lord have mercy on me

High school students don't, as a rule, cry in response to the material that is presented to them in their cinderblock, sheetrock, or portable classrooms. I could feel today, however, that some of my students were on the verge of tears. Thinking back to the fall, I knew a number of students who had been through their own close experiences with death. But it wasn't just they who were clearly affected. Art, after all, speaks to everyone, regardless of how near you have been to the art's subject matter.

I gave my students a copy of the song after they had heard it a couple times. We went through it, stanza by stanza, and talked about how that stanza worked for them—the repetitions, the variations of repetition, the word choices, the sheer presence of the sounds that Wilkins makes as he sings. That "mmmm" sound is a sound made between closed lips. It seems like feeling trying to get out and it seems like feeling trying to restrain itself and it seems like someone meditating on his feelings—all at the same time. My students have talked about sound all year long, but they were taken aback to see how much could occur within such a simple sound.

I had my students write a response piece to Wilkins' song. This is some of what a student named Pete Terzio wrote. Pete prides himself on his mellowness and is not one to let his feelings show: "I have never heard anything quite like Robert Wilkins' song. All I know right now is that I need to hear more such songs. I don't know where I've been that I never heard this music and these lyrics. When he sings 'but I can't / Mmmm get her back' it pretty much breaks your heart. I read some Greek tragedies in World Lit last year and I have to say that I thought of someone like Antigone when I heard this song. It's all so basic and simple and real. It's elemental. You feel how 'lonesome' that church bell is. You feel 'that song my / Baby used to sing.' The repetitions just grab hold of you and put you under his spell. It's like he's talking to himself more than he's singing to you. It all makes me wonder what is going on in America that a young person like me would never even know this stuff existed. I mean is this part of our history or what? I'd thank you, Mr. P., but I can't stand brownnosers."

I stay with the blues for a full week. All along, I stress that I am showing them a few leaves on a very big tree. I show them the Smithsonian collections of blues songs and we look at some latter-day blues by contemporary African American poets. There's so much material that I feel I am on a very fast moving tour bus. Like a tour guide, I am indicating to them what exists. That's what a certain amount of teaching is—indicating what exists and what students can put into their lives if they want to. I make sure, for all the brevity of the tour, that they get a glimpse of how sly the blues can be, how full of worldly, sardonic humor: "It may look funny / Funny as can be / We got eight children, baby / Don't none of 'em look like me."

april 24

elementary

I like to work a day in the elementary school each year. Given the enthusiasm of the ten-year-olds with whom I do poetry, I could work a lot of days with them. Their eagerness concerning poetry always wakes me up. High school students try to act blasé and self-possessed—been there, done that (although, of course, they haven't). Ten-year-olds are right in the center of imaginative being. They are the natural poets the romantics used to make a big deal about. They always will be.

My preference is to not talk a lot of conceptual talk about poetry, but rather to show them a poem and get them writing poetry. I like to use models just as I do with my high school students. Again, I find the children are eager to jump in, eager to try. Poetry excites them. They sense that it is—somehow and someway—a different sort of thinking and writing. They intuit that it is associative thinking and, as children, they tend to be comfortable with that. The world of childhood legends and myths and tales is, after all, full of associative thinking. Things happen because they want to happen not because of various grown up "reasons."

Today I used a poem that I found in a book by John Haines, a poet who lived in Alaska for many years. It's a wonderfully simple, direct poem:

The Long Rain

Rain falls
in the quiet woods.

Smoke hangs
above the evening fire,
fragrant with pitch.

Alone, deep
in a willow thicket,
the olive thrush
is singing.

I put the poem on an overhead projector and read it to the children. We talk, first of all, about the words in the poem. I ask them if they know what *pitch* is. Usually, they do. I ask them if they know what a *thrush* is. Usually, they don't. Then we talk about what happens in each of the stanzas (I use that word with them and see if they know it). We talk about the things that are happening in each stanza. We talk about the different senses that come into the poem: how there's a smell in the second stanza and there's a sound in the third stanza.

I talk with them about how being a poet depends on being attentive. Anyone can be a poet if he or she is willing to pay careful attention to the world. I ask them to tell me what is going on at that very moment in the room they are in. A lot of the time, the kids don't mention the noisy heater blowing air. They have become so used to its sound that they don't hear it. When I call attention to it or the light coming through the windows or the teacher's ivy plant on top of a filing cabinet, I can feel them taking in the notion of attentiveness.

I tell them that a poem like the Haines poem is a container. It's a moment and it contains some things that are happening in that moment. After all, a lot is going on at any moment. I remind them of the room we are in and how many different things are going on in the room. Then I tell them that I want them to use the poem as a model for a poem they are going to write. Their poem is going to be about something they know about—their evening meal. I tell them the old-and-true saw that writers write about what they know about. They know about their houses and their lives.

I think it's very important for the kids to have a structure to use. They don't have to worry about how to put the poem down on the page. Indeed, by using Haines' three-stanza structure, they are internalizing a basic way of organizing a free verse poem. "Three things are going to happen in your poem," I say. Sometimes the kids notice how Haines builds the poem from two lines to three lines to four lines. They ask if they can do that and I tell them that they can if they want to. I tell them the basic thing is that I want them to think about all the different things that go on at their dinner table and write down three of them. I keep the poem up on the overhead as they write so that can refer to it. I see them look up as they write. They are studying Haines' poem closely: This is how the poet did it and now they are writing a poem. I love it.

While they write, I keep up an intermittent patter. I know some teachers want there to be utter silence when students write, but I have found that kids take what they need from me and tune out the rest. I talk about using all the senses, I talk about details (how about those peas?), I talk about who might be in the dining room or kitchen. Is the TV on? Are pets around? How do people eat? My remarks tend to help students who have a hard time getting going or students who get stuck. In a sense I'm their guide and I'm talking them into the world of poetry. I mix in periods of silence with my remarks.

When we share poems, I am very prompt about praising them. There almost always is some word or phrase that deserves mention. When I talk them into the poem I may call attention to clichés or obvious statements. I tell them, for instance, that I know that they are eating food at the dinner table. They don't have to say that. They can tell me instead, if they want, about specific foods. When they tell me in their poem about the spicy chicken or the icky gravy I praise them for their detailing. Again, when I talk them into the poem I talk about how much writers like strong verbs and vivid adjectives. The children hear this from their classroom teachers in their "regular" writing. It's not a big leap for them.

Here are two poems I got today:

My Supper Table

The butter oozing into the instant mashed potatoes.

The thirds and fourths coming my way.

My sister refusing to eat lima beans.
Whining every day and
Yelling, "You know I hate lima beans."

My Kitchen

The steam's floating to the ceiling
From the stove.

Water swishes on the plates
As the dirty plates get
Clean to eat off.

The cat meows to have his tuna.

After school I talk with the teachers who have hosted me. They write along with the students and have been putting more and more poetry into their classrooms. One thing they remark upon frequently is that students who otherwise (to quote one of them) "won't pick up a pencil," write poetry eagerly. I think that in any classroom there are a number of students who naturally take to poetry. Their minds work that way: They are essentialists; they see in terms of images; they like to think about words as words, and they feel the physical nature of words. They like how poetry taps into their feelings about life. They are associative thinkers by instinct. It makes sense. Poetry has been around forever for some good reasons. Ten-year-olds are part of that.

april 28

native american

As a teacher, one issue that I am always mulling over is how much information to provide my students about any given poem. I'm thinking, for instance, of the ethnic identity of the poet. Identity, to my mind, is a two-way street. In one direction, it affirms a background that is crucial for feeling the poem's depth. All human beings are circumstantial creatures and those circumstances have very real consequences for the art that people make. In the other direction, I am wary of pigeonholing an artist by a tag—racial, ethnic, or otherwise. Art is particular not categorical. Indeed, many artists protest vigorously when they are slotted into categories. I once heard a woman poet speak who was very angry at finding her books in the section of the bookstore devoted to women's literature. She felt she was a poet—period. She didn't want to be considered, as she put it, "a hyphenated artist."

I don't pretend to have the answers to these delicate considerations, but I try to vary my entryways when I am presenting poems. Sometimes I will make a specific statement. When, for instance, we looked at a poem earlier in the year that alluded to Wounded Knee, I mentioned that, according to a recent book I read, the United States government signed 378 treaties with Native Americans and broke every one of them. It's not information that my students are eager to hear, but I'm not here to avoid realities. I'm here to confront them. I wanted to bring in something from the world of information and let that resonate in their reading of the poem.

Other times I simply present the poem with a modicum of introduction and let my students draw their own conclusions from the poem. This happened today when I did a poem by Mary Tallmountain, an Athabascan activist, fiction writer, and poet. The poem is called "The Last Wolf":

> The last wolf hurried toward me
> through the ruined city
> and I heard his baying echoes
> down the steep smashed warrens
> of Montgomery Street and past
> the ruby-crowed highrises
> left standing
> their lighted elevators useless
>
> Passing the flicking red and green
> of traffic signals
> baying his way eastward
> in the mystery of his wild loping
> gait
> closer the sounds in the deadly
> night
> through clutter and rubble of quiet
> blocks
>
> I hear his voice ascending the
> hill
> and at last his low whine as he
> came
> floor by empty floor to the room
> where I sat
> in my narrow bed looking west,
> waiting
> I heard him shuffle at the door and
> I watched
>
> He trotted across the floor
> he laid his long gray muzzle
> on the spare white spread
> and his eyes burned yellow
> his small dotted eyebrows quivered
>
> Yes, I said.
> I know what they have done.

One advantage of the formalist approach is that my students never know the angle from which I am going to approach the poem. They know they have to attend to the actuality of the poem on the page very carefully because that is what the artist did.

One advantage of the formalist approach is that my students never know the angle from which I am going to approach the poem.

Poems aren't envelopes with messages in them. Poems are all of a piece. What I asked them today was why there weren't any periods in the poem until the last stanza. What, as I less than eloquently put it, is with that?

It's not an easy question and I let them ponder it. Sometimes their responses aren't what we conventionally call answers in the classroom. Nor should they be. What they are doing is talking out the poem. They are trying to articulate matters that, to some degree, defy articulation. What Jill Gretsch said seems representative: "Things happen and happen. It's the end of the world—or at least a real big mess—and things aren't hanging together anymore. I mean literally things are *smashed* and *ruined*. So why should there be punctuation? It's sort of dream-like, too. And the way people have acted is all of a piece. Why punctuate it with periods? So when you get to the periods at the end of the poem, they really feel like periods. This is the end. That's what a period is, right? It's an end. There's a ton of finality there. Oh, it's sad, Mr. P. It makes me want to cry. There need to be wolves."

The student next to Jill, Beth Swift spoke right away while putting a hand on Jill's shoulder: "There do need to be wolves. It matters. I mean I've never seen a wolf and I know they are very wild creatures, but that's what it's about isn't it—that they are wild creatures? We need wild creatures. We can't just be cities, cities, cities. We can't just be *highrises*. And the more we destroy the wild creatures, the more we are destroying ourselves. That's what the poem is saying, isn't it? It's because there's only one wolf left that the cities are destroyed. It's not that the wolves destroyed the cities. It's that the brutality and—what's the word I want?—*indifference* that destroyed the wolves has also destroyed where people live. If you persecute nature, then you are persecuting people because people are part of nature." Beth stopped. I could see she was thinking about what she said. One reason for us to talk about poems is that we say things we didn't know we had inside us. This seemed like one of those moments.

I stayed with it. "Are there any groups that think that people are, in Beth's words, part of nature?" Silence. Then Luray Peacock raised her hand. She sits out back and has an out-back-kid's persona, on the quiet and wary side. When, periodically, I move her up front she's still like that. She said: "People who live on the earth are aware of that. People who feel that all creatures are precious feel that. To me, from what I've read in here and just picked up on my own, a lot of Native American people feel that way. I think they feel that creatures have spirit and you have to pay attention to their spirits. And that the earth has spirit. Everything does really. We don't notice it, but what do we notice? We're mostly thinking about what the cafeteria is going to have for lunch or where everybody's going this Saturday night. We're the *they* in the poem." Pause. "I like this poem a lot. I'm going to tell it to my sister and my mom."

I asked if there were other thoughts about the question but there were none. Luray had them all thinking to themselves, thinking about who the *they* in the poem was. I was okay with that. I gave them some homework to do in their poetry journal. "Look up," I said, " the word *Athabascan* and write down what it means. Also, write down the origins of the word *wolf*."

april 30

dictionaries

I collect dictionaries and am always on the prowl at yard sales and such for them. My classroom has all sorts, including a number of unabridged dictionaries I picked up for what seemed to me to be embarrassingly low prices. To my students my penchant for dictionaries seems, to put a kind spin on it, somewhat odd. They are used to a monolithic entity called "the dictionary." As to what actual dictionary they are using, well that is really beside the point as far as they are concerned. Any dictionary will do: "They all have the same words in them, right, Mr. P.?"

Part of being in my classroom over the course of a year is to learn that they may have, more or less, the same words in them, but how those words are treated does vary. I don't shy away from having my students look up the same word in a couple of dictionaries. I encourage it and mandate it at times.

It's not something they are used to doing. Many of them, as they candidly inform me, stopped looking up words in grade school: "You can pretty much tell from the other words what's going on. It's a bother to take time and look up a word." One wonderful thing about working with young people is how they don't hesitate to puncture any illusions you may be carrying around.

In my classroom, because we are looking closely at poems, dictionary use is a given. What I find is that familiarity breeds amity. It stops being a big deal to look up a word because it's routine. If we don't know a word, we look it up. There are no ifs, ands, or buts about it. We do it and we talk about our findings. We actively discuss words as words. Poets do it all the time. Part of getting my students to think like poets is to immerse them in the medium of language. I want them to be curious about language and enjoy that curiosity.

I also find that a significant number of students don't know how to use a dictionary. I mean that they have problems with alphabetical arrangement; they don't understand etymologies; they don't bother with pronunciation because it daunts them; they don't know the various abbreviated labels; and they tend to think the first meaning closes the door as far as meaning is concerned. I go over all these issues with them, including the alphabet. After all, it's a bit tricky how abbreviations and acronyms are handled in the dictionary. Going over these issues routinely puts everyone at ease. What is the order for "la," L.A.," and "LA"?

It probably goes without saying that I am always looking words up and telling my students what I find. We don't have vocabulary tests in my classes. Instead, we use dictionaries on a daily basis. I'm not trying to get my students to artificially remember a certain number of words for a certain amount of time so that they can then forget those words. I am trying to put my students on an amicable basis with the English language. I am trying to get my students to feel that it is a joy to be articulate and that the dictionary abets that joy. Needless to say, all of my students do not buy into my vision, but significant numbers of them really take to the dictionary use. I suspect in many cases they wanted to but felt strange admitting it. Or their natural curiosity is simply getting a chance to go to work. The dictionary, to use a currently popular word, "empowers" them.

Part of their work in their poetry journals is to look up words and write down definitions. Periodically I check their journals to see if they are doing this in terms of poems they get in and out of class. Also I assign various dictionary assignments. For instance, I will have students look up the word *fascism* and write a response piece about the differences in defining the word. How are the differences correlated to the age and scope of the dictionary? When did the word enter the language? Where did it come from? What are the crucial words, in their opinion, that are used to define *fascism*? Are those words repeated from one dictionary to another? I do this regularly with all sorts of "big" words. It gets students thinking.

Or I have students focus on a word that is used often, but somewhat sketchily such as *charisma*. Again, I have them look in a couple of dictionaries and note the different definitions. What is the primary meaning and what is the secondary meaning of the word? Have the positions of primary and secondary meaning changed over time? How do they think the word should be used? Who in their opinion has this quality?

Or I take a very common word such as *cap*. I first ask students to list all the meanings they can think of that the word has. They generate a list with their own definitions. Then we go to the dictionary and look up all the meanings of the word. This tends to be revelatory because students don't focus on how much can be in the simplest words. When I ask them how many different definitions of the word there are in a dictionary such as *The American Heritage Dictionary of the English Language*, third edition, and I tell them that there are nine separate definitions for the word *cap* as a noun and that there are various related definitions under those definitions, they are very surprised. To say that they don't go around thinking about words would be an understatement. It's part of my day-in, day-out job to do something about that. The question I pose is whether they are in charge of their language or their language is in charge of them. As I tell my students, if you are using the same words over and over, if you swear at the drop of a hat, if you avoid words because you don't know them, if you are afraid of language, then language is in charge of you.

Dictionary Work

1. Check different dictionaries for definitions of abstract/subjective words such as *fascism* or *freedom* or *soul*. Compare and contrast. Be sure to focus on etymology.
2. Check different dictionaries for definitions of words that are commonly used but not necessarily well-defined, such as *charisma* or *serendipity*. Compare and contrast.
3. Consider all the meanings of an ordinary word. Do they have anything in common?

It's not a coincidence that my students consistently do well on the vocabulary parts of the various standardized tests, including the SATs. In some cases, they become real devourers of words, so to speak. School doesn't focus on language per se. Language is always a tool and, usually, it's a dull and blunt one. The dictionary work and the all-around high profile that words have in my classroom focus students on how they use language—not just in terms of "who" and "whom" or "that" and "which" or "farther" and "further" (and we do look at such issues)—but in terms of what each of them is doing with words. Poetry facilitates this naturally. My students start to understand how much they can choose their language.

I have a sign in my room that I copied out of a pre-World War II *Webster's International Dictionary*: "The dictionary is really an all-knowing special teacher whose services are always available." Amen.

may 1

justice

May Day as a political event has faded. As a boy, I stared at front pages filled with thousands upon thousands of marchers and soldiers and arms and reviewing stands filled with dignitaries. I was appalled and impressed by worlds in which I really couldn't imagine living, but could hardly dismiss either. For my students, *com-*

munism is just a word they are usually at a loss to define. When I ask them what *USSR* stands for, I don't get a quick response. Often I don't get any response.

Certainly my students are not political in any conventional sense of the word. They don't much care about taxes and balanced budgets and various economic debates that constitute a good deal of political life in the United States. Presidential elections are basically popularity contests as far as they are concerned. It's not that my students feel politically disenfranchised. It's that politics seems one more consumer topic, something to buy or not buy.

What my students do care about passionately is justice. It may be a situation around school in which someone is accused of some wrongdoing, or it may be a situation in society-at-large, or it may be something going on in the family. Adolescents are keen to feel slights. They are somewhere between childhood and adulthood and, though that "somewhere" can be hard to define on any given day, they are very sensitive to being slighted. Another way of saying this is that they tend, as young people, to be idealists. Justice is one of their ideals.

How poetry engages social issues is a tricky matter. It's all too easy to proclaim the truth of one's attitudes and beliefs. It's all too easy to write predictable sentiments that ask to be applauded because they are virtuous. It's all too easy to pat oneself on the back for being a sensitive person. What I am looking for in poetry that deals with social issues is "moral imagination"—the ability to present a situation without a lot of overbearing commentary. What I often find is not so much imagination as self-righteousness.

As much as the kids tend to be passionate about justice, they tend to be passionate about hypocrisy also. They can tell when someone is trying to snow them, outfox them, talk down to them. They are, for all their idealism, very wary characters. Our principal could tell you. You think long and hard when you are instituting a change because how you present it matters enormously. They are quick to tell you when they don't think you are living up to their standards.

When I present poems to my students that deal with issues of justice, I don't hang out a flag about it. We look at specific poems rather than general categories and I like the issues to emerge from the discussions of the art of the poem. To my mind, the poem we did today by the American poet Robert Winner is artful. I've used it a number of times and it has always gotten a strong response. It's called "Segregated Railway Diner—1946":

> I sat down in the colored section
> in my sixteen-year-old's gesture.
> He sat facing me in his life.
>
> A thin smile licked his lips
> and disappeared in the corners. Outside,
> gray unpainted cabins, red clay yards
> where black men and their calico women
> watched the slick trains pass—
>
> It buried me, that smile. It said
> I didn't know enough to sit with him
> in that lacerated corner.
>
> He studied his plate when the captain came over,
> M.P. face the color of butcher's meat—
> rapping me on the shoulder with a heavy pencil,
> arm grip steering me to my assigned seat.

Today I wanted to choose the word through which we entered the poem. I chose the word *in* as it appears in the second and third lines. "*In*, huh?" Brandon Wang asked me. "You're really getting into the vocabulary, Mr. P. I would have bet you would have picked *lacerated*. Shows to go you."

I decided to stay with Brandon. "And what can you say about *in*, Brandon?" Brandon is sharp, so sharp he gets bored and cranky sometimes. I wasn't at all sure where he would go with my simple word.

"Yeah, I do have some words to say about that little preposition." Brandon smiled briefly. He was winding up and I better be ready to catch. "Here's the story. This guy is a soldier and he's stationed somewhere in the South. He's our age, which means he doesn't know everything, but he thinks he knows everything." Pause again. Brandon is letting the self-reference sink in. The other kids get it. "Now the thing is—he is visiting. He is just stationed there and then he will be stationed somewhere else and then, eventually he will be back home in his white-guy life. So he isn't *in* anything. He is *in* his *gesture*. But a gesture is just a gesture. It's not a place where you live. It's like when you tell someone you'll support that person. Well, that's cool but what is it? It's one thing to fly a flag and another thing to go to war. So the black guy is there and he is *in* his life. He is sitting there in that segregated diner and it is no gesture. That's his life and he is in it. He isn't going visiting. He's there. Right? *The slick trains pass,* but he's not on those trains. That's what *in* is about." Brandon looked around. Mouths were not open, but everyone was respectful. He had said a mouthful.

"So can I go down to the gym and shoot hoops, Mr. P.? I've made my contribution."

You gotta love it, how they are always looking for an angle. Brandon stayed put and we talked about more words—including *lacerated.* We talked about the details, such as the color words. We talked about being sixteen and making such a gesture. That's where we ended and I had them write a response piece: What do you think about the narrator? Do you see yourself in the narrator? I could feel their feelings moving into their pens as they wrote in their journals. They aren't indifferent to justice, those sixteen-year-olds. They are eager to test it.

may 5

free verse

My work with poetry in the classroom is cumulative. I expect my students to be able to demonstrate certain abilities by the end of the year. One is the ability to look at a free verse poem and be able to say how it is a free verse poem. They can't do this by negative definition: It's not written in meter, so it must be free verse. They have to talk about the qualities that distinguish free verse.

A lot of my students walk in with the notion that anything outside of meter and rhyme is not poetry. They walk out with a lot more complex notion of what a poem can be. In this regard I feel I have done some real work. I have met many an educated adult who snorted when I mentioned the notion of free verse and assured me that wasn't poetry. It seems equivalent to me to saying that painting has to be representational. It just ain't so.

Accordingly, I assign a poem to my students and have them write a response piece that focuses on how the free verse in the poem works. That, of course, is always the emphasis in my class—how the poem works rather than what the poem is about. If you tell how it works, you engage the mysteries of form and content and, inevitably, will wind up saying a great deal as to what the poem is about. By this point in the year, if someone walked in and asked the question at the beginning of a discussion, "Now what does the poem mean?" my students would shake their heads in wonder, as if to say, "What kind of question is that? Grow up. This is art."

Accordingly, I assign a poem to my students and have them write a response piece that focuses on how the free verse in the poem works. That, of course, is always the emphasis in my class—how the poem works rather than what the poem is about.

The poem I used for the free verse response piece is by the contemporary American poet Kim Addonizio. It's called "Bird":

> He finds it in the yard
> one morning. Small, stunned,
> still breathing. But before
> he can do anything
> (what could he do?)
> T.J. and Spoon squat
> down next to him. T.J.
> flips it over: dark eyes,
> legs drawn up. Spoon takes it
> and hurls it at the fence.
> *Fly, you sucker,* he says.

What I have recorded in my journal is a composite of the discussions that we had based on my students' written work. My questions were the usual, simple, direct questions: "What words in the poem stand out?" "How is the poem lineated?" "How much detailing is there in the poem?" Some of the things that my students called attention to were:

How the run-on lines don't let you rest and how important that is to the poem. It's a harsh scene and a very real scene—the bird is *still breathing*. There's no time to pause. It all happens in a sort of flash yet the poet breaks it down so you feel it happen. As an example of this, many students chose the third line's *But before. . . .*" They aren't very big words, but they put the reader squarely in the situation and they begin in the middle of a line. No respite is allowed. As a student noted, "I've been in this poem. I've seen birds when they're hurt and there's no time out. You don't understand what's going on because you aren't a bird and a bird can't talk to you. You feel you need to do something."

The shortness of the lines contributes to the sense of urgency. Everything is going by quickly. The poem doesn't feel composed the way a longer line can feel composed and thoughtful. The poem "just happens."

There aren't big words in the poem. Its title is a one-syllable word and that says a lot about how the poem works. It's about a simple scene that acts on your nerves and feelings. A student observed that "a lot of longer words tend to be thought words where physical words tend to be short. I get the feeling right away in the first line when all the words are one syllable."

When lines comprise a whole phrase or clause, the poet has a good reason for doing so. Students pointed to the next to the last line—*and hurls it at the fence.* It's a case of forcing the reader to take it all in at once. Breaking down the line would "delay what can't be delayed."

Free verse is suited to the present tense and this poem shows it. It's not in the past tense because it isn't being thought about or described later. It's now. It's happening and free verse is like life—you don't know exactly what is going to happen next. Again, it "just happens" because there is no pattern (as in metrical verse). One person is there and then two other people show up and before you know it one of those people has done something with the bird. "You could say a lot about this but nothing you could say is equal to what the guy does when he throws the bird." This was John Vasco talking, a moody kid who when he is there is really there. He went on: "You know what I mean? I like this poem because she doesn't put a lot of comments on it about how that was a nasty thing and I'm sorry for the bird and that kind of stuff. I mean this isn't Joseph Poindexter the Third who is throwing the bird. It's some dude named *Spoon.* He's just a dude. He's probably never thought twice his whole life about anything. I'd bet on it." John smiled slightly. "Poets think twice—and more than twice—about things but guys named *Spoon* do not." Pause. "That's why it hurts. It's not just the bird. It's that a whole lot of people don't think twice."

Sometimes I stand there in the front of the room in my worn-out Dockers and seen-better-days shirt and I am *stunned* to use a word in the poem. We are talking about so-called formal issues of art, but that's the beauty of art: It's all of an emotional piece. I love how my students go right after the poem and how they don't condescend to it. It's not Shakespeare but the world of Spoon isn't Shakespeare. My students read Shakespeare on other days. As for free verse, it comes to seem like water and air to them. It's natural but they realize its naturalness can be carefully calibrated. They know the poet didn't just put the lines down and say, "Good enough." They know that art works in quiet yet forceful ways. That's one way it is art.

may 8

rhyme

I touch now and then on rhyme during the year when we look at lyrics or traditional poems. Many of my students walk into the class with something like a fixation about rhyme. Rhyme equals poetry and vice versa. It's part of my job to disabuse them of that notion. As I like to explain it, rhyme works like a funnel. There are all the possible word choices in the world available when you write a poem, but when you turn to rhyme the choices are narrowed radically. That tube-like protrusion that is the bottom part of the funnel is very thin. Rhyming easily becomes more about rhyming than it is about the poem you are trying to write.

I'm not constitutionally opposed to rhyme. I just want my students to see how extensive their options are beyond the world of rhyme and how rhyme easily creates artificiality. It tends to turn poems into misshapen creatures that obey the needs of what rhyming words are available rather than what needs to be said in the poem. There is only so much that can be done with *love* in terms of *your glove, Heavens above, the look of,* and so on.

To my taste, one area where rhyme sparkles is wit. The thrill of linking two words that might not seem to go together is considerable. Also the self-awareness of a witty rhymer is a pleasure in its own right. The writer knows that rhyme is something of a joke and that's great—the writer capitalizes on rhyme's wackiness. In the hands of such a writer, rhyme takes on a genuine *joie de vivre*. It revels in its energies and it delights in making fun of itself. Those lugubrious, predictable rhymes of adolescence (*blue* and *true, death* and *breath*, for instance) have no part in the light-footed doings of inspired, playful rhyme.

What's come to be called the American songbook, the lyrics of the great pop composers of the twentieth century, is a bottomless trove of unrepentant rhyme. It startles me that my students tend to know absolutely nothing about it. The cultural amnesia of the United States (to say nothing of the wages of commercialism) is frightening sometimes. The songs of Irving Berlin and Cole Porter and Johnny Mercer and so many others form a remarkable, distinctly American heritage. Yet my students, most of whom listen to vast amounts of music, have never heard "I Get a Kick out of You." Alas.

I spend a couple days this time of year playing some tunes and looking at some lyrics with my students. I challenge them to try their own hands at some of the themes the songwriters tackle. By this time of the year, they can appreciate how rhyme works because they have a feeling for poetry's other resources. They have some perspective on rhyme's obsessive quality. And they get a kick out of seeing what light fingers can do with rhyme.

Cultural references date quickly and that's part of what I am teaching my students when I look at a lyric such as Cole Porter's "You're the Top." When the indefatigable Porter rhymes *Shakespeare sonnet* with *Bendel bonnet* or *Jimmy Durante* with *Dante*, there are blank looks. Bendel? Durante? Say what? On the other hand, there is much delight when products such as Ovaltine or Pepsodent surface in the song. Similarly, they enjoy it hugely when Porter wrenches his rhymes as in *Russia* with *usher* or fools around with pronunciation as in *thoist* and *foist*.

What delights them the most is Porter's over the top energy. "The guy doesn't give up, does he?" Denise Concannon sagely observed today. They can't believe that "You're the Top" goes on for as long as it goes on. It astonishes them and that's not an easy thing to do with young people at the beginning of the twenty-first century. It's a big salute to Porter's art.

It's also a delightful writing prompt. I have my students write their own "You're the Top" using references from their own world, as in "You're J. Crew / You're My mom's beef stew" or "You're Ralph Lauren / You're my lover calling again." You get the idea. We work individually on rhymes and then assemble them for a class poem. It gets zany.

> I have my students write their own "You're the Top" using references from their own world.

Because I am intrigued by the issue of cultural references and how they date or don't date, I like to throw a variety of songs at my students. One I have used is by the great, African American songwriting team of Noble Sissle and Eubie Blake. The tune is called "Baltimore Buzz" (Baltimore was Blake's hometown) and I have transcribed the verse first and then the refrain:

> There have been a thousand raggy, draggy dances
> That are danced in ev'ry hall,
> And there have been a thousand raggy, draggy prances
> That are pranced at ev'ry ball.
> But the bestest one that "wuzz"
> Is called the Baltimore Buzz,
> So

> First you take your babe and gently hold her,
> Then you lay your head upon her shoulder,
> Next you walk just like your legs were breaking,
> Do a fango like a tango,
> Then you start the shimmy to shaking.
> Then you do a raggy, draggy motion
> Just like any ship upon the ocean,
> Slide
> And then you hesitate,
> Glide
> Oh, honey, ain't it great!
> You just go simply in a trance
> With that Baltimore Buzzing dance.

A lot of my students are ready to get up and start moving and grooving when they hear this stuff. I've talked with Cheryl Cormier, one of our phys. ed. teachers, about getting together and combining some movement things she does with poetry. For now we move in our seats and talk about the proficiency of Noble Sissle at rhyming. My students called attention to how he varied his rhyme schemes, how some lines were shorter than others, how he rhymed successive words, how he rhymed a word within a line with a word at the end of a line, how he rhymed words that ended with an accent and words that didn't. It seemed to them that a lot of what could be done with rhyme was being done within the confines of one song.

As often happens, some of the lyric's parlance quickly entered the annals of classroom lore. When the final period class walked in and I asked them how they were doing, a number of them replied in chorus, *raggy and draggy*. You can't keep a good rhyme down. Poetry has been defined as inspired play and as serious play. Sometimes it's just plain play: "You just go simply in a trance."

may 12

skills

School teaches skills and as part of my ongoing assessment of poetry in the classroom I have my students write about the skills they believe they have developed over the course of the year. We brainstorm various skill areas and then my students write about them. I tell them to write about only those improvements that they feel have genuinely happened to them. "Tell the truth" is a motto in our class. They know this assignment is not about telling me what they think I want to hear.

Here are some remarks:

Listening: "Everyone tells you that you're not listening, but they don't ask you why you aren't listening. So much of school is 'same old, same old.' If I know what's being said ahead of time, I'm not interested in listening. Hearing the poems each day has gotten me to enjoy listening. I don't know what that poem is going to be and I've got to listen hard if the poem is going to happen for me. And I want it to happen so I listen. I find myself listening more carefully in our class and other classes. Not that it's all worth hearing but I listen more. I think it's a good habit to develop."

Spelling: "If someone had told me I would get into spelling, I would say, 'You are sick, man.' But it's happened. I get a kick out of learning to spell all the new words we get in the poems. When we take dictation I know you are going to check our notebooks for spelling and after not caring for a couple of weeks, I started to try (probably because you were taking points off my dictations for poor spelling). Then it became a pride thing for me. And it makes me understand what I'm writing down better. Sometimes words are just like the juice from canned peas that runs all over my plate. I don't know where those words are going when I try to spell them. I'm not going back to middle school to enter the spelling bee but I do like it."

Being still: "I tend to drift around in my mind. I have a hard time focusing some days. I have a lot on my mind, I guess. But when I hear the poems, I can relax. It's hard to explain but it's like a door opens and I can walk in and just be there. It's comfortable."

Vocabulary: "I don't know if I know more words but I have more interest in words. Does that make sense? I mean that I don't walk around using all the words I discover in our poems but I could use them. I can see myself using them. I can see the point of having a bigger vocabulary. I don't mean to impress people that you are some kind of big-shot brain but to say what you want to say. That's what the poets do, they say what they want to say and nothing stops them. Whatever the word is, they nail it. I like that, how they nail it."

Dictionary: "I hadn't even used a dictionary for a couple of years. No teacher ever made me do it and if a teacher doesn't make me, then I don't do it. That's how school works for me. You made us do it and I thought this is little kids' stuff. I'm still not crazy about it (it's such a big book and the print is so small) but it feels good when I learn a word and can apply that word to the poem. I'm doing something. You wouldn't believe what's in the dictionary. Every kind of word and thing. You'd believe it, Mr. P., but most people don't ever use one. I think the school should give us all dictionaries."

Analysis: "When a teacher used to ask us to write about a poem, I'd want to go to the bathroom and spend the period there. What did I know about a poem? Now, though, I can write about a poem. I can do that because I understand all I have to do is look at the words and start writing about the words. That's a load off my mind. It's not like I'm going around in life with people asking me about poems. It's a school thing. But it's a load off my mind because I'm not afraid. It's pretty stupid when you think about it, to be afraid of a poem, but there I was. I can even think about what words I want to write about first."

Writing poems: "I wrote a couple poems in grade school but I got sick of rhymes and stuff. When I started this year, I thought I wouldn't like it. But I do like it. I really like it and I'm not ashamed to like it. I feel better when I write poems. It's not that every poem I write is about heavy stuff. They aren't. I just feel better to be able to write a poem. It's cool to look down and see what you did when you let yourself go and you don't force it. I'm going to keep writing poems. No one is stopping me."

Writing prose: "I can see that writing poems has helped my prose. In a poem you can't beat around the bush and in prose I used to beat around the bush a lot. I had this idea that the more words I used, the more the teacher would be impressed. The sad thing is I think it did impress some of my teachers. Anyhow, now I enjoy looking over a paragraph and tightening it up: every word has to justify itself. My history essays and reports are much more to the point. I think poetry helped me."

Reading: "It's not a big thing to read a poem. Most of them are just a page or so. It's that you have to read them really carefully. Really carefully. I think that I forgot how to read carefully. When you read novels and stuff, you just read along and you get the drift of things. When you read a poem, you have to be there with every word. So poetry sort of woke me up because I couldn't skip words or just tune out. It's like what my dad calls 'honest work.' My dad is big on honest work, believe me."

Understanding: "I understand how poems work. I didn't use to. I used to think they were hieroglyphs. I understand that there's no hidden meaning and that poems aren't problems with answers printed in the back of the book. I understand that a poem is something you quoted to us one day that stayed with me—'a clear expression of mixed feelings.' (Don't ask me to tell you who said it.) That means that the language is precise but there is a lot of feeling in the language. You can't expect to add up the words and get some kind of even number. Poems always add up to an odd number. That's why they are poems. I understand that poetry is an art and that you can talk about it the way you talk about a work of art. So you understand it, the way you understand a work of art. You can say and write things about it that tell how it works as art. I'm gassing on but you get the idea."

Discussion: "It's cool when we talk. People have such different things that they find in the poems and I never know what you are going to ask us. I like that and I like it even better when you ask us to come up with questions for discussion. I like being the teacher—some. I'd never want to grade papers or anything though. Anyhow I like how we just keep finding new things to talk about in the poem. It feels effortless. Sometimes I get really excited though I try not to show it. You have to be cool."

I can't see myself sending these remarks to a group of statisticians, but they certainly cheer me up. I have shared them with my colleagues and I get more and more interest in what the students call "Mr. P.'s poetry thing." Poetry doesn't just feed spirits; it sharpens minds. It promotes literacy in the most concrete fashion possible—word by word students grapple with language. When they do it daily, it starts to become second nature. Poetry becomes their touchstone for language use. This doesn't take away from their ability to communicate in all the mundane ways. They can write a better business letter or a technical description (our head of curriculum is wild about tech writing) because they feel more responsibility about words. They get that sense of responsibility by attending to the "best words in the best order."

may 15

literacy

It seems to me that there are two subtexts to what I do with poetry. One is feeling. That seems pretty straightforward. Poems engage our emotions and when we talk about a poem, we wind up talking about our feelings. Objectivity is a prelude to talking about a poem as we engage the rudiments and fine points of the poet's art.

212 ■ A SURGE OF LANGUAGE

We can talk, for instance, in detail about the assonance in any given poem. Where our talking and writing ends, however, is in the domain of intensity. No one likes a dull poem. A student of mine once noted that poetry is "shaking all over." I buy that. The classical texts are as full of palpable feeling as any contemporary poem. Poetry has always thrived on engagement.

The other subtext is literacy. It's one of those words that pop up on workshop days and typically is enveloped in some program or another. "Systems will save us," might be the slogan. For my part, I don't think systems are saviors. I don't think poetry is a savior either. What I do think is that poetry can get kids addressing their issues about language in remarkable ways.

Let me tell you about James Smith. He came into my classroom this year with the tag of "reluctant reader." That's school talk for low reading skills and no interest in making them better. He's gotten passed along from year to year on the basis of his personality and coping skills. He's a savvy kid in terms of bluffing it and faking it and pretending to make an effort. Anyone who thinks "dumb" kids are dumb hasn't been in a school for very long.

When we first started reading poems out loud, I explained that reading out loud was about trying. If you didn't get a word, the teacher would help. I told the class that I didn't want people hollering out the right word and I didn't want so much as a snicker about anyone's reading. Respect is everything and respect extends across the board. All I wanted from the reader was an effort.

I remember when James' turn came up to read. I could feel his anxiety and I joked with him that I wasn't grading him. He stumbled badly on many words and I let him stumble in places and in places I jumped in. I wanted him to have ownership and I also wanted him to know I wasn't indifferent to his plight. He got through the eight lines of the poem. It wasn't pretty, but I could feel his relief and a tinge of pride. He knew he wasn't being singled out. Reading aloud was part of the classroom experience. James' individual educational program didn't note any issue such as dyslexia. James simply read at a low (fourth-grade) level.

I pointed out to the kids after James read that misreading is an integral part of poetry. This raised more than a few eyebrows. I went on to explain that poets are aware of words that are within words. For instance, *dying* is inside *drying* and a poet may want us to misread in the sense that the two words are so close together. Or a poet may listen to how people read a poem for words that are left out in the reading or changed. Many times these changes are beneficial to the poem in that the reader has instinctively felt something was "off" in the poem—perhaps sound or rhythm or grammar.

This usually leads to someone saying, "You mean it's okay to misread poems? I thought every word mattered. That's what you teach us, Mr. P." And that's true—every word does matter. What's important to understand is that every word is the result of a fair amount of consideration. Sometimes the conscious mind does the considering and sometimes the unconscious mind does it. How the mind apprehends words when it encounters them in a poem is something of a mystery. The mind may feel a word is there when it isn't or that a word wants to be another word or that a word doesn't belong in the poem.

What I tell my students is that this misreading is a good thing in that it allows us to feel the shadows of a poem, how a poem is not prose but more like a sculpture. It's put together and our whole being responds to how it's put together. It's not just words on a page. It's an organism and everything is working with everything else. Our reading mind intuits that.

This has important implications for students such as James because literacy is, as far as poetry is concerned, interactive. Words aren't inert. Words are shaped into a poem and reading is about apprehending those shapes. A two-syllable word is different from a three-syllable word, not only because it's a different word, but also because the syllable count affects the rhythm of the line the word is in. Hence, all reading of poems is exploratory and kinesthetic.

When the likes of a James stumbles, I point out how creative the stumbling can be, that when poets are looking for words they want to stumble to a degree. They are finding their way through the dense woods of language and all help is appreciated. "It could be that word," I will say when a misreading comes up. This quickly changes perceptions about reading. We confirm the right word on the page, but the person who has misread hasn't committed a humiliating sin. On the contrary, we are in my room to entertain language and the slips that are made in reading are part of that entertaining.

I talked with James after school the day he first read. After he beat around the bush for a certain amount, he said he knew how to read, but was uncertain because he never heard himself read. He said that words were in his head but not on his tongue. "My head and tongue don't go together," were his exact words. He went on to say that no one had asked him to read aloud for "a lot of years" and that he "got lost in books." "Too many words for me to say." He smiled shyly.

I, of course, told James that we all were on the same page with a poem quite literally, that we never got to the bottom of the words and that reading the words in a poem was more like scouting than reading. We were getting a feeling for the words when we read aloud and if a reader didn't get all the words that was okay. We were considering the words and misreading was just one more way to consider words.

James looked at me with something like incredulity. "Do you mean it's okay when I mess up? You mean it's not a bad thing? You mean that it's part of the whole deal?" I started talking pretty volubly about poetry and how it worked differently from prose because I could see James was shaken. Something had appeared on his horizon—as a reader—that he never knew was there.

We ended up reading a poem. I read a line, then James read a line. He wasn't fully at ease—Rome is rarely built in a day in a classroom—but he was sensing that he was reading something that was, at once, challenging and comforting. Poetry didn't care for correctness in the sense of reading leading to something called *understanding*. Poetry was words that wanted to be engaged as words.

It goes without saying that I think poetry is a vital key to literacy and a neglected one. Poetry frees kids up to experience words as words rather than words as signs that are always leading somewhere else. Language disappears for a lot of kids because they do not feel the words as words. The words for a lot of kids are baffling because we don't let our students wallow in language. Poetry is all about wallowing. It wants you to feel each word and it wants you to feel the aura around each word. It refuses to subjugate words to higher ends. James

> Poetry frees kids up to experience words as words rather than words as signs that are always leading somewhere else.

intuited this and so have many of my students over the years. What was once a chore and a threat becomes something like a pleasure. To hear a teacher say "I like that word you came up with" is a good shock. The burden of being a poor reader is no longer the same burden. I want, of course, my students to read correctly, but I want them to feel how deep the waters of language are and how poetry is alert to those depths. Poetry enables what I like to call "deep literacy."

may 19

traditions

When I went to college I learned about the great poets and I'm glad I did. I can't imagine my life without the presence of Shakespeare and Blake and Yeats and Dickinson and so many others. Unfortunately, those figures existed the way genius tends to exist—amid darkness a bright, piercing light that can never be accounted for. I revered the lights, but had no sense of any tradition to convey to my students beyond these are a bunch of geniuses we throw together under the rubric of British literature or American literature or World literature.

What the recent decades have taught me is that there are a lot of other poems out there by a lot of other people and that kids need to know those poems exist. The various fat anthologies of African American writing and women's writing or the Beats or writers from one or another section of the United States or Native American writers have shown me how rich the tapestry of literature really is. It's changed me permanently.

It's not that I still don't gravitate to the great writers because I do. It's that I am able to see writing as a whole more. We write to feel for ourselves and for others. That seems to me to be the basic soil of writing and when I read through the various anthologies I am reminded of that soil. When someone is telling you to be someone else, when someone is telling you that your perceptions lack validity, when someone is denying you the right to be taken seriously as a writer, the act of writing takes on a significance that goes well beyond the clichés of individual self-expression. It's not that individuality is blocked out. On the contrary, it emerges more strongly as the individual sees him or herself as part of a context that touches his or her life profoundly. The woman does not speak for all women nor does the African American speak for all African Americans. *All* is often a silly word. The writer does acknowledge the genuineness of being a woman or an African American and that acknowledgement as it translates into art makes a great difference.

I have found my students comfortable with writers who express their own concerns in expected ways—female students gravitating to female writers and students enjoying writers who come from the same area of the United States that they live in— and in unexpected ways. My students are predominantly Caucasian, but their interest in African American literature can only be described as *avid.* They are, to my mind, hungry for other worlds and African American literature portrays such worlds to them.

I ask my students to do a semiformal (about as formal as I am able to get) paper for me at the end of the year that asks them to spell out as best they can what their own poetic tradition would look like. America is about choice and I ask my students to explore and choose. They can list writers whom we have studied. Indeed, I make a point of having each student include either Whitman or Dickinson (or both if the student desires) as a part of the tradition. They are the seminal figures of American poetry and I want my students to express their feelings about them. It's their heritage and heritage matters.

Guidelines for Your Poetic Tradition Paper

1. Consider poets you have encountered during the year and choose some (at least five) of them to begin your paper with.
2. Note similarities (and dissimilarities) among the poets you have chosen.
3. Write specifically about the chief features of each poet's art.
4. Include some poets (at least three) whom you have not encountered this year. Look in anthologies for possibilities.
5. Include at least two poets who are from a different ethnic/racial background than your own. Also at least two

poets from the opposite gender.

6. Write about your feelings in terms of what these poets mean to you—your tradition. As you do this stay focused on the poems.

7. How do the poems that you have chosen tell who you are?

Beyond the writers we have looked at, I ask my students to dig in the anthologies and individual volumes in my classroom and in the library and come up with other poets who make a difference to them. This is part of an ongoing process where I have students write down poems by other poets in their poetry journals. They are used to doing this and used to exercising the right of their own taste.

They go all over the place. Many students gravitate to the formal poets of the nineteenth century. Paul Laurence Dunbar is a favorite. They love the precision of his language and his command of meter. They are fascinated that one man could write poems in both literary English and in African American dialect. A few years ago a student did a beautiful poster that illustrated Dunbar's poem "We Wear the Mask." I still have it up in my room.

As part of the paper I ask students to supply some biographical background concerning each artist. I'm not, as I am quick to tell them, interested in a report, but I am interested in how a student thinks that the writer's life meshes with the writer's poetry. For my students, thinking about the life of an African American artist in the nineteenth century is a remarkable event. To say it is something that they had not considered would be an understatement.

They also go to the seminal feminist poets. I have received many papers on the likes of Rich, Plath, and Sexton. What strikes me is how eager my students are to find foremothers. It isn't that each of these students is a card carrying feminist. Some are, some are careful to distance themselves. What they tend to share, however, is a real pride in the fierce integrity of the poems. I still recall a student coming up to me holding Sexton's *Complete Poems* and saying, "Have you read this, Mr. P? Have you read this? I wish everyone could read this." She proceeded to read "The Wifebeater" by Anne Sexton. Her voice contained anger, sadness, and an intensity that went beyond words.

One other place my students go is to the Beats. Although for me the Beats are not ancient history, they are to my students. There is an ethos to the Beats that draws my students like moths to light. I think, based on what students write and say, that the Beats represent for many of them what I would call "The Figure of the Poet." That's to say the Beats were the latest incarnation of Romanticism and my students respond deeply to that mystique.

According to that mystique, the poet is someone who is not at ease with society, who passionately desires to be free, who is willing to say whatever he or she chooses to say and damn the consequences, who is looking for new ways to say those things and takes nothing at face value, who values the authenticity of experience, who is not afraid to make a fool of him or herself. No wonder adolescents gravitate to such a figure. It is the figure of the adolescent in a positive sense—not as a fledgling, awkward adult, but as a powerful force in his or her own right. It is the figure of the Seeker, the Idealist, the Iconoclast. It is the figure who lives life like a Poet with a very capital *p*.

For some students their awareness of the Beats serves as a genuine lifeline. In their imaginations the open road beckons and many days they need that sense because a lot of life seems, with its standardized tests, social rites, and college application essays, very mapped out. Of course, they are young and the wages of being a writer are far from clear to them. That Jack Kerouac ended up as a paranoid, abusive drunk is not on their radar. Nor should it be. His life remains a particular life rather than an allegory.

I think of what one student quoted last year in her paper. She read the essay by Ann Charters that prefaces the *Portable Beat Reader* and quoted from it in her paper. What struck her was a remark by the critic Northrop Frye who spoke of writers as trying "to produce out of the society we have to live in, a vision of the society we want to live in." In a relatively new nation that has not acquired many traditions and that relentlessly commercializes and streamlines the ones it has (what happened to Lincoln's birthday?), that vision of "the society we want to live in" has powerful resonance for young people. They are quick to include themselves in the *we*. I like that readiness on their part. Poetry is vision we can share. The heritages and traditions that move us will vary but the awareness of how much is out there that can move us seems precious.

may 22

my poems

I write poetry too. I do the writing I assign to my students as a matter of course. I always have been a believer that teachers should be writers. If we don't, as teachers, practice what we preach, then it doesn't mean a whole lot. We would be like scientists who talk about experiments but don't actually perform them. I know it means a great deal for my students to see my writing because they have told me so many times. It's not that I'm a great poet or that I enjoy some exalted status as a writer because I am the adult in the room. It's that I too am grappling with the art and am trying in my own way to write some genuine poems. I think they feel some pride in knowing that their teacher thinks writing is important enough for him to be expending real energy on it.

I don't share everything I do. It depends on the situation. Sometimes I want to put my work out there—usually as an indication of a different approach or emphasis—and sometimes I want the kids to be focused totally on student work. Over the course of the year, we did a couple of poems that stem from interactions with places on earth. The assignment was to be walking or hiking or biking or running or whatever physical motion you want to describe with someone. As always, I wanted my students to make me feel the place, the experience of it. I wrote "Nonesuch River":

> We walk the bank of the Nonesuch River
> through Scarborough Marsh heading toward Pine Point.
> We wind with the tidal stream through grey-green
> raspy tussocks and pungent mud-flats.
> Where the ground goes flat in salt marshes
> creeping and laced with creeks seeping
> down to the sea, it billabongs and oxbows.
> And you are with me walking nowhere
> along the Nonesuch talking about nothing much.
> I know now the river is us lost
> in its sluggish confusions, some brackish
> and muddy delay before surrendering,
> lost in turning back upon itself in
> circling hesitation where the land comes

> to its knees flattening on its own slow
> flow down to the sea, lost in the coiled
> channel labyrinths, a tangle of ropy
> second thoughts and third thoughts caught
> fast in the dark knot of deadwater pools.
> Come to the last marshes and grass quivers,
> the salt sharp and sweet, the pine islands
> harboring deep scents and shade, the Nonesuch
> loses its urge. It will be like this one day.
> Even rivers that come rippling full-bodied,
> brimming to their mouths, pushing into rising
> tides, send up standing waves that curl,
> whitecap, crane and bend back, wavering before
> the merge with anything so large or final.

We talked about this one in class. First we started at the usual place—words that might not be familiar. That meant we talked about *billabong* ("An Australian word, huh? Interesting.") and *oxbows* and the name of the river and how names are given to places on earth and what they signify. They thought that I was talking about *nonesuch* in *a bigger sense*, that the river is without equal because no place equals another place. Of course, there were some students who simply insisted that a name is a name is a name. "Leave it at that," in the words of Susan Takimoto in my last period class.

I asked my students what the salient elements of the poem were. A number of students focused on sound and pointed to internal rhymes (*stream* and *green*, *creeping* and *seeping*). Other students focused on the lines and how they seemed to enact the winding nature of the river. We talked about syntax and how the use of *Come* at the beginning of a sentence threw them off and whether that was a good thing (mixed response on that one). We talked about whether the reader needed to know more about who *we* constituted. That's always a topic of discussion—pronouns and whether they need to be backgrounded more in the poem. Again the reaction was mixed. Some people thought more would get in the way; others thought it was too vague—"like the people didn't matter in a way."

I prize this sort of discussion. Quite honestly it's better than a lot of what I get from adult writing groups I have been in. The kids start pulling for what the poem can be and aren't inhibited about saying where the poem can go and what it can do. Adults, particularly those who don't have much grounding in the art of poetry, often are content with niceties. Niceties grow tiresome when you are looking to make a poem better.

The poems I show my students are inevitably windows into who I am. As one student put it about "Nonesuch River," "That's a sad poem." I didn't argue the point. It is sad, though I think, as is always the case with poems, that other feelings are there also. It's a representative poem for me in the sense that I have told my students that if you boil poetry down to its essence, you wind up with three ingredients—beauty, mortality, and heartbreak. It's not the stuff of situation comedy or everyday banter, but it is the stuff of poetry. Kids recognize that. Their feelings are right out there many days: Love is very much on their minds. The topic that they would write about endlessly is breaking up and how hard it is. They have a difficult time getting beyond the clichés, but then who doesn't?

I have had poems published in little magazines and have them in my classroom for my students to see. I'm sporadically ambitious about wanting to try to do a chapbook of some sort. I have been to a couple of writing conferences in the summer and have corresponded with other poets. It's a way of life, an approach to existence, and it has nothing to do with fame. As more than one student has remarked, "How famous could any poet be?" That's hard for some of the kids to understand—that I do it because I want to do it. They tend to think instrumentally—you do something to attain something. But a lot of the kids do get it. When a student asks me, "How's the writing going, Mr. P.?" it's really everything I could ask for.

may 27

memorial day

Immediately before and after Memorial Day I do poems that deal with war. I think Memorial Day is a very important holiday and the tone of much of our nation concerning that day pains me. I like a long weekend as much as anyone but I feel it's very important that we remember those who have given their lives for their country. "Very important" is really an understatement. I think it's crucial that we take time out and meditate on what war is and on those who have fought.

Perhaps I am particularly aware of this, as I, through a series of circumstances, became involved in putting out flags on soldiers' graves in a nearby small town. The stones go back to the Civil War and in front of some of them are resolute little metal markers denoting G.A.R., the Grand Army of the Republic. There are stones for soldiers who fought in World Wars I and II, the Korean War, and the Vietnam War. I inevitably start thinking about them and their wives (who sometimes also served) and their children and their parents.

It's been a sobering experience. I had a student deferment at the tail end of Vietnam and have no experience with the military. When I stand in one of the small cemeteries that date back to mid-nineteenth century, I feel more feelings than I can describe. One that I feel, for sure, is that these men once lived and that their lives ended prematurely, violently, and far from home. Another I feel is that they tried in one way or another to be brave and deal with their circumstances as best they could.

I wonder what they would make of the United States they fought for. Some parts of it remain recognizable, but so much has changed since Shiloh and Antietam. Perhaps that's the fate of life on earth. Even in a lifetime, we experience changes that leave us feeling bewildered. It's not patriotism, per se, that I find myself dwelling on. It's the habit of reflection and meditation, of personally honoring what others have gone through. Too many days, I feel we don't want to be bothered as we pursue our fun. Our inwardness gets lost in the shuffle.

One of the poems I have used with my classes is Bruce Weigl's "Surrounding Blues on the Way Down." It hails from the Vietnam War:

> I was barely in country.
> We slipped under rain black clouds
> Opening around us like orchids.
> He'd come to take me into the jungle
> So I felt the loneliness
> Though I did not yet hate the beautiful war.
> Eighteen years old and a man

Was telling me how to stay alive
In the tropics he said would rot me—

Brothers of the heart he said and smiled
Until we came upon a mama san
Bent over from her stuffed sack of flowers.
We flew past her but he hit the brakes hard,
He spun the tires backwards in the mud.
He did not hate the war either,
Other reasons made him cry out to her
So she stopped,
She smiled her beetle-black teeth at us.
In the air she raised her arms.

I have no excuse for myself.
I sat in that man's jeep in the rain
And watched him slam her to her knees,
The plastic butt of his M-16
Crashing down on her.
I was barely in country, the clouds
Hung like huge flowers, black
Like her teeth.

Ever since I encountered this poem in the mid-1980s, I have admired it. It typifies a lot of what I am trying to teach my students about the careful use of words and how a poem plays one word off against another. It seems much simpler than it is and it shows how straightforward, declarative sentences can add up to powerful effect.

For my students' part, they don't know much about the Vietnam War. "I got an *A* on that unit but I don't remember much. We lost," is a lot of what I hear. So be it. Poems offer windows into experiences that facts can never touch. It's not to deny facts (slippery as they are), but to acknowledge the place of poetry.

We talked about flowers and what they were doing in the poem. Plainly they were part of the local flora and fauna. But what about the *beautiful war*? What was that? What did that have to do with flowers? What was happening at the end of the poem? How is it that the flowers are associated with blackness? That's a lot to think about and it took us time to talk it out. What I felt in all my classes was how much they wanted to talk it out, how important the poem instantly became to them. They walked into the room not knowing the poem or thinking about Vietnam, but in minutes they were there and they didn't want to leave. They wanted to stay with it until they had said what they needed to say.

Various remarks always stay in my head for a time and, sometimes, for longer than a time. One was written by Darius Harrison, a little guy who plays point guard and can, in his own words, "jump to the moon." He wrote that because "someone is a soldier doesn't mean that someone stops being a person. It means a person keeps noticing all of life but maybe more and maybe more deeply because you could die at any time. The war brings men together as brothers and the beauty of flowers remains as the beauty of flowers. The tragedy is that there are bad things inside us and war lets them come out. Maybe they come out anyway but war lets men do it. It makes men hate beauty because war is so awful. Beauty is unbearable. I think that's why the soldier attacked that woman. He didn't hate her. He hated the beauty." He read his response to the class. Normally he smiles a little, sly half smile after he says something that indicates he knows he is cool. He didn't smile. He was staring straight ahead; then he bowed his head. I let the silence be there for a while, then—the way teachers do—I started talking.

june 2

way of life

I always seem to have mixed feelings during these last days of school. Part of me is delighted. I love being outside and when the last bell of the day rings I want to tear out the door and put on my running shoes. Part of me, however, wants to linger in my room and today that's what I did. I just walked around and looked at the desks, desk by desk. Then I sat by the bookcase and started pulling books and journals out. Then I started leafing through student portfolios. Very quiet time, just the clock and me.

Poetry is a way of life and at the end of the school year I feel that very strongly. It speaks to the value of imagination. Once upon a time—in the nineteenth century—that word was considered vital to the human endeavor. As a writer back then put it, what electricity was to nature imagination was to people. We live through our imaginations and poetry makes that force palpable.

Or as Emerson said of Thoreau, "He knew the worth of the Imagination for the uplifting and consolation of human life."

Still, I wonder, the way many teachers wonder, what I have imparted to my students. My students are in a hurry—for school to be out, for their lives to get to the next place their lives are going—and it's hard to tell what exactly is sticking to that blur that is adolescence. I wonder whether poetry will become part of their lives. I know, because I have been teaching for a while, that in some cases it does stick. I hear from old students and occasionally get a poem. It isn't necessarily from the students that were most taken, at the time, with what I was doing.

To make a place for poetry isn't hard. A poem doesn't take a lot of time. The issue is more of what to do with poems. By that, I mean our tendency in school is inevitably to reduce the poem to a core or kernel of meaning and triumph by demystifying the poem. "There," we say, "we have made the poem comprehensible." Which is to say, we have pushed the poem aside for something else, something easier to deal with. We have slain the hydra of art.

I realize that the society I live in is uneasy about poetry and when June comes along and the kids leave, I feel that all the more strongly. I create a little world in the classroom, the way any classroom teacher does. I like doing that, but I know there's a bigger world out there. After all, that's where poetry comes from. When I sit—the way I did this afternoon—and end up with their poems and responses to poems, I am moved. They aren't by any stretch of the imagination great (though some, as I have noted throughout the course of the year, would surprise anyone as to how very good they are), but they are tremendously real. They register the ache and thrill of being.

In a world besotted with entertainment, we tend to lose both of those feelings. The ache, of course, is pushed aside or, when it is taken up, sentimentalized or rationalized. I joke with the kids that we still, as a society, haven't grown up enough to accept our two genius poets from the nineteenth century, Emily Dickinson and Walt Whitman. The ache of mortality that both poets powerfully engaged remains strangely forbidden.

As to the thrill, we tend to confuse it with sensationalism, with cheering, with special effects, with novelty. We want to control the often erratic pulse of life and poetry knows that you can't control it. It's much more important to feel it in all its endless manifestations. Poetry is one way of apprehending that thrill. We take the thrill of being alive for granted but it gets buried. The kids intuit that. They can feel it coming on, the great snows of adult responsibility and knowingness and muddling through. Part of them thinks that high school will go on forever and part of them—a part they don't often confess to—knows that it is passing very quickly and that those decisions that will determine their lives have begun already.

It's hard for me to imagine a world in which poetry was more available. I know the nineteenth century was such a world. You went to school and half the English curriculum was poetry. I know people memorized poems and read poems in journals and news-papers. I know that famous poets sold lots of books and that there were reader groups devoted to poetry. I know that poetry was quoted and read aloud at all sorts of occasions. No graduation, for instance, would have been a graduation without someone reading a poem. (We do read a poem at our graduation.)

I'm not nostalgic, however. I know the wounds of the twenti-eth century run deep and I know my students are, for better and for worse, the inheritors of those wounds. It wasn't that the nine-teenth century was a picnic. It's more, to my mind, that modern experience shook human faith and poetry was part of faith. Poets in modern times had to deal with that shaking and they did. Schools, however, and society at large, I think, didn't want to know about that shaking. They didn't, as they say nowadays, want to go there. And so prose took over. The world of the realistic, workaday word triumphed.

My students, however, know that the world has been shaken. It's not that many of them read the papers or watch the news. It's that the music and the social fraying—at home, in their town, in their nation, on their planet—and the advent of a mass, techno-logical society are not reassuring. When they discover that poetry exists and they see that poetry is being written in their own world and that they can write poetry, they feel a kind of reassurance that the glossy, glowing perks can never provide. The word, after all, is very old and my students feel some of that ancientness when they tap into poetry. It's primal. As I noted earlier in this journal, it's conservative in the deep sense of holding onto experience. Words, as they conserve meanings, do hold onto our experiences and poetry is the keenest way that words can be words. As I sat in my classroom and put away those portfolios, I was happy for that.

Anthologies

Here are anthologies found on Mr. P.'s classroom bookshelf, A to Z:

The Short Shelf (Utterly Essential)

Contemporary American Poetry. Donald Hall, ed., Penguin Books.

Good Poems, Garrison Keillor, ed., Viking.

I Feel a Little Jumpy Around You: Paired Poems by Men and Women, Naomi Shihab Nye and Paul B. Janeczko, eds., Simon and Schuster.

Looking for Your Name: A Collection of Contemporary American Poems, Paul B. Janeczko, ed., Orchard Books.

Poetry 180, Billy Collins, ed., Random House.

The Rattle Bag, Seamus Heaney and Ted Hughes, eds., Faber and Faber.

Reflections on a Gift of Watermelon Pickle . . . and Other Modern Verse, Stephen Dunning, ed., Scott, Foresman & Co.

The Space Between Our Footsteps, Naomi Shihab Nye, ed., Simon and Schuster.

The Voice That is Great Within Us, Hayden Carruth, ed., Bantam.

The Long Shelf (Very Worthwhile)

The Breath of Parted Lips: Voices from the Robert Frost Place, CavanKerry Press.

Chief Modern Poets of England and America, Gerald DeWitt Sanders, John Herbert Nelson, and M.L. Rosenthal, eds., Macmillan.

Contemporary Poetry of New England, Robert Pack and Jay Parini, eds., Middlebury College Press.

The Crystal Cabinet: An Invitation to Poetry, Horace Gregory and Marya Zaturenska, eds., Collier Books.

Every Shut Eye Ain't Asleep: An Anthology of African Americans Since 1945, Michael S. Harper and Anthony Walton, eds., Little, Brown and Company.

A Fine Excess: Fifty Years of the Beloit Poetry Journal, Marion K. Stocking, ed., The Beloit Poetry Journal Foundation, Inc.

The Jazz Poetry Anthology, Sascha Feinstein and Yusef Komunyakaa, eds., Indiana University Press.

Letters to America: Contemporary American Poetry on Race, Jim Daniels, ed., Wayne State University Press.

Line Drives: 100 Contemporary Baseball Poems, Brooke Horvath and Tim Wiles, eds., Southern Illinois University Press.

Mid-Century American Poets, John Ciardi, ed., Twayne Publishers.

New Poets of England and America, Donald Hall and Robert Pack, eds., the World Publishing Company.

One Hundred Poems from the Chinese, Kenneth Rexroth, trans., New Directions Publishing Corporation.

Orpheus & Company: Contemporary Poems on Greek Mythology, Deborah DeNicola, ed., University Press of New England.

The Oxford Book of English Traditional Verse, Frederick Woods, ed., Oxford University Press.

The Oxford Book of Twentieth-Century English Verse, Philip Larkin, ed., Oxford University Press.

The Oxford Illustrated Book of American Children's Poems, Donald Hall, ed., Oxford University Press.

The Penguin Book of Contemporary Irish Poetry, Peter Fallon and Derek Mahon, eds., Penguin Books.

The Penguin Book of Women Poets, Carol Cosman, Joan Keefe, and Kathleen Weaver, eds., Penguin Books.

A Poem a Day, Karen McCosker and Nicholas Albery, eds., Steerforth Press.

Poetry in English, Warren Taylor and Donald Hall, eds., Macmillan.

Poetry of the New England Renaissance, 1790–1890, George F. Whicher, ed., Holt, Rinehart and Winston.

Poetry Speaks: Hear Great Poets Read Their Work from Tennyson to Plath, Elise Paschen and Rebekah Presson Mosby, eds., Sourcebooks MediaFusion.

The Poets' Grimm: 20th Century Poems from Grimm Fairy Tales, Jeanne Marie Beaumont and Claudia Carlson, eds., Story Line Press.

The Random House Book of Poetry for Children, Jack Prelutsky, ed., Random House.

Real Things: An Anthology of Popular Culture in American Poetry, Jim Elledge and Susan Swartout, eds., Indiana University Press.

Strong Measures: Contemporary American Poetry in Traditional Forms, Philip Dacey and David Jauss, eds., Harper & Row.

Sunflower Splendor: Three Thousand Years of Chinese Poetry, Wu-chi Liu and Irving Yucheng Lo, eds., Anchor Books.

Sweet Nothings: An Anthology of Rock and Roll in American Poetry, Jim Elledge, ed., Indiana University Press.

Touching the Fire: Fifteen Poets of Today's Latino Renaissance, Ray Gonzalez, ed., Anchor Books.

Urban Nature: Poems About Wildlife in the City, Laure-Anne Bosselaar, Milkweed Editions.

Verse and Universe: Poems About Science and Mathematics, Kurt Brown, ed., Milkweed Editions.

The Vintage Book of Contemporary American Poetry, J.D. McClatchy, ed., Vintage.